SILVER EDITION

P9-CJF-183

Mosaic 1

READING

Brenda Wegmann

Miki Knezevic

Lawrence J. Zwier
Contributor, Focus on Testing

Pamela Hartmann
Reading Strand Leader

Mosaic 1 Reading, Silver Edition

Published by McGraw-Hill ESL/ELT, a business unit of The McGraw-Hill Companies, Inc., 1221 Avenue of the Americas, New York, NY 10020. Copyright © 2007 by The McGraw-Hill Companies, Inc. All rights reserved. No part of this publication may be reproduced or distributed in any form or by any means, or stored in a database or retrieval system, without the prior written consent of The McGraw-Hill Companies, Inc., including, but not limited to, in any network or other electronic storage or transmission, or broadcast for distance learning.

ISBN 13: 978-0-07-340639-8 (Student Book)
ISBN 10: 0-07-340639-2
1 2 3 4 5 6 7 8 9 10 VNH 11 10 09 08 07 06

ISBN 13: 978-0-07-333740-1 (Student Book with Audio Highlights)
ISBN 10: 0-07-333740-4
1 2 3 4 5 6 7 8 9 10 VNH 11 10 09 08 07 06

Editorial director: Erik Gundersen
Series editor: Valerie Kelemen
Developmental editors: Mary Sutton-Paul, Terre Passero
Production manager: Juanita Thompson
Production coordinator: Vanessa Nuttry
Cover designer: Robin Locke Monda
Interior designer: Nesbitt Graphics, Inc.
Artists: Burgundy Beam
Photo researcher: Photoquick Research

The credits section for this book begins on pages iv and 256 and is considered an extension of the copyright page.

Cover photo: David Samuel Robbins/CORBIS

www.esl-elt.mcgraw-hill.com

The McGraw-Hill Companies

A Special Thank You

The Interactions/Mosaic Silver Edition team wishes to thank our extended team: teachers, students, administrators, and teacher trainers, all of whom contributed invaluably to the making of this edition.

Macarena Aguilar, **North Harris College**, Houston, Texas ■ Mohamad Al-Alam, **Imam Mohammad University**, Riyadh, Saudi Arabia ■ Faisal M. Al Mohanna Abaalkhail, **King Saud University**, Riyadh, Saudi Arabia; Amal Al-Toaimy, **Women's College, Prince Sultan University**, Riyadh, Saudi Arabia ■ Douglas Arroliga, **Ave Maria University**, Managua, Nicaragua ■ Fairlie Atkinson, **Sungkyunkwan University**, Seoul, Korea ■ Jose R. Bahamonde, **Miami-Dade Community College**, Miami, Florida ■ John Ball, **Universidad de las Americas**, Mexico City, Mexico ■ Steven Bell, **Universidad la Salle**, Mexico City, Mexico ■ Damian Benstead, **Sungkyunkwan University**, Seoul, Korea ■ Paul Cameron, **National Chengchi University**, Taipei, Taiwan R.O.C. ■ Sun Chang, **Soongsil University**, Seoul, Korea ■ Grace Chao, **Soochow University**, Taipei, Taiwan R.O.C. ■ Chien Ping Chen, **Hua Fan University**, Taipei, Taiwan R.O.C. ■ Selma Chen, **Chihlee Institute of Technology**, Taipei, Taiwan R.O.C. ■ Sylvia Chiu, **Soochow University**, Taipei, Taiwan R.O.C. ■ Mary Colonna, **Columbia University**, New York, New York ■ Lee Culver, **Miami-Dade Community College,** Miami, Florida ■ Joy Durighello, **City College of San Francisco**, San Francisco, California ■ Isabel Del Valle, **ULATINA**, San Jose, Costa Rica ■ Linda Emerson, **Sogang University**, Seoul, Korea ■ Esther Entin, **Miami-Dade Community College**, Miami, Florida ■ Glenn Farrier, **Gakushuin Women's College**, Tokyo, Japan ■ Su Wei Feng, Taipei, Taiwan R.O.C. ■ Judith Garcia, **Miami-Dade Community College**, Miami, Florida ■ Maxine Gillway, **United Arab Emirates University**, Al Ain, United Arab Emirates ■ Colin Gullberg, **Soochow University**, Taipei, Taiwan R.O.C. ■ Natasha Haugnes, **Academy of Art University**, San Francisco, California ■ Barbara Hockman, **City College of San Francisco**, San Francisco, California ■ Jinyoung Hong, **Sogang University**, Seoul, Korea ■ Sherry Hsieh, **Christ's College**, Taipei, Taiwan R.O.C. ■ Yu-shen Hsu, **Soochow University**, Taipei, Taiwan R.O.C. ■ Cheung Kai-Chong, **Shih-Shin University**, Taipei, Taiwan R.O.C. ■ Leslie Kanberg, **City College of San Francisco**, San Francisco, California ■ Gregory Keech, **City College of San Francisco**, San Francisco, California ■ Susan Kelly, **Sogang University**, Seoul, Korea ■ Myoungsuk Kim, **Soongsil University**, Seoul, Korea ■ Youngsuk Kim, **Soongsil University**, Seoul, Korea ■ Roy Langdon, **Sungkyunkwan University**, Seoul, Korea ■ Rocio Lara, **University of Costa Rica**, San Jose, Costa Rica ■ Insung Lee, **Soongsil University**, Seoul, Korea ■ Andy Leung, **National Tsing Hua University**, Taipei, Taiwan R.O.C. ■ Elisa Li Chan, **University of Costa Rica**, San Jose, Costa Rica ■ Elizabeth Lorenzo, **Universidad Internacional de las Americas**, San Jose, Costa Rica ■

Cheryl Magnant, **Sungkyunkwan University**, Seoul, Korea ■ Narciso Maldonado Iuit, **Escuela Tecnica Electricista**, Mexico City, Mexico ■ Shaun Manning, **Hankuk University of Foreign Studies**, Seoul, Korea ■ Yoshiko Matsubayashi, **Tokyo International University**, Saitama, Japan ■ Scott Miles, **Sogang University**, Seoul, Korea ■ William Mooney, **Chinese Culture University**, Taipei, Taiwan R.O.C. ■ Jeff Moore, **Sungkyunkwan University**, Seoul, Korea ■ Mavelin de Moreno, **Lehnsen Roosevelt School**, Guatemala City, Guatemala ■ Ahmed Motala, **University of Sharjah**, Sharjah, United Arab Emirates ■ Carlos Navarro, **University of Costa Rica**, San Jose, Costa Rica ■ Dan Neal, **Chih Chien University**, Taipei, Taiwan R.O.C. ■ Margarita Novo, **University of Costa Rica**, San Jose, Costa Rica ■ Karen O'Neill, **San Jose State University**, San Jose, California ■ Linda O'Roke, **City College of San Francisco**, San Francisco, California ■ Martha Padilla, **Colegio de Bachilleres de Sinaloa,** Culiacan, Mexico ■ Allen Quesada, **University of Costa Rica**, San Jose, Costa Rica ■ Jim Rogge, **Broward Community College**, Ft. Lauderdale, Florida ■ Marge Ryder, **City College of San Francisco**, San Francisco, California ■ Gerardo Salas, **University of Costa Rica**, San Jose, Costa Rica ■ Shigeo Sato, **Tamagawa University**, Tokyo, Japan ■ Lynn Schneider, **City College of San Francisco**, San Francisco, California ■ Devan Scoble, **Sungkyunkwan University**, Seoul, Korea ■ Maryjane Scott, **Soongsil University**, Seoul, Korea ■ Ghaida Shaban, **Makassed Philanthropic School**, Beirut, Lebanon ■ Maha Shalok, **Makassed Philanthropic School**, Beirut, Lebanon ■ John Shannon, **University of Sharjah**, Sharjah, United Arab Emirates ■ Elsa Sheng, **National Technology College of Taipei**, Taipei, Taiwan R.O.C. ■ Ye-Wei Sheng, **National Taipei College of Business**, Taipei, Taiwan R.O.C. ■ Emilia Sobaja, **University of Costa Rica**, San Jose, Costa Rica ■ You-Souk Yoon, **Sungkyunkwan University**, Seoul, Korea ■ Shanda Stromfield, **San Jose State University**, San Jose, California ■ Richard Swingle, **Kansai Gaidai College**, Osaka, Japan ■ Carol Sung, **Christ's College**, Taipei, Taiwan R.O.C. ■ Jeng-Yih Tim Hsu, **National Kaohsiung First University of Science and Technology**, Kaohsiung, Taiwan R.O.C. ■ Shinichiro Torikai, **Rikkyo University**, Tokyo, Japan ■ Sungsoon Wang, **Sogang University**, Seoul, Korea ■ Kathleen Wolf, **City College of San Francisco**, San Francisco, California ■ Sean Wray, **Waseda University International**, Tokyo, Japan ■ Belinda Yanda, **Academy of Art University**, San Francisco, California ■ Su Huei Yang, **National Taipei College of Business**, Taipei, Taiwan R.O.C. ■ Tzu Yun Yu, **Chungyu Institute of Technology**, Taipei, Taiwan R.O.C.

Authors' Acknowledgements

We are pleased to be part of the McGraw-Hill team presenting this fifth *silver* edition of *Mosaic* which we feel is distinctive, with its greater development of reading strategies, critical thinking skills and interactive tasks promoting oral and written fluency. We wish to thank Tina Carver and Erik Gundersen for their effective research which laid the foundation for this edition, and Erik in particular for his guidance and responsiveness throughout the process. We are grateful to Pam Hartmann for helpful advice and to our excellent editors: Mari Vargo who gave us a good start, Mary Sutton-Paul who assisted us in finishing up a significant part, and most especially to Terre Passero who directed, encouraged and cajoled us with infinite patience and many inventive suggestions which were incorporated into the book. We are also indebted to Anne Knezevic, for her expert ESL advice and the contribution of excellent materials, Dennis McKernan and Andrew Jovanovic for their computer assistance, and to Dr. Anne Fanning for recommending the speech of Wangari Maathai, used in Mosaic 2. We would also like to thank Larry Zwier for his superb contribution to the Focus on Testing segments and to Dr. Jessica Wegmann-Sánchez for her creative ideas and technical assistance in designing activities and exercises. Finally, we wish to express our deep appreciation of ESL/EFL teachers who spend countless hours teaching their students English, a language of international communication. Better communication leads to richer understanding of others' lives and cultures, and hopefully to a more peaceful co-existence.

—Brenda Wegmann, Miki Prijic Knezevic

Photo Credits

Page 3: © Digital Vision/Getty Images; 5: © The McGraw-Hill Companies Inc./Ken Cavanagh Photographer; 6 (top): © Karl Weatherly/Getty Images; 6 (bottom): © Doug Menuez/Getty Images; 12 (top left): © PhotoDisc/PunchStock; 12 (bottom left): © Digital Vision; 22 (bottom right): © Michael Newman/PhotoEdit; 13 (left): © Tim Pannell/CORBIS; 13 (right): © Ryan McVay/Getty Images; 14: © image100/PunchStock; 20: © Kevn O'Hara/Age Fotostock; 21: © Jeff Greenberg/PhotoEdit; 27: © Jon Feingersh/zefa/CORBIS; 31: AP/Wide World Photos; 35: © Reuters/CORBI; 36: © Victor Fraile/Reuters/CORBIS; 40: © Don Farrall/Getty Images; 44: AP/Wide World Photos; 51: © Christian Liewig/CORBIS; 57: © Simon Marcus/CORBIS; 61: © BananaStock/PunchStock; 65: © The McGraw-Hill Companies, Inc./Jill Braaten, photographer; 68: © Richard Nowitz/Getty Images; 72 (left): © Bettmann/CORBIS; 72 (right): © Stephen Frink/CORBIS; 79: © Thinkstock Images/JupiterImages; 82 (top): © Digital Vision; 82 (bottom): © BananaStock/JupiterImages; 83: © Anthony Bannister, Gallo Images/CORBIS; 84: © C Squared Studios/Getty Images; 93: © Jeff Greenberg/PhotoEdit; 94: Courtesy of the authors; 103: © Royalty-Free/CORBIS; 107: © Joshua Lott/Reuters/CORBIS; 118: © Sucheta Das/Reuters/CORBIS; 129: © Big Cheese Photo RF/fotosearch; 133: © Pitchal Frederic/CORBIS SYGMA; 138: © Image Source/PunchStock; 141: © Bettmann/CORBIS; 145: © Underwood Pohto Archves/Superstock; 150: © Barry Sweet/The Image Works; 153: © Owen Franken/CORBIS; 156: © Bettmann/CORBIS; 162 (top): © John Van Hasselt/CORBIS SYGMA; 162 (bottom): © CORBIS; 163 (top): © Andrew Holbrooke/CORBIS; 163 (bottom): © G.Racinan/Witness/CORBIS SYGMA; 164: © Caroline Penn/CORBIS; 173: © Ed Kashi/CORBIS; 177: © Rafael Macias/Photo Researchers; 178: © Ben Schnall/Archive Photos/Getty Images; 182 (both): © José Fuste Raga/zefa/CORBIS; 186: © Diego Gómez/epa/CORBIS; 187: © Jamal Saidi/Reuters/CORBIS; 188: © Ruben Eshuis Photography; 192: © Bettmann/CORBIS; 197: Digital Vision/Getty Images; 201 (top): © PhotoLink/Getty Images; 201 (bottom): © Dr. Parvinder Sethi; 207: © image100/PunchStock; 210: © Bettmann/CORBIS; 217: © Stockbyte/Punchstock Images; 221: © Digital Vision/Getty Images; 224: © Bettmann/CORBIS; 230: AP/Wide World Photos; 233: © William Whitehurst/CORBIS; 236: © Peter Dazeley/zefa/CORBIS; 243: © Joshua Ets-Hokin/Getty Images.

Table of Contents

Welcome to Interactions/Mosaic Silver Edition

Interactions/Mosaic **Silver Edition** is a fully-integrated, 18-book academic skills series. Language proficiencies are articulated from the beginning through advanced levels <u>within</u> each of the four language skill strands. Chapter themes articulate <u>across</u> the four skill strands to systematically recycle content, vocabulary, and grammar.

NEW to the Silver Edition:

- **World's most popular and comprehensive academic skills series**—thoroughly updated for today's global learners
- **New design** showcases compelling instructional photos to strengthen the educational experience
- **Enhanced focus on vocabulary building, test taking, and critical thinking skills** promotes academic achievement
- **New strategies** and practice for the TOEFL®iBT build invaluable test taking skills
- **New "Best Practices" approach** promotes excellence in language teaching

NEW to Mosaic 1 Reading:

- **All new content:** Chapter 2 Teamwork and Competition
- **Enhanced design**—featuring larger type and 50% more instructional photos—ensures effective classroom usage
- **Transparent chapter structure**—with consistent part headings, activity labeling, and clear guidance—strengthens the academic experience:
    Part 1: Reading Skills and Strategies
    Part 2: Reading Skills and Strategies
    Part 3: Tying it All Together
- **Dynamic vocabulary acquisition program**—systematic vocabulary introduction and practice ensures students will interact meaningfully with each target word at least four times
- **New focus on vocabulary from the Academic Word List** offers additional practice with words students are most likely to encounter in academic texts
- **Line numbering and paragraph lettering** in reading passages allows students and teachers to easily find the information referred to in activities
- **Expanded audio program** includes all reading selections, vocabulary words, and selected listening activities to accelerate reading fluency
- **New *Vocabulary index*** equips students and instructors with chapter-by-chapter lists of target words

---

* TOEFL is a registered trademark of Educational Testing Service (ETS). This publication is not endorsed or approved by ETS.

Interactions/Mosaic
Best Practices

Our Interactions/Mosaic Silver Edition team has produced an edition that focuses on Best Practices, principles that contribute to excellent language teaching and learning. Our team of writers, editors, and teacher consultants has identified the following six interconnected Best Practices:

Making Use of Academic Content

Materials and tasks based on academic content and experiences give learning real purpose. Students explore real world issues, discuss academic topics, and study content-based and thematic materials.

Organizing Information

Students learn to organize thoughts and notes through a variety of graphic organizers that accommodate diverse learning and thinking styles.

Scaffolding Instruction

A scaffold is a physical structure that facilitates construction of a building. Similarly, scaffolding instruction is a tool used to facilitate language learning in the form of predictable and flexible tasks. Some examples include oral or written modeling by the teacher or students, placing information in a larger framework, and reinterpretation.

Activating Prior Knowledge

Students can better understand new spoken or written material when they connect to the content. Activating prior knowledge allows students to tap into what they already know, building on this knowledge, and stirring a curiosity for more knowledge.

Interacting with Others

Activities that promote human interaction in pair work, small group work, and whole class activities present opportunities for real world contact and real world use of language.

Cultivating Critical Thinking

Strategies for critical thinking are taught explicitly. Students learn tools that promote critical thinking skills crucial to success in the academic world.

Highlights of Mosaic 1 Reading Silver Edition

New design showcases compelling instructional photos to strengthen the educational experience.

Interacting with Others
Questions and topical quotes stimulate interest, activate prior knowledge, and launch the topic of the unit.

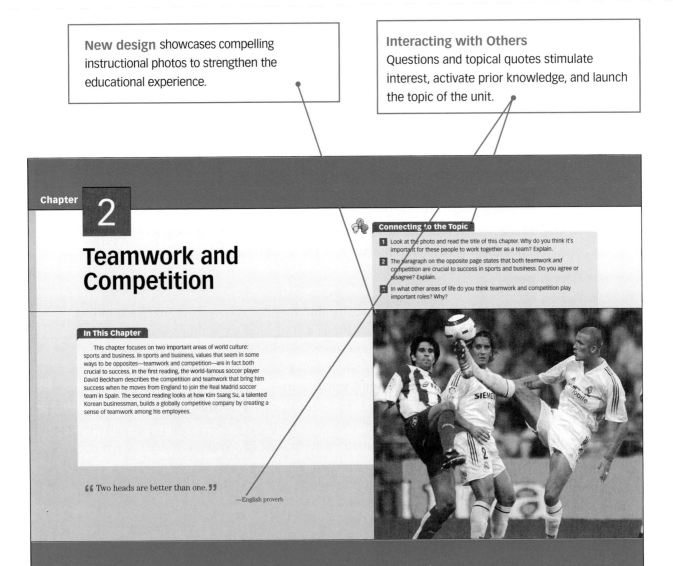

Chapter

2

Teamwork and Competition

Connecting to the Topic

1. Look at the photo and read the title of this chapter. Why do you think it's important for these people to work together as a team? Explain.

2. The paragraph on the opposite page states that both teamwork *and* competition are crucial to success in sports and business. Do you agree or disagree? Explain.

3. In what other areas of life do you think teamwork and competition play important roles? Why?

In This Chapter

This chapter focuses on two important areas of world culture: sports and business. In sports and business, values that seem in some ways to be opposites—teamwork and competition—are in fact both crucial to success. In the first reading, the world-famous soccer player David Beckham describes the competition and teamwork that bring him success when he moves from England to join the Real Madrid soccer team in Spain. The second reading looks at how Kim Ssang Su, a talented Korean businessman, builds a globally competitive company by creating a sense of teamwork among his employees.

❝ Two heads are better than one. ❞

—English proverb

Activating Prior Knowledge
Prereading strategies and activities place the reading in context and prompt the student to read actively.

Making Use of Academic Content
Magazine articles, textbook passages, essays, and website articles explore stimulating topics of interest to today's students.

Part 1 Reading Skills and Strategies

Eat Like a Peasant, *Feel* Like a King

Before You Read

Strategy

Using Headings to Preview
Picking out the headings in an article is one form of previewing. It improves comprehension by helping you see the organization and major ideas. Headings are usually of two kinds: they present or illustrate the main idea of a section, or they give a small detail to catch the reader's interest. The ones that tell the main idea are the most helpful.

1 Using Headings to Preview The article on pages 81–84 begins by introducing its subject. Answer the questions about headings.

1. After the introduction, there are two headings. List them below.
Introduction

2. In this story, which heading tells the main idea of the section?

3. Judging from the headings, what do you think you will read about in Sections 2 and 3?

2 Getting Meaning from Context Guess the meaning of words from their context by following these instructions.

1. The only uncommon word in the title is *peasant*. To infer its meaning, notice how it is in a parallel construction with the word *king*: "Eat Like a _____, Feel like a _____." A parallel construction is used either for comparison or for contrast. So *peasant* means either something very similar to *king* or something very different. With this clue in mind, read the sentence on lines 44 to 48, and tell what you think is meant by a *peasant diet*. How does this relate to the title?

---

with a Greek salad, sprinkled with olive oil, and a New Zealand kiwi fruit for dessert.

B   An eclectic menu, to be sure. But it could contain some of the world's healthiest dishes. Miso soup, according to recent Japanese research, may help prevent cancer, as may cabbage. Salmon, olive oil, and the garlic in pesto can all help fight heart disease. Even kiwi is rich in fiber, potassium, and vitamin C. In the last few years, nutritionists have been studying such international superfoods—dishes from around the globe that may hold the key to healthy eating. They're building on research that began in the '40s and '50s, when researchers first realized that a country's diet is intimately connected to the health of its people.

▲ A healthy meal has lots of vegetables

C   Since then, an explosion of medical studies has produced a flood of information on diverse human diets—from the Inuit of the Arctic to the Bushmen of Africa's Kalahari Desert. But the globe-trotting researchers have done more than discover the best features of each country's cuisine. They've also demonstrated broad nutritional principles that apply to people all over the world. And their clearest finding is a sobering one.

D   In many countries, they've found, the healthiest diet is simple, inexpensive, traditional fare—precisely the diet that people abandon as they move into affluence. Japanese immigrating from the high-carbohydrate Pacific to high-fat America have a greater risk of heart disease the more westernized their diet becomes. The same pattern holds for developing nations that emerge from poverty into prosperity. Poor people who can't get enough to eat are at risk, of course, whatever their diet. But as a country's food becomes richer, the scourges of poverty (infectious disease and malnutrition) are replaced by the "diseases of civilization" (arteriosclerosis, certain cancers, obesity).

▲ A "fast food" meal is often unhealthy.

E   The simple, ideal diet—often called the "peasant diet"—is the traditional cuisine of the relatively poor, agrarian countries. It's usually based on a grain (rice, wheat, corn), fruits and vegetables, small amounts of meat, fish, eggs or dairy products, and a legume.

Target Vocabulary is highlighted in blue in the first reading selection of each chapter to aid vocabulary acquisition.

Enhanced focus on vocabulary building promotes academic achievement.

Organizing Information
Graphic organizers provide tools for organizing information and ideas.

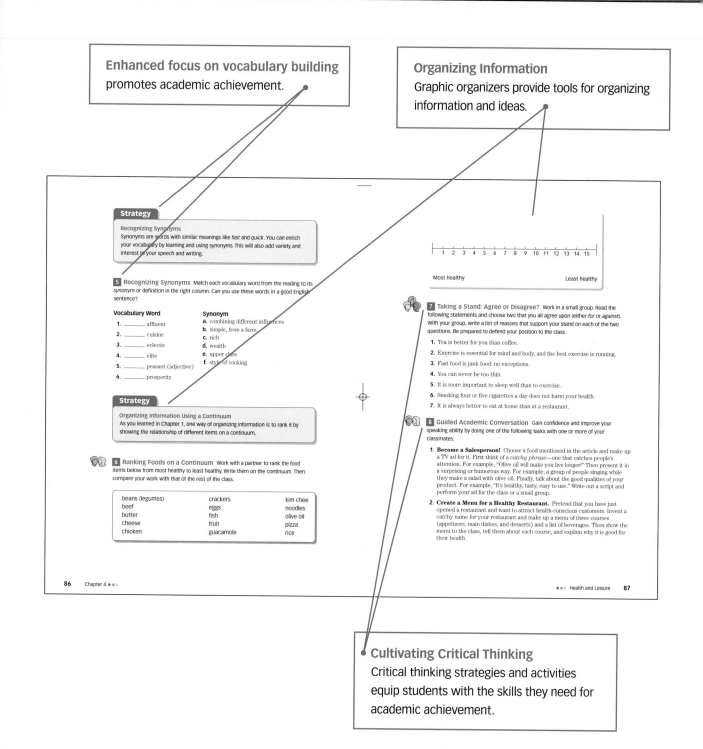

Recognizing Synonyms
Synonyms are words with similar meanings like *fast* and *quick*. You can enrich your vocabulary by learning and using synonyms. This will also add variety and interest to your speech and writing.

5 Recognizing Synonyms Match each vocabulary word from the reading to its *synonym* or definition in the right column. Can you use these words in a good English sentence?

Vocabulary Word
1. _____ affluent
2. _____ cuisine
3. _____ eclectic
4. _____ elite
5. _____ peasant (adjective)
6. _____ prosperity

Synonym
a. combining different influences
b. simple, from a farm
c. rich
d. wealth
e. upper class
f. style of cooking

Strategy

Organizing Information Using a Continuum
As you learned in Chapter 1, one way of organizing information is to rank it by showing the relationship of different items on a continuum.

6 Ranking Foods on a Continuum Work with a partner to rank the food items below from most healthy to least healthy. Write them on the continuum. Then compare your work with that of the rest of the class.

beans (legumes)	crackers	kim chee
beef	eggs	noodles
butter	fish	olive oil
cheese	fruit	pizza
chicken	guacamole	rice

1 2 3 4 5 6 7 8 9 10 11 12 13 14 15

Most healthy   Least healthy

7 Taking a Stand: Agree or Disagree? Work in a small group. Read the following statements and choose two that you all agree upon (either *for* or *against*). With your group, write a list of reasons that support your stand on each of the two questions. Be prepared to defend your position to the class.

1. Tea is better for you than coffee.
2. Exercise is essential for mind and body, and the best exercise is running.
3. Fast food is junk food: no exceptions.
4. You can never be too thin.
5. It is more important to sleep well than to exercise.
6. Smoking four or five cigarettes a day does not harm your health.
7. It is always better to eat at home than at a restaurant.

8 Guided Academic Conversation Gain confidence and improve your speaking ability by doing one of the following tasks with one or more of your classmates.

1. **Become a Salesperson!** Choose a food mentioned in the article and make up a TV ad for it. First think of a *catchy phrase*—one that catches people's attention. For example, "Olive oil will make you live longer!" Then present it in a surprising or humorous way. For example, a group of people singing while they make a salad with olive oil. Finally, talk about the good qualities of your product. For example, "It's healthy, tasty, easy to use." Write out a script and perform your ad for the class or a small group.

2. **Create a Menu for a Healthy Restaurant.** Pretend that you have just opened a restaurant and want to attract health-conscious customers. Invent a catchy name for your restaurant and make up a menu of three courses (appetizers, main dishes, and desserts) and a list of beverages. Then show the menu to the class, tell them about each course, and explain why it is good for their health.

Cultivating Critical Thinking
Critical thinking strategies and activities equip students with the skills they need for academic achievement.

Scaffolding Instruction
Instruction and practice with new language structures helps students increase their reading fluency.

New strategies and activities for the TOEFL®iBT build invaluable test-taking skills.

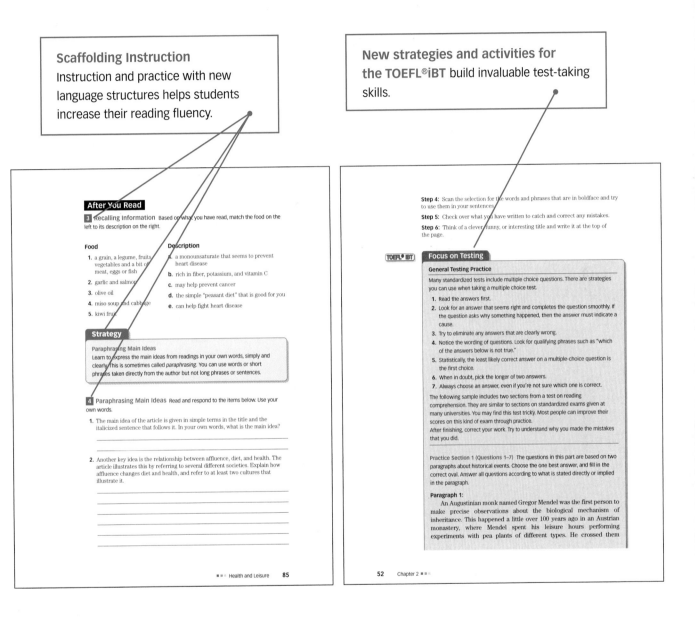

After You Read

3 **Recalling Information** Based on what you have read, match the food on the left to its description on the right.

Food

1. a grain, a legume, fruits, vegetables and a bit of meat, eggs or fish
2. garlic and salmon
3. olive oil
4. miso soup and cabbage
5. kiwi fruit

Description

a. a monounsaturate that seems to prevent heart disease
b. rich in fiber, potassium, and vitamin C
c. may help prevent cancer
d. the simple "peasant diet" that is good for you
e. can help fight heart disease

Strategy

Paraphrasing Main Ideas
Learn to express the main ideas from readings in your own words, simply and clearly. This is sometimes called *paraphrasing*. You can use words or short phrases taken directly from the author but not long phrases or sentences.

4 **Paraphrasing Main Ideas** Read and respond to the items below. Use your own words.

1. The main idea of the article is given in simple terms in the title and the italicized sentence that follows it. In your own words, what is the main idea?

_____

2. Another key idea is the relationship between affluence, diet, and health. The article illustrates this by referring to several different societies. Explain how affluence changes diet and health, and refer to at least two cultures that illustrate it.

_____
_____
_____
_____
_____

■ ■ ■ Health and Leisure **85**

Step 4: Scan the selection for the words and phrases that are in boldface and try to use them in your sentences.

Step 5: Check over what you have written to catch and correct any mistakes.

Step 6: Think of a clever, funny, or interesting title and write it at the top of the page.

TOEFL® iBT **Focus on Testing**

General Testing Practice

Many standardized tests include multiple choice questions. There are strategies you can use when taking a multiple choice test.

1. Read the answers first.
2. Look for an answer that seems right and completes the question smoothly. If the question asks why something happened, then the answer must indicate a cause.
3. Try to eliminate any answers that are clearly wrong.
4. Notice the wording of questions. Look for qualifying phrases such as "which of the answers below is not true."
5. Statistically, the least likely correct answer on a multiple-choice question is the first choice.
6. When in doubt, pick the longer of two answers.
7. Always choose an answer, even if you're not sure which one is correct.

The following sample includes two sections from a test on reading comprehension. They are similar to sections on standardized exams given at many universities. You may find this test tricky. Most people can improve their scores on this kind of exam through practice.
After finishing, correct your work. Try to understand why you made the mistakes that you did.

Practice Section 1 (Questions 1–7) The questions in this part are based on two paragraphs about historical events. Choose the one best answer, and fill in the correct oval. Answer all questions according to what is stated directly or implied in the paragraph.

Paragraph 1:
    An Augustinian monk named Gregor Mendel was the first person to make precise observations about the biological mechanism of inheritance. This happened a little over 100 years ago in an Austrian monastery, where Mendel spent his leisure hours performing experiments with pea plants of different types. He crossed them

52 Chapter 2 ■ ■ ■

Scope and Sequence

Critical Thinking Skills	Vocabulary Building	Focus on Testing
Interpreting cultural differences Ranking for social acceptance (on a continuum) Synthesizing group discussion and reporting on it Expressing an opinion Synthesizing Internet content: taking notes and presenting results Supporting your ideas with details in writing	Understanding the meaning of words from context Analyzing suffixes Making new words by adding suffixes Understanding compound words (with and without hyphens) Getting the meaning of words from context and structure Analyzing the prefixes *non-* and *anti-* Focusing on words from the Academic Word List	**TOEFL® IBT** Analyzing points of contrast on tests
Using a graphic organizer (chain of events diagram) to identify the sequence of events Recognizing implied feelings Taking a stand for or against a proposal Synthesizing Internet content: taking notes and presenting results Choosing adjectives to describe people in writing	Figuring out idiomatic expressions and specialized terms Learning sports-related vocabulary Inferring the meaning of words from context Understanding metaphors Using compound adjectives Inferring meaning of words as synonyms or antonyms Focusing on words from the Academic Word List	**TOEFL® IBT** Using strategies to correctly answer multiple choice questions
Presenting ideas effectively in a group Summarizing a group opinion Comparing past and present generations Synthesizing Internet content: taking notes and presenting results Summarizing by listing key points in writing	Matching words to their definitions Identifying antonyms Focusing on words from the Academic Word List Reviewing vocabulary through pantomime	**TOEFL® IBT** Answering vocabulary questions

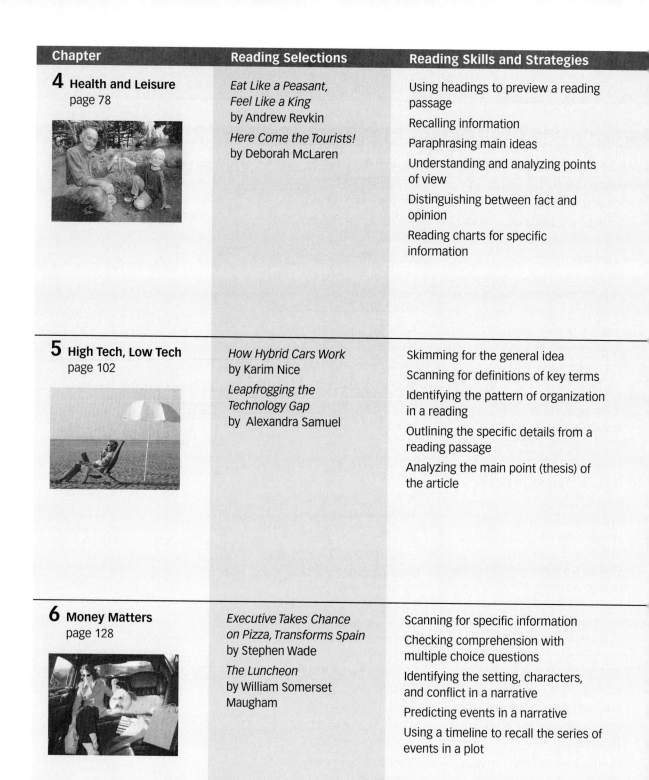

Critical Thinking Skills	Vocabulary Building	Focus on Testing
Using a graphic organizer (a continuum) to rank items Taking a stand by agreeing or disagreeing Analyzing points of view Using a Venn diagram to compare answers from an interview Reaching a group consensus and writing an opinion statement Synthesizing Internet content: taking notes and presenting results Structuring an argument to support an opinion in writing	Getting meaning from context Recognizing synonyms Scanning for vocabulary Focusing on words from the Academic Word List	Analyzing compound words on vocabulary tests
Filling out a chart for comparison Comparing opinions Choosing a favorite theme-related item and researching it Creating a study outline Interviewing and using a graphic organizer (Venn diagram) to compare answers Synthesizing Internet content: taking notes and presenting results Selecting strong examples to support a point of view in writing	Inferring the meaning of expressions from context and vocabulary Inferring the meaning of specialized terms Understanding compound words Analyzing compound adjectives with hyphens Focusing on words from the Academic Word List	TOEFL® IBT Using a computer effectively on tests
Comparing opinions Synthesizing Internet content: taking notes and presenting results Analyzing the actions and outcomes of a situation and presenting an alternative solution through a skit Solving problems related to the theme Using a cluster diagram to help organize ideas for a writing task	Recognizing word families Getting the meaning of words from context Focusing on words from the Academic Word List	Reading between the lines on reading comprehension tests

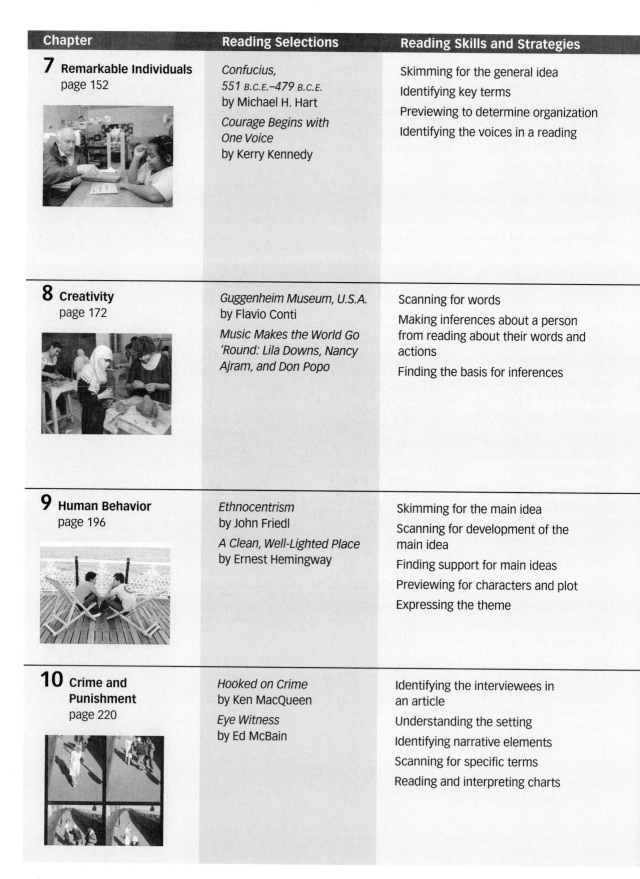

Critical Thinking Skills	Vocabulary Building	Focus on Testing
Supporting or disproving a general statement with facts Expressing an opinion Using a graphic organizer (a continuum) to rank leaders Comparing ideas Synthesizing Internet content: taking notes and presenting results Using a Venn diagram to compare and contrast two topics in writing	Figuring out meaning from structure clues: compound words, prefixes and suffixes Forming new words from the same word family Matching words to their definitions Using expressive synonyms Creating new words using noun suffixes Focusing on words from the Academic Word List	**TOEFL® IBT** Understanding sentence-insertion questions tests (Reading: *The Most Dangerous Jobs in the U.S.*)
Expressing and comparing opinions and interpretations Summarizing group discussions and reporting them to the class Identifying points of comparison Synthesizing Internet content: taking notes and presenting results Selecting and ordering descriptive details when writing about art	Understanding the vocabulary of shapes and forms Inferring the meaning of adjectives and adverbs from structure clues and context Choosing synonyms or definitions for strong verbs Matching words to their definitions Focusing on words from the Academic Word List	Thinking twice about tricky test questions
Comparing opinions Analyzing love poems (Readings: three poems) Making inferences about characters Synthesizing Internet content: taking notes and presenting results Writing a dialogue	Using prefixes to build new words Scanning for words with clues Focusing on words from the Academic Word List Getting the meaning of words from context	**TOEFL® IBT** Answering questions on tests about an author's purposes or attitudes (Reading: *Gestural Ethnocentrism*)
Reporting opinions Using a graphic organizer (storyboard) to summarize the plot Interpreting a scene from the plot in a group skit Synthesizing Internet content: taking notes and presenting results Using a summary of an event to connect to a personal viewpoint in writing	Getting the meaning of specialized terms from context Inferring the meaning of adjectives from context and structure Focusing on words from the Academic Word List Identifying spelling variations Matching descriptive adverbs to their context	**TOEFL® IBT** Understanding prose summaries on tests (Reading: *Privatized Prisons*)

1

New Challenges

In This Chapter

People take on the challenge of learning English for many reasons. For example, it may help them advance in their career, it is used internationally for science and business, and it is the most common language on the Internet. To improve their skills, students of English often study or work in one of over 45 countries. In this chapter, we will look at two popular destinations. The first reading gives useful information about the United States and some of the customs and attitudes of its people. The second reading presents facts about Canada and discusses the qualities that visitors will find in Canadians that make them different from their neighbors to the south.

" A person who can not tolerate small difficulties can never accomplish great things. **"**

—Chinese proverb

Connecting to the Topic

1. Look at the photo below. What's happening? Where do you think this photo is taking place?

2. The quote on the opposite page mentions tolerating "small difficulties." What kinds of small difficulties do you think the man in the photo has had to tolerate in order to become a successful athlete?

3. This chapter examines some of the typical greetings in different parts of the world. How do you think greeting someone from a different culture could present a "new challenge"?

First Impressions

Before You Read

Strategy

Reading Without Knowing Every Word

The articles in this book contain many words that you know, along with a number of words that you do not know. This is not surprising. Linguists tell us that, for historical reasons, English has a larger vocabulary than any other known language. Practice the important skill of reading without knowing the meaning of every word by following these three steps:

- Look over the article quickly, paying attention to the title and the headings of the sections. Try to get a general idea of the contents of each section.

- Read the article for the main ideas. Certain words have been highlighted for you to work on later, but for the moment, skip these and any other words you do not understand. Do not slow yourself down by looking up words in a dictionary. Keep going.

- Do the exercises that follow the reading, referring back to the article, and reading all or parts of it, as necessary. Two or three quick readings are better for understanding than one slow one.

Introduction

The following selections are taken from *Living in the U.S.A.*, a book written by Alison Raymond Lanier and updated after her death by Charles William Gay.

- What purpose do you think the authors had for writing this book?
- What do you know about the United States?
- Do you expect to be surprised by some of the facts given about that country and its people?

Read

1 **Reading Without Knowing Every Word** Read the following article by practicing the steps from the Strategy Box above. Pay attention to the key vocabulary in bold blue type and try to use it in the exercises and activities. Key words have been put in bold blue type to aid you in Part 1, but not in Part 2.

First Impressions

Size

A   It is difficult to really experience or "feel" the size of the United States. To get the full impact you should realize, for example, that it takes 48 hours (two entire days and two long nights) to travel by train from Chicago to Los Angeles, rolling along hour after hour across wheat fields, mountains, and deserts. 5

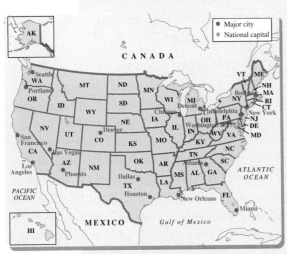

▲ Map of the U.S.

B   Another way to think about it is to compare distances in the United States with others more familiar to you. For example, New York to Washington, D.C. is about the same as London to Paris or Nairobi to 10 Mombasa or Tokyo to Kyoto; New York to Los Angeles is farther than Lisbon to Cairo or Moscow to Montreal or New Delhi to Rome.

Climate

C   Naturally, with such distances, the climate 15 in the **continental** United States is also one of great extremes. From New England and New York through Chicago and much of the Midwest and Northwest, temperatures vary from subzero in winter to the high 90s (Fahrenheit) or over in summer. 20

D   The South and Southwest have warmer weather, though even these sections have **occasional** frosts and periods of moderate cold. Generally, summers are likely to range from 70° F to 100° F (21° C to 38° C), and many areas can be quite humid. However, air conditioning is so widespread that you can expect most office 25 buildings and homes to be kept at relatively **comfortable** temperatures.

Americans in Motion

E   Americans are **restless**. Most travel whenever they get the chance. They crowd onto trains, buses, and planes. In increasing numbers, they hike with packs on their backs or ride bicycles, 30 heading for the mountains, seashore, or national parks.

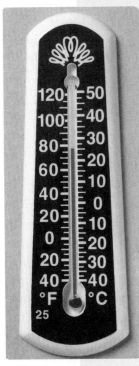

▲ Fahrenheit temperatures are shown on the left compared with Celsius on the right.

▲ Biking is a popular sport in the U.S.

Blunt Speech

F   Don't think that Americans are being rude if we tend to speak in monosyllables or answer with a mere "O.K.," "Sure," or "Nope" or greet you with "Hi." Our **brevity** is not a **personal** insult, though to those accustomed to formal phrases, we seem **blunt**. American **informality** has become more **desirable** than formal expressions of greeting or farewell. 35 40

A Do-It-Yourself Society

G   The United States is a **do-it-yourself** country. We generally carry our own bags, take our laundry to the laundromat, stand in line at the grocery store, or shine our own shoes, whoever we may be—lawyer, professor, bank president, or corporate executive. Anyone who can afford the high cost of service in this country and wants to pay for it, may. But there is absolutely no social **stigma** in doing one's own daily **chores**, no matter how **menial**. In fact, Americans take pride in do-it-yourself accomplishments and may devote a great deal of their **leisure** time to projects around the home. Huge warehouse stores that cater to do-it-yourself tasks have been built throughout the country. 45 50

▲ Americans take pride in do-it-yourself projects.

H   Many Americans who could afford **household** help or a **driver** or a **gardener** do not employ them. They prefer family privacy, independence, and freedom from **responsibility**, all of which are at least partially lost when one has help in one's home. 55

I   Houses interest Americans greatly. They spend much of their time thinking and reading and talking about the design of houses, their decorations, how to improve them. Many weekend hours are passed in do-it-yourself projects around the house. People also love to look at each other's houses. Since they would **thoroughly** enjoy visiting and examining a house in another country, they **assume** that you will probably have the same desire. Don't be surprised, therefore, if you are shown the entire house from top to bottom, including bathrooms and closets! Don't make the mistake of **refusing**: the whole house may have been cleaned especially for you! 60 65 70

Because people in the United States have come from so many **nationalities**, there is a far wider range of what is **acceptable** than in some countries where the **inhabitants** have grown up with a common 75 **heritage**. As a result, no one needs to feel awkward or uncomfortable in following his or her own customs. Although Americans are noticeably informal, if you prefer somewhat greater **formality**, feel free to act in your own way. This will be acceptable to those around you.

Source: "First Impressions" *Living in the USA* (Alison R. Lanier and Charles William Gay)

After You Read

2 **Recalling Information** Mark each of these sentences with a *T* (for true) or *F* (for false). Correct the false statements to make them true. Remember to read the article (or parts of it) again if you have trouble with it. If you can do this activity, you have read well enough for your present purpose.

1. __T__ The United States has a varied geography, including fields, mountains, and deserts.

2. _____ Its continental climate is basically moderate.

3. _____ Its people are not very active and spend most of their time reading books.

4. _____ They are rude and like to insult others with simple direct words.

5. _____ Americans are very interested in their homes and love to show them off, even to people they don't know very well.

6. _____ Americans spend a lot of time thinking and talking about projects to fix up their homes.

7. _____ They send their servants to huge warehouse stores to buy decorations for their houses.

8. _____ Americans come from many different nationalities.

9. _____ They generally prefer formality and do not like people to be informal.

Strategy

Analyzing Paragraphs for the Main Idea and its Development
An important skill for reading is finding the main idea, which is often stated directly. In most cases, a sentence or two states the main idea. This sentence is usually (but not always) the first sentence of the paragraph. The other sentences develop the paragraph in these ways:

1. by giving examples or details to illustrate the main idea

2. by expanding upon it with related ideas

3. by expressing an emotional reaction to the main idea

3 Analyzing Paragraphs for the Main Idea and its Development
Read the questions below about the previous reading.

1. Is the main idea in the first sentence of each of the first five sections of the reading?

2. The first three sections develop the main idea in the same way. Which way is that? Choose 1, 2, or 3 in the Strategy Box on page 7.

3. The fourth section also does it that same way, but finishes up with one other way in the last sentence. Which way does it finish up? Choose 1, 2, or 3 in the Strategy Box on page 7.

4. What punctuation mark indicates an emotional reaction? Look through the rest of the article and find the section that uses method 3 (expressing an emotional reaction) to finish up. What are the first four words of that paragraph?

Strategy

Understanding the Meaning of Words from Context
The *context* of something is its surroundings or situation. The context of a word is what goes before it and after it. You can often guess the meaning of a new word by reading past it to the next sentence. If the meaning is still unclear, read the sentence before the word. If necessary, read the whole paragraph. Then go back and try to understand the word again.

4 Understanding the Meaning of Words from Context
Choose the best definition for each word below. If you don't remember the context, go back to the reading and look for the words in bold (darker type).

1. *blunt*   **a.** loud and rude   **b.** short and direct   **c.** personal and formal

2. *stigma*   **a.** new rule   **b.** good word   **c.** negative mark

3. *leisure*   **a.** not working   **b.** work   **c.** family

4. *chores*   **a.** tasks   **b.** accounts   **c.** pastimes

5. *menial*   **a.** difficult   **b.** attractive   **c.** low

6. *thoroughly*   **a.** somewhat   **b.** completely   **c.** possibly

7. *assume*   **a.** doubt   **b.** believe   **c.** fear

8. *refusing*   **a.** saying yes   **b.** saying no   **c.** not saying anything

9. *heritage*   **a.** history and tradition   **b.** physical appearance   **c.** economics and class

ANALYZING SUFFIXES

A suffix is a letter or group of letters put at the end of a word to form a new word. For example, suffixes can make a noun (person, place, or thing) out of a verb (action word) or an adjective (a word that describes a noun) out of a noun. Learning common suffixes can help you to increase your vocabulary.

You will work with these six suffixes in the exercise below:

-able	(comfortable)
-al	(logical)
-ant	(consultant)
-er	(reader)
-ity	(tranquility)
-less	(helpless)

5 **Analyzing Suffixes** Study the meanings of the following suffixes and fill in the second example for each one. The first one is done as an example.

1. **-able**

   The suffix *-able* means relating to the action of a verb. It makes adjectives out of verbs. Something you can love is *loveable*.

   A house you can afford is an *affordable* house.

2. **-al**

   The suffix *-al* means relating to some object or thing. It makes adjectives out of nouns. Things that relate to nature are *natural* things.

   A job you get for only one season of the year is a _____ job.

3. **-ant**

   The suffix *-ant* means a person who does the action of the verb. It makes nouns out of verbs. A person who serves is a *servant*.

   A person who applies for something is an _____. (Note: the spelling changes here—add a *c* before the suffix.)

4. **-er**

   The suffix *-er* means a person who is capable of doing the action of the verb. It makes nouns out of verbs. A person who can bake is a *baker*.

   A person who can teach is a _____.

5. **-ity**

   The suffix *-ity* means the state or condition of some quality. It makes a noun out of an adjective. A material that is elastic has *elasticity*.

   People who are cordial are known for their _____.

6. **-less**

   The suffix *-less* means "without." It makes adjectives out of nouns. A situation without hope is a *hopeless* situation.

   A person who is causing no harm is a _____ person.

6 **Making New Words by Adding Suffixes** Form words used in the reading by adding suffixes from the list on page 9. Check your answers by finding the words in the reading. The first sentence is an example and is not from the reading.

1. A person who *settles* (comes to live) in a place is a _____*settler*_____.

2. A person who *gardens* (works in a garden) is a _____. (line 54)

3. A person who *drives* is a _____. (line 54)

4. A chair that gives a lot of *comfort* is a _____ chair. (line 26)

5. Some groups of people are *formal*. They are known for their

_____. (line 78)

6. Other groups of people are *informal*. They are known for their

_____. (line 38)

7. The people who *inhabit* a region are the _____ of that region. (line 75)

8. We *accept* certain ways of acting. Those ways are _____ to us. (line 74)

9. They take that trip only on certain *occasions*. They take an

_____ trip. (line 22)

10. A quality we all *desire* to have is a _____ quality. (line 39)

11. Some information relates especially to just one *person*. It is his or her

_____ information. (line 36)

12. We are *responsible* for our employees. They are our _____. (line 57)

13. Many Americans participate in numerous activities without much *rest*. They

are a _____ people. (line 28)

14. Weather patterns that affect a whole *continent* are _____ weather patterns. (line 16)

15. A speaker sometimes gives a *brief* speech. If we are tired, we appreciate his or

her _____. (line 35) (Notice that there is a spelling change in

this one.)

16. Part of our identities relate to our *national* origins. We call them our

_____. (line 74)

Strategy

Understanding Compound Words

Some English words are made up of smaller words joined together. Sometimes these words contain hyphens and sometimes they don't. To understand them, look at the words and break them into their smaller parts. Then you can usually guess their meaning, especially if you also find clues in the context.

Examples:

do-it-yourself (project): this is a project you have to do on your own

bedroom: the room with a bed, the room for sleeping

7 **Understanding Compound Words** Guess the meanings of the words in italics below by looking at each individual word and the general context. Write the meanings in the blanks.

Compound Words With Hyphens

1. Kim wanted to buy a CD with some *easy-listening* music.

   music that is soft and easy to listen to

2. My friend can't go out until he finishes his *to-do* list.

   _____

3. The bookstore has a big section of *self-help* books.

   _____

4. Her brother always helps people out; he's a real *do-gooder*.

   _____

Compound Words Without Hyphens

1. Chicago is an *overnight* train trip from New York.

   a train trip that continues through the night

2. Air conditioning is *widespread*.

   _____

3. They do not use long formal expressions of greeting or *farewell*.

   _____

4. People in the U.S. go to the mountains, *seashore*, or national parks to hike.

   _____

5. Many Americans do not have *household* help.

   _____

8 **Around the Globe** Working with a classmate, look at the photos in each section below to find out more about customs in the United States and around the world. Take turns reading aloud the descriptions that accompany the photos. Then follow the directions and answer the questions after each section.

A. Meeting and Greeting

A   In some cultures, such as Japan and Korea, people bow to each other when they meet. In others, they put their palms together in front of their faces and incline their heads. (This is called *namaste* in India and *wai* in Thailand.) In Russia, France, Italy, and many other parts of Europe, as well as in Latin America, people touch each other when they meet, embracing (hugging) and often exchanging a quick kiss on one or both cheeks. Muslims greet each other with a *salaam* greeting. This means that they bow, sometimes touching their foreheads with the palm of their right hand, and say "Salaam Alaikum!" or a similar phrase wishing peace to each other. (*Salaam* means peace.) In the English-speaking world (Australia, Britain, Canada, New Zealand, and the U.S.A.), the usual custom is to shake hands, but sometimes people don't, preferring to just nod and smile. A casual "Hi" or "How ya' doin'?" or "Hello, there" often takes the place of a formal handshake, but it means the same thing. If a person extends her or his hand in greeting, then it is polite to shake hands.

▲ In parts of Europe and Latin America, people often kiss each other on the cheek when they meet.

▲ In the English-speaking world, people usually shake hands when they meet, particularly in formal situations.

▲ In some parts of the world, people often touch each other when they meet.

Look at the photos on page 12 and discuss the following:

1. What is happening in each photo? Where is the greeting taking place?

2. What do you think of these ways of greeting?

3. Which one is similar to the customs in your culture?

4. With your partner, practice greeting each other as they do in English-speaking cultures, and also in some other way. Introduce yourself by saying, "My name is _____ .What is your name?" This is acceptable and often appreciated in English-speaking cultures. After learning the name of a person, say "Pleased to meet you!" or "Nice meeting you!"

B. Social Distance

B   The "comfort zone," or the distance people stand from each other when they talk, varies among different cultures. Asians stand quite far apart when they talk. Greeks, Arabs, and South Americans stand quite close together. Often, they move closer as the conversation heats up. Americans and Canadians are somewhere in the middle. Studies show that they feel most comfortable in conversation when standing about 21 inches apart from each other.   25

▲ The "comfort zone" is different for various cultures.

Look at the photos above and discuss the following:

1. What are the people doing and where do you think the conversation is taking place?

2. How far apart do people usually stand when having a conversation in your culture?

3. Stand up and play the role of two people talking about the weather. First pretend you are in an Asian country, then in Greece, and then in the United States. Which distance feels most comfortable to you? Why?

9 Asking Personal Questions What questions are polite for a first meeting? This varies greatly depending on where you live. Look at the following questions. Every one of them is polite in some cultures. Decide which ones would be polite and which would be impolite for a first meeting in your culture.

1. Where are you from?

2. How much did you pay for your jacket?

3. What do you do for a living?

4. How much money do you make?

5. Are you married?

6. How old are you?

7. Do you have any children?

8. What is your religion?

10 Politeness Look at the questions in Activity 9 again. Circle the questions that are impolite in your culture. Half of them are generally considered impolite in American culture. Check (✓) those that you think are impolite in the U.S. (Answers at the bottom of this page.) Discuss the questions below.

1. Are there more that are impolite in your culture or in U.S. culture?

2. In your opinion, what is the man in the photo thinking? What do you think he will say to the woman? Will he answer her question?

3. What can you say if someone asks you a question you don't want to answer?

Answers to 9, Personal Questions, above:
Questions 2, 4, 6, and 8 are generally considered impolite in American culture.

11 Talking About Preferences The reading passage, *First Impressions,* describes some American customs and attitudes. Of course, these would not apply to all Americans. There are cultural preferences and personal preferences. In small groups, talk about the following U.S. customs and attitudes. Which do you each agree with personally, and why? In general, should you "do as the Americans do" if you live in the U.S.?

1. the use of air conditioning in homes and public buildings

2. hiking with backpacks in the mountains

3. blunt speech

4. informal dinners in private homes

5. informality in the workplace

6. doing things for yourself and not having live-in servants in your home

Strategy

Using a Continuum
A *continuum* is a diagram, like the two below, used to show different amounts or degrees of something; in this case, degrees of acceptance. You will use these diagrams in the next exercise.

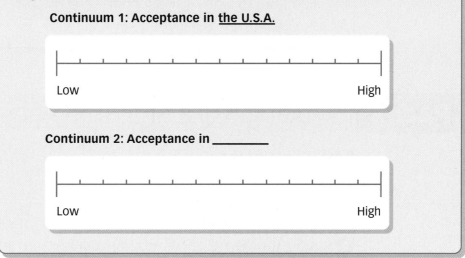

Continuum 1: Acceptance in <u>the U.S.A.</u>

Low　　　　　　　　　　　　　　　　　High

Continuum 2: Acceptance in _____

Low　　　　　　　　　　　　　　　　　High

12 Using a Continuum: Rating Social Acceptance Work in a small group and read the situation and the list of actions on page 16. Discuss and rate the acceptance of each action and mark it from *Low* to *High* on each continuum diagram in the strategy box above. Continuum 1 represents the U.S. and Continuum 2 represents a culture with which your group is familiar. Base your ratings on the article you have read and on your knowledge of the other culture.

Situation: Imagine that you are a fairly wealthy professional man or woman and you want to do the actions below. How acceptable would they be in the U.S.? How acceptable would they be in another culture? Rate each action and write the letter on each continuum above.

Actions:

   a. Answering in short words like "Nope" or "Sure"

   b. Asking a person how old he or she is

   c. Asking someone how much money he or she makes

   d. Digging in your garden

   e. Driving your own car

   f. Hiking with a backpack

   g. Inviting someone over to your house

   h. Painting your fence by yourself

   i. Refusing to look at someone's home

   j. Saying to someone: "Do you have any children?"

   k. Saying to someone: "What is your religion?"

   l. Shining your own shoes

   m. Speaking bluntly

   n. Telling a couple you'd like to see their new bathroom

   o. Washing your own clothes

   p. Wearing shorts or jeans and a t-shirt

Part 2   Reading Skills and Strategies

My Country

Before You Read

1 **Getting the Meaning of Words from Context and Structure** Working by yourself or with a partner, guess the meaning of the following italicized words or phrases and underline the correct definition for each. To help guess the meaning, determine if it has a suffix, if it's a compound word, and if you can examine how it is used in context.

1. Berton says that to a stranger the land must seem *endless*. (line 1) *Endless* means (full of variety / <u>stretching out in all directions</u>).

2. It is the *vastness* of Canada that surprises people. (line 4) *Vastness* means (beauty / large size).

3. The *observant* visitor will note some differences. (line 8) This means the visitor who (looks around / talks a lot).

4. The national *makeup* (line 9) refers to the Canadian (economy / character).

5. Berton talks about the American *melting pot*. (line 10) This means a society of people who become very (similar / different).

6. In July and August, eastern Canadians suffer in the heat and *humidity*. (line 17) *Humidity* means (wetness / dryness).

7. A *newcomer* (line 10) is someone who (wants to arrive / has just arrived).

8. Canada did not have a civil war, but it did have some *uprisings*. (line 27) Uprisings are (big revolutions / small battles).

9. The *lawmen* (line 31) are (robbers and murderers / sheriffs and policemen).

10. The author says that Americans are more *outgoing* than Canadians. (line 48) This means they are not as (shy / loud) as Canadians.

11. The *French-style* cooking of Quebec (line 61) means food prepared (for French people / in the French way).

Read

Strategy

Finding the Implied Main Idea of a Paragraph
Sometimes the main idea of a paragraph is not stated directly in one sentence. The main idea is *implied* (suggested by the facts, details, and ideas about the topic). A main idea brings together all or most of the different parts of the paragraph. It does not express just one part.

Introduction
The following excerpts are from a book by Pierre Berton, one of Canada's leading writers and a popular TV personality who wrote over 50 books before he passed away in 2004 at the age of 84. He was best known for his books on Canadian history. In this selection, Berton gives his personal reply to the question so often asked by visitors: "What is the difference between Canadians and Americans?"

- What do you know about Canadians?
- In what ways do you think they are different from Americans?

2 Reading an Article: Finding Implied Main Ideas Practice the skill of finding implied main ideas by analyzing the first five paragraphs of the following reading selection on pages 18–21. Most of its paragraphs do not have one sentence that describes the main idea. The main ideas are implied. Read each paragraph and the three phrases that follow it. Choose the phrase that best expresses the main idea.

▲ The North American continent consists of Canada, the United States and Mexico.

My Country (excerpts)

A   To a stranger, the land must seem endless. A herring gull, winging its way from St. John's, Newfoundland, to Victoria on the southern tip of Vancouver Island, will travel as far as the distance from London to Baghdad. It is the vastness that startles the imagination of all who visit my country.

5

1. What is the main idea of the paragraph above?

   (A) Canada is strange and surprising.
   (B) Canada is very, very big.
   (C) Canada is hard to know.

B   Contrary to common belief, we do not live in snow-covered cabins far from civilization. Most of us inhabit cities that do not seem to differ greatly from those to the south of us. The observant visitor, however, will note some differences. The variety of our national makeup is, I believe, more pronounced than it is in the American melting pot. A newcomer in the United States quickly learns to cover up his or her origins and become an American. A newcomer to Canada manages to keep something of the culture and customs of his or her ethnic background.

2. What is the main idea of the paragraph above?
- (A) Canadians appear to others as simple people who inhabit snow-covered cabins in the woods.
- (B) Canadians live in almost exactly the same way as Americans live but really there are differences.
- (C) All Canadians seem alike but they have more variety in their customs and culture than Americans.

C   Traditionally, the stranger has thought of Canada as a mountainous, snow-swept land. Certainly it can get very cold in Canada. Few non-Canadians understand that it can also get very hot. The eastern cities suffer in the humidity of July and August, and people actually die each year from the heat. In Victoria, roses bloom on Christmas Day.

3. What is the main idea of the paragraph above?
- (A) It can get very cold in Canada.
- (B) It can get very hot in Canada.
- (C) Roses can bloom on Christmas Day.

D   Where temperature is concerned we are a country of extremes; and yet, as a people, we tend toward moderation and even conservatism. Non-Canadians think we are the same as our American neighbors, but we are not really like the Americans. Our temperament, our social attitudes, our environment, and our history make us a different kind of North American.

4. What is the main idea of the paragraph above?
- (A) People think Canadians are like Americans, but Canadians are really more conservative and moderate.
- (B) Canada is a country of extremes, both in its temperatures and in the character of its people.
- (C) The Canadian temperament is like the American one because of social attitudes, environment, and history.

E First, there is the matter of our history. It has been called dull because it is not very bloody. We are, after all, the only people in all the Americas who did not separate violently from Europe. We have had three or four small uprisings but no revolution or civil war. 25

5. What is the main idea of the paragraph above?
- Ⓐ Canadian history is dull.
- Ⓑ Canadian history is bloody.
- Ⓒ Canadian history is not violent.

▲ The Royal Canadian Mounted Police (RCMP) has been an important force in keeping order in Canada.

F We were slow to give up our colonial ties to England. While the Americans chose freedom, we chose 30 order. Our lawmen are appointed from above, not elected from below. The idea of choosing town marshals and county sheriffs by vote to keep the peace with guns never fitted into the 35 Canadian scheme of things. Instead, we invented the North West Mounted Police. The Canadian symbol of the Mountie, neat and clean in his scarlet coat, contrasts with the American 40 symbol of the lawman in his open shirt and gun-belt. The two differing social attitudes persist to this day. In the United States, the settlers moved across the continent before law—hence the "wild" west. In Canada, the law 45 came first; settlement followed.

G Outward displays of emotion are not part of the Canadian style. We are, after all, a northern people. The Americans are far more outgoing than we are. One reason for this, I think, is the very real presence of nature in our lives. Most of us live within a few hours' drive of the wilderness. No 50 Canadian city is far removed from those mysterious and silent places that can have such an effect on the human soul.

H There is another aspect of my country that makes it unique in the Americas, and that is our bilingual and multicultural[1] makeup. (Canada has

---

[1]The original text said *bicultural*, but this has been changed to *multicultural* because in 1971, Canada's official policy changed from biculturalism to multiculturalism, although it still kept its two official languages. Canada was the first country in the world to establish an official government policy that recognizes and celebrates the heritages of all its peoples. This policy is defined as "multiculturalism within a bilingual framework."

two official languages, English and French, and in its largest province, a 55 majority of the inhabitants speak French almost exclusively.) It gives us a picturesque quality, of course, and that certainly helps tourism: Visitors are attracted to the "foreignness" of Quebec City, with its twisting streets and its 60 French-style cooking. But there is also a disturbing regional tension. Quebec has become a nation within a nation, and the separatist movement is powerful there.

▲ The main languages of bilingual Canada are English and French.

Canadians are not anti-American. We 65 watch American television programs. We tend to prefer American-made cars over the European and Asian products. We welcome hundreds of thousands of American tourists to our country every 70 year and don't complain much when they tell us that we're exactly the same as they are.

Of course, we're not the same. But the visitor may be pardoned for thinking so when he or she first crosses the border. The buildings in our 75 cities are designed in the international styles. The brand names in the supermarkets are all familiar. It is only after several days that the newcomer begins to sense a difference. He cannot put his finger on that difference, but then, neither can many of my fellow Canadians. The only thing we are really sure of is that we are not Americans. 80

Source: *My Country* (Pierre Berton)

After You Read

3 **Checking your Comprehension** Mark the following statements *T* (true) or *F* (false), according to Pierre Berton. Correct the false statements to make them true.

1. _____ Most Canadians live in snow-covered cabins far from civilization.

2. _____ In Canada, newcomers keep more of their original country's customs and culture than do newcomers in the United States.

3. _____ Canada is a very cold country, even in the summertime.

4. _____ The history of Canada is more bloody and violent than the history of the United States.

5. _____ Generally speaking, Canadians are more conservative than Americans.

6. _____ The "wild west," with its guns and sheriffs with open shirts, was an important part of American and Canadian history.

7. _____ Canadians express their emotions more openly than Americans do.

8. _____ The United States has only one official language, but Canada has two.

9. _____ In general, Canadians are anti-American, and Americans are anti-Canadian.

10. _____ Canadian buildings, food, and businesses look very different from those in the United States.

Strategy

Analyzing the Prefixes *Non-* and *Anti-*

A prefix is a group of letters at the beginning of a word that changes its meaning. Learning the meaning of some of the common prefixes, such as *non-* and *anti-*, can expand your vocabulary and reading comprehension.

- The prefix *non-* means "not."
- The prefix *anti-* means "against."

In the reading *My Country*, there are two words with hyphens that have the prefixes *non-* and *anti-* in them: *non-Canadians* and *anti-American*. (These prefixes are also used at times without hyphens.) So *non-Canadians* are "people who are not Canadians." Being *anti-American* means being "against Americans or things associated with Americans."

4 **Analyzing the Prefixes *Non-* and *Anti-*** Using the examples in the Strategy Box above as models, write definitions for the following words:

1. nonresidents _____

2. anti-anxiety pills _____

3. an antiwar protest _____

4. a nonviolent group _____

5. non-Germans _____

6. non-Mexicans _____

7. an anticommunist _____

8. nonvoters _____

9. antimonopoly laws _____

10. nonpayment _____

5 **Analyzing Four More Suffixes** Here are more common suffixes to add to your knowledge of English words. Study them and fill in the second example for each one.

1. **-ation**

   The suffix *-ation* means the "process or condition of some action or quality." It makes nouns out of verbs. If a couple is in the process of separating, they are going through a *separation.*

   If you are in the process of *decorating,* you are involved in _____.

2. **-ful**

   The suffix *-ful* means "full of or characterized by a certain quality." It makes adjectives out of nouns. Something full of beauty is *beautiful.*

   Something that can cause a lot of *harm* is _____.

3. **-ment**

   The suffix *-ment* means "something that results from the action of a verb." It makes nouns out of verbs. The things that people accomplish are *accomplishments.*

   The group of people who *govern* are members of the _____.

4. **-ous**

   The suffix *-ous* means "having or being full of some quality." It makes adjectives out of nouns. People who are full of fury become *furious.*

   A moment that is full of *glory* is a _____ moment.

6 **Making New Words by Adding Suffixes** Form words used in the reading by adding suffixes from the previous activity. Check your answers by finding the words in the reading. Line numbers are given in parentheses.

1. Our surroundings are our *environs.* Everything that is around us is our _____. (line 23)

2. Some countries are hard to *imagine.* It is difficult to see them in our _____. (line 4)

3. The head of that corporation has a lot of *power,* and he also has many _____ friends. (line 64)

4. Some people are *moderate.* They show _____ in their reactions. (line 20)

5. The place that *settlers* come to live is a _____. (line 46)

6. Many of the people who want to separate from their nation are on the *move* and hope to build a strong separatist _____. (line 64)

7. North America is filled with *mountains,* and its _____ regions attract many tourists. (line 14)

8. Certain natural spots seem full of *mystery* and their _____ atmosphere can have a strong effect on the human soul. (line 51)

7 **Focusing on Words from the Academic Word List** Read the paragraphs below from the reading in Part 2. Write the most appropriate word from the box in each of the blanks. One word is used twice. Do NOT look back at the reading right away; instead, first see if you can remember the vocabulary. Check your answers on page 20.

attitudes	displays	scheme	symbol
contrasts	removed	style	

F   We were slow to give up our colonial ties to England. While the Americans chose freedom, we chose order. Our lawmen are appointed from above, not elected from below. The idea of choosing town marshals and county sheriffs by vote to keep the peace with guns never fitted into the Canadian _____ of things. Instead, we invented the   5
1
North West Mounted Police. The Canadian _____ of the
2
Mountie, neat and clean in his scarlet coat, _____ with
3
the American _____ of the lawman in his open shirt and
4
gun-belt. The two differing social _____ persist to this
5
day. In the United States, the settlers moved across the continent before   10
law—hence the "wild" west. In Canada, the law came first; settlement followed.

G   Outward _____ of emotion are not part of the Canadian
6
_____ . We are, after all, a northern people. The Americans
7
are far more outgoing than we are. One reason for this, I think, is the very   15
real presence of nature in our lives. Most of us live within a few hours' drive of
the wilderness. No Canadian city is far _____ from those
8
mysterious and silent places that can have such an effect on the human soul.

8 **Guided Academic Conversation** In small groups, discuss three of the following four topics. Make sure that everyone in the group contributes to the discussion. Choose one person to report the group's ideas to the class.

1. **The effects of history on national character.** What countries in the Americas did not separate violently from a European colonial power? According to one of the writers in this chapter, what effect did this have on the character of the people? What wars or periods of violence do you know about that have had an effect on the character of a nation?

2. **The power of language.** How many official languages does Canada have? In your opinion, does it make a country weak or strong to have more than one official language? What other countries do you know of that have more than one official language? Are there any countries that you think should change their language policy?

3. **Actions of newcomers.** Does a newcomer to your culture have to cover up his or her origins? Do different groups keep some of their own culture or customs? There is an English proverb that says, "When in Rome, do as the Romans do." What do you think this means? Do you agree with it or not? Explain.

4. **The climate factor.** In your opinion, is there a connection between climate or geography and national character? Do these connections exist in your country? In large countries, how do you think that the character of the people changes with the region?

TOEFL® IBT

Focus on Testing

Analyzing Points of Contrast on Tests

The TOEFL® iBT often asks questions about points of contrast in a reading. These contrasts are usually between two ideas. Questions might also be about differences between events, styles, or groups of people.

To analyze points of contrast:

1. Fix firmly in your mind the two things that are being considered.

2. Look carefully for the ways in which the two are different. These are the points of contrast.

3. For each point, ask yourself exactly how the two things are different from each other.

4. Try to see how the many points of contrast add up to an overall idea.

Practice Analyze the points of contrast in the following paragraph from "My Country" by Pierre Berton. Read the paragraph. Then mark an X to indicate whether each point relates to Canadian or American society.

We were slow to give up our colonial ties to England. While the Americans chose freedom, we chose order. Our lawmen are appointed from above, not elected from below. The idea of choosing town marshals and county sheriffs by vote to keep the peace with guns never fitted into the Canadian scheme of things. Instead, we invented the North West Mounted Police. The Canadian symbol of the Mountie, neat and clean in his scarlet coat, contrasts with the American symbol of the lawman in his open shirt and gun-belt. The two differing social attitudes persist to this day. In the United States, the settlers moved across the continent before law—hence the "wild" west. In Canada, the law came first; settlement followed.

	Canadian	American
1. freedom rather than order	————	————
2. the neat and clean Mountie	————	————
3. order instead of freedom	————	————
4. sheriffs elected by vote	————	————
5. keeping the peace with guns	————	————
6. lawmen appointed from above	————	————
7. settlement before law	————	————
8. law before settlement	————	————
9. lawmen in scarlet coats	————	————
10. the "wild" west	————	————

9 **What Do You Think?** Read the paragraph below and in small groups discuss the questions that follow.

What to Wear?

When you travel to a new country, it's often difficult to decide what clothes to pack in your suitcase. If you are going on a business trip, chances are a man will bring a suit and tie, and a woman, a business suit. But what would you wear if you are doing business in the tropics? What would you wear to a wedding in India or Korea? What would you wear to a job interview in England or Australia? What would you wear to a barbecue in Canada? What would you wear to a dinner party in Japan? Although the world has become more casual, and less formal, there are still certain dress codes that should be followed.

▲ In many American companies, people dress informally.

1. What would be the best sources to go to to find out what to wear to a certain occasion in a certain country?

2. Have you ever been in a situation where you wore the wrong clothing and felt out of place? Explain.

3. Is there an international outfit for casual wear? What do you think is the most popular item of clothing in the world?

Part 3 Tying It All Together

1 Making Connections Read the questions below and choose one that interests you. Work by yourself to answer that question by finding facts and opinions on the Internet or in books at the library. Report your findings to the class.

1. Choose England, Ireland, Scotland, or some other country where English is spoken, and find information about its regional cooking. What are some special dishes from different regions? Give their names, key ingredients, and a brief description of them.

2. Choose Australia, New Zealand, India, or some other country where English is spoken. What are some of the most famous and interesting national parks in the country, and where are they located? What activities do people participate in? How do the seasons influence the activities?

3. If you were going to live in the U.S., where would you like to live? In what state and in what city or region? Give facts and statistics about this place, along with a physical description, and explain why you would like to live there.

4. If you were going to live in Canada, where would you like to live? In what province and in what city or region? Give facts and statistics about that place, along with a physical description, and explain why you would like to live there.

Responding in Writing

WRITING TIP: USING DETAILS TO SUPPORT YOUR IDEAS

Details are small points. They serve as examples or illustrations of a larger idea and make it convincing and understandable. For example, if you say, *Tornadoes can be very destructive*, you can then describe houses that have fallen down and trees with their roots in the air. These details support your main idea.

---

2 **Writing a Paragraph Using Details**   Write a clear paragraph in English about something you have learned in either Part 1 or Part 2 of this chapter. Follow these steps:

Step 1: Choose *one* of the following beginnings (depending on which part of the chapter you have chosen). Fill in the blank with a country you know well.

  A. From what I have learned in this chapter, I would say that living in the U.S. is different from living in _____ because . . .
  B. From what I have learned in this chapter, I would say that Canada is different from _____ because . . .

Step 2: Complete the sentence you chose by stating the *main reason* you find the life style described in Part 1 (or in Part 2) different from the one in another country.

Step 3: Go back to the selection you are discussing and reread it quickly, making a list of the *details* (small points) that illustrate or give examples of your reason.

Step 4: Choose the three or four details that are the most interesting or convincing.

Step 5: Write a sentence about each one.

Step 6: Check over what you have written. Do all the sentences support your main idea? Change any that do not seem right.

Step 7: Look at the spelling, grammar and vocabulary. Make your paragraph as correct, clear, and interesting as you can.

Self-Assessment Log

Read the lists below. Check (✓) the strategies and vocabulary that you learned in this chapter. Look through the chapter or ask your instructor about the strategies and words that you do not understand.

Reading and Vocabulary-Building Strategies

- ❑ Reading without knowing every word
- ❑ Analyzing paragraphs for the main idea and its development
- ❑ Understanding the meaning of words from context
- ❑ Analyzing suffixes
- ❑ Understanding compound words
- ❑ Using a continuum
- ❑ Getting the meaning of words from context and structure
- ❑ Finding the implied main idea of a paragraph
- ❑ Analyzing the prefixes *non-* and *anti-*

Target Vocabulary

Nouns

- ❑ attitudes*
- ❑ brevity*
- ❑ chores
- ❑ displays*
- ❑ driver
- ❑ environment*
- ❑ formality
- ❑ gardener
- ❑ heritage
- ❑ humidity
- ❑ imagination
- ❑ informality
- ❑ inhabitants
- ❑ lawmen
- ❑ makeup
- ❑ melting pot
- ❑ moderation
- ❑ movement
- ❑ nationalities
- ❑ newcomer

- ❑ non-Canadians
- ❑ responsibility
- ❑ scheme*
- ❑ settlement
- ❑ stigma
- ❑ style*
- ❑ symbol*
- ❑ uprisings
- ❑ vastness

Verbs

- ❑ assume*
- ❑ contrasts*
- ❑ refusing
- ❑ removed*

Adjectives

- ❑ acceptable
- ❑ anti-American
- ❑ blunt
- ❑ comfortable

- ❑ continental
- ❑ desirable
- ❑ do-it-yourself
- ❑ endless
- ❑ French-style
- ❑ household
- ❑ leisure
- ❑ menial
- ❑ mountainous
- ❑ mysterious
- ❑ observant
- ❑ occasional
- ❑ outgoing
- ❑ personal
- ❑ powerful
- ❑ restless

Adverb

- ❑ thoroughly

*These words are from the Academic Word List. For more information on this list, see www.vuw.ac.nz/lals/research/awl.

Chapter

Teamwork and Competition

In This Chapter

This chapter focuses on two important areas of world culture: sports and business. In sports and business, values that seem in some ways to be opposites—teamwork and competition—are in fact both crucial to success. In the first reading, the world-famous soccer player David Beckham describes the competition and teamwork that bring him success when he moves from England to join the Real Madrid soccer team in Spain. The second reading looks at how Kim Ssang Su, a talented Korean businessman, builds a globally competitive company by creating a sense of teamwork among his employees.

❝ Two heads are better than one. **❞**

—English proverb

Connecting to the Topic

1 Look at the photo and read the title of this chapter. Why do you think it's important for these people to work together as a team? Explain.

2 The paragraph on the opposite page states that both teamwork *and* competition are crucial to success in sports and business. Do you agree or disagree? Explain.

3 In what other areas of life do you think teamwork and competition play important roles? Why?

Beckham: An Autobiography

Before You Read

Strategy

Figuring Out Idiomatic Expressions and Specialized Terms

An *idiomatic expression* is a group of words with a meaning that is different from the meaning of each individual word, such as *get the drift* of something, which means to *understand the general idea* of something. Learning expressions like these will help you to understand conversations and read informal writing in English.

Specialized terms are the words associated with a particular area of knowledge; for example, in this chapter, sports terms. Readings and discussions relating to sporting events include their own specialized vocabulary. For example, you might hear this in a soccer game: *go for goal*, which means to *try and kick the ball in the net and get a goal, or a point.*

Often you can figure out the meanings of these words from their context.

1 **Getting the Meaning of Idiomatic Expressions from Context**

In the first reading, David Beckham and his coauthor use a number of common idiomatic expressions. Read the sentences below from Beckham's autobiography and try to figure out the closest meaning for the underlined idiomatic expressions in each sentence. Use the hints below each sentence to help you.

1. I took a knock or two during my first year in Madrid.
Hint: Usually to *knock* means to hit something, or it refers to the noise made when you hit something hard, such as *knocking on a door.* So, for someone to *take a knock or two* means:
  - (A) to leave quickly and with a lot of noise
  - (B) to knock on many doors, asking for help
  - (C) to have a hard time and to have problems
  - (D) to hit back at all the people who attack you

2. With the standards set by the club, you could never say you were in a comfort zone at Manchester United (the name of the team Beckham had played with before).
Hint: A *zone* means a particular area or space. So, to be *in a comfort zone* means:
  - (A) to feel safe and relaxed
  - (B) to feel nervous and worried
  - (C) be in the right part of the city
  - (D) to be on the wrong side of the field

3. Now I'd been <u>whisked off</u> to a new club in a new country . . .

Hint: *Whisk* means to move rapidly in a brushing or whipping motion, as when you are cooking and you *whisk* the eggs with a special wire utensil. To be *whisked off* means:

- Ⓐ to brush yourself off and get ready for something new
- Ⓑ to decide to leave everything behind and go far away
- Ⓒ to be told to accept a new position
- Ⓓ to be moved to a new place very quickly

4. Now I'd been whisked off and <u>didn't really have a clue</u> what was coming next.

Hint: When a detective tries to solve a murder, he or she looks for *clues* that will lead to a solution. To *not have a clue* means:

- Ⓐ to feel positive about the future
- Ⓑ to not know what to do
- Ⓒ to understand that life is always a mystery
- Ⓓ to search hard for the answer to a question

5. I was <u>bracing myself</u> for the challenge . . .

Hint: A *brace* is a device for keeping something firmly in place, such as a metal frame used to hold the pieces of a chair together while it is being glued, or a device for someone with a back problem to hold his or her back straight. To *brace oneself* means:

- Ⓐ to stop thinking about the future
- Ⓑ to stop thinking about the past
- Ⓒ to find a way to escape
- Ⓓ to prepare for something unknown or difficult

6. I'm confident in my own ability but, that summer morning at the training ground, there was a little <u>twist in the pit of my stomach</u>: it felt as though I'd arrived in Madrid with something to prove.

Hint: To *twist* means to turn or bend. So, a *twist* is something that has been turned or bent. The *pit* here means the deepest part. So, you may imagine from the context of the phrase above that to have a *twist in the pit of one's stomach* means:

- Ⓐ to feel very sick after eating some bad food
- Ⓑ to be in good shape and have strong stomach muscles
- Ⓒ to feel very nervous and uncomfortable
- Ⓓ to be happy and feel confident

7. The next day, I didn't need to understand the articles to <u>get the drift</u> of the headlines.

Hint: To *drift* means to be moved in one direction by a current, as in a river or ocean, and *get* means to grab or catch. To *get the drift of* something, then, means:

- Ⓐ to understand the general idea
- Ⓑ to understand completely
- Ⓒ to change the meaning of something
- Ⓓ to read a newspaper article

8. Almost from kick-off you could tell it was going to be our night.
   Hint: Notice that the use of "our" in the expression implies *belonging*, meaning that the night will belong to *our team*. From the context, it was going to *be our night* means:

   Ⓐ it was going to be late before the game would end
   Ⓑ it was going to get dark very soon
   Ⓒ we were going to lose that game
   Ⓓ everything was going to go well for us

9. I celebrated with a new set of teammates who'd already done everything they could to make me feel at home . . .
   Hint: Usually people feel relaxed and at ease in their own homes. So, to make someone *feel at home* means:

   Ⓐ to cause someone to think about childhood
   Ⓑ to help someone to feel comfortable
   Ⓒ to force someone to think about returning home
   Ⓓ to influence someone to be good

2 **Getting the Meaning of Specialized Terms from Context** Read the sentences and phrases from the reading in the column on the left. Match the underlined phrase with the correct definition in the column on the right.

1. _e_ Carlos took me off ten minutes into the second half.	**a.** hit the ball with my chest
2. _____ Almost from kick-off you could tell it was going to be our night.	**b.** hit, when the player connects with the ball in any way
3. _____ Ronaldo got away down the left wing . . .	**c.** kick the ball across the field
4. _____ I was thinking: he'll not cross it here.	**d.** move in front of other players
5. _____ He's bound to cut in . . .	~~**e.** removed me from the game~~
6. _____ and go for goal.	**f.** the center of the playing field
7. _____ He swung it over, through, and I could tell it was going to miss out Guti . . .	**g.** the left side of the field when facing the other team's net
8. _____ at the near post.	**h.** the player in charge of defending the net
9. _____ I could see the goalkeeper coming to challenge . . .	**i.** the side of the net nearest to the player
10. _____ My first touch of the game, . . .	**j.** the start of the game
11. _____ I chested the ball off . . .	**k.** to not reach
12. _____ to someone in midfield . . .	**l.** to try to put the ball in the net

Read

3 **Reading Without Knowing Every Word** As you read "Beckham: An Autobiography,"pay attention to the key vocabulary in bold blue type and use it in the activities that follow.

Reading Tip

Learning Sports-Related Terms
Learning sports-related terms will help you to read the second half of the selection in which Beckham describes playing two soccer matches. It can also prepare you to discuss team sports, to understand sports broadcasts, or to play sports with English-speaking teammates.

Introduction
The following reading passage is from the autobiography of David Beckham, from England, one of the world's most famous soccer players at the beginning of this millennium. He and his wife, Victoria Caroline Adams Beckham ("Posh Spice" of the musical group *The Spice Girls*) have three sons: Brooklyn (born 1999), Romeo (born 2002), and Cruz (born 2005). In this selection, he has just moved from England, where he had

▲ David Beckham

been playing for ten years on the Manchester United soccer team, to Spain to play on the Real (pronounced ray-AL) Madrid team. The Real Madrid players have the nickname "galacticos" (a Spanish word deriving from "galaxy," and so implying *huge*) because almost every player on the team is a world star. The story is written in British English and describes how Beckham and his new team competed in the seasonal soccer tournament in Spain.

- How do you think Beckham was feeling after moving to a new team in a new country? Why?

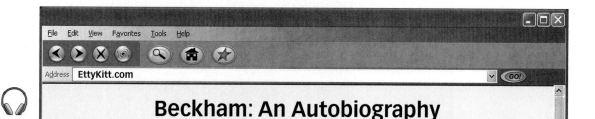

File Edit View Favorites Tools Help

Address **EttyKitt.com** GO!

Beckham: An Autobiography

A   I **took a knock or two** during my first year in Madrid. With the standards set by the club, you could never say you were **in a comfort zone** at Manchester United. But for 15 years, Old Trafford (stadium) had been home for me, as a soccer player at least. I knew how things worked and understood exactly what was expected of me. Now I'd been   5 whisked off to a new club in a new country and **didn't really have a clue** what was coming next. I was **bracing myself** for the challenge: unfamiliar surroundings, a different language, and another way of life. Soccer's soccer wherever you're playing it, of course, but I was pretty sure that training at Real would be very different to what I'd grown used 10 to back home. How much of what I'd learnt so far, as a player and as a person, was going to be of any use to me here?

B   It didn't help matters that I'd had some of the Spanish paper talk translated for me. Although I got the feeling that, in England, people wanted me to do well, some of the pundits here were saying that 15 Florentino Perez had just signed me to help the club shift replica shirts.* I'm confident in my own ability but, that summer morning at the training ground, there was a little **twist in the pit of my stomach**: it felt as though I'd arrived in Madrid with something to prove. For a start, I had the prospect of lining up alongside the *galacticos*. 20

C   I was still pretty nervous when the balls came out and we got down to training. Was it because of what other people might have been saying or was it me feeling a bit unsure of myself?

D   We had a *friendly*† against Valencia at the Mestella (Stadium) that didn't go well for me or the team. Then we were away to Real Mallorca 25 (Stadium) and just never found a shape or pattern. Worse for me, Carlos‡ **took me off** ten minutes into the second half. The next day, I didn't need to understand the articles to **get the drift** of the headlines. Basically, people were saying: *Is that it? If it is, what's he doing in Spain?*

▲ The Real Madrid soccer team

E   Everything that had gone wrong in Mallorca seemed to come right at   30
the Bernebeu (Stadium). Almost from **kick-off** you could tell it was
going to **be our night**. Raul and Ronaldo both scored and then, about a
quarter of an hour from the end, Ronaldo got away down the **left wing**. I
was on my way forward, but I was thinking: he'll not **cross it** here. He's
bound to **cut in** and **go for goal**. He swung it over, though, and I could   35
tell it was going to **miss out** Guti at **the near post**. As I jumped, I could
see the **goalkeeper** coming to challenge and just concentrated on
keeping my eyes open. It was a fantastic cross. I was in the right place
for the ball to hit me on the head and go in, without me having to direct it
at all. I could hardly believe it was happening. My first game at the   40
Bernebeu and I've just scored my first goal for Real Madrid.

F   The other players all rushed over towards me. Roberto Carlos
hugged me and lifted me off the ground. I think the rest of the team
understood what the moment meant to me. The Real crowd had been
great with me all night, never mind what doubts I'd had beforehand. My   45
first **touch** of the game, I **chested** the ball off to someone in **midfield**—
a simple touch to a team-mate—and the fans were all up on their feet
clapping and cheering.

G   I'd been so unhappy during my last few months at Old Trafford. Now,
in those few seconds as I celebrated with a new set of teammates who'd   50
already done everything they could to make me **feel at home**, I knew for
sure that by moving to Madrid, I'd done the right thing.

Source: "Football La Vida" from *Both Feet on the Ground: An Autobiography* (David
Beckham with Tom Watts)

---

*The word *pundits* refers (somewhat humorously) to journalists who think they know
everything. They are suggesting that the manager Florentino Perez has brought Beckham
to the team only because he is famous and his name will help sell t-shirts with the team
name on them.
†A *friendly* is British slang for a match that does not count as part of the season's
competition.
‡Carlos Queiroz, the coach of Real Madrid at the time.

After You Read

Strategy

Using a Graphic Organizer to Follow the Sequence of Events
One important element of any story is the plot, a series of events (or chain of
events) that lead to the story's conclusion. Following the various events in the
order (sequence) they occur is necessary for an overall understanding of the story.
In Activity 4, you will use a graphic organizer called a *chain of events diagram* to
take notes on key events from David Beckham's autobiography.

4 **Finding the Sequence of Events** Read the sentences below about the events described by Beckham in his autobiography. Then look through the reading to find the sequence (order) in which they occur. Write the letter for the event in the chain of events dagram below in the order in which they appear in the story. Write one letter in each box. Using a graphic organizer of this type helps to organize and retain information.

Key Events in the Selection from Beckham's Autobiography:

A. Beckham plays a great game at the Bernebeu stadium.

B. Public opinion seems to be asking what Beckham is doing in Spain, based on his poor performance so far.

C. A *friendly* [a non-official game] against the Valencia team at the Mestella stadium goes poorly for Beckham and his team.

D. Beckham leaves England and arrives in Spain to work with the Real Madrid team.

E. The crowd loves Beckham, and the fans clap and cheer for him.

F. The Spanish newspapers suggest that the team manager only signed on Beckham in order to sell more replica shirts (i.e. team merchandise).

G. A game at the Real Mallorca stadium goes poorly for Beckham and his team.

Beginning: First Event

Chain of Events Diagram

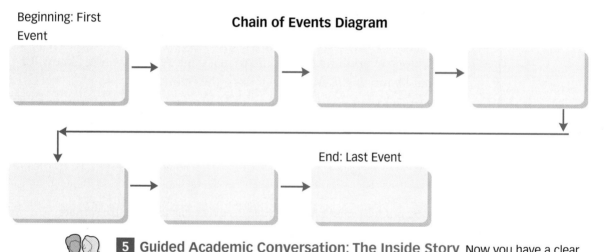

End: Last Event

5 **Guided Academic Conversation: The Inside Story** Now you have a clear picture of the sequence of events in Beckham's autobiography. He also describes his reactions to these events, what he is feeling inside.

Work with a classmate and follow the steps below.

1. Discuss Beckham's moods and emotions and how they change.

2. Number from 1 to 7 on a piece of paper and make a list of the seven events (in brief form) from Activity 3, leaving space between them.

3. After each event, write a brief description of how Beckham feels and why. Use words and expressions from the article as much as possible.

4. Finish up with a concluding sentence about the overall change in this man.

5. After you finish, compare your list with those of other classmates.

No, no, no! Not among yourselves!

▲ "Fight, team, fight!"

 6 Practicing Speaking by Doing Tasks Gain confidence and improve your speaking ability by doing one of the following tasks with a partner. Later, your teacher may ask you (or one of the other pairs) to role-play for the class.

1. *"Madrid Tonight" . . . and Three Months Later*

You are scriptwriters for the popular Spanish radio show *Madrid Tonight*. Make up two sets of interview questions for Beckham: 1) for when he first began with the Real Madrid soccer team and 2) for three months later. One person then plays the role of the radio announcer and the other the role of Beckham for the first interview. Change roles for the second interview.

2. *Only for Sports Fans: The Quick Draw*

This activity is for those who have some knowledge about soccer or have a very analytical mind. Pretend you are a coach, and draw a diagram of the field, players, goal, etc. on a sheet of paper to illustrate what happened in the play a quarter of an hour from the end of the game at the Bernebeu that was so important to Beckham. (See lines 33–41.) Then explain out loud in your own words to a partner what happened, pointing to the parts of your illustration as you give your explanation of this play. The partner then gives an explanation, using his/her drawing. Compare your drawings. Are they the same? Were your explanations similar?

3. *Tell Us Your Story!*

Have you ever felt that something (a sports game, a social event, a school assignment, or something else) was not going in your favor only to succeed in the end, as Beckham did here? Tell the story. This is the basis for the Spanish TV show, *Tell Us Your Story!* and you are the guest. (If nothing like this has ever happened to you, you can make up a story.) Be sure to tell about your emotions as well as the events, and don't be afraid to be "dramatic." Your classmate will be the TV host who introduces you and asks you questions. After you finish, reverse roles and start over.

7 **What Do You Think?** Read the paragraph and discuss the questions that follow.

The Olympics

▲ The Olympic Games are based on an ancient ritual that started in Greece.

The Olympic games are based on an ancient ritual started in Greece some time in the ninth Century B.C.E. (Before Common Era, referring to the year 1.) The modern Olympic games began again in 1896 and, except for one cancellation during WWII, have continued every four years until the present time. Winter Olympics are two years behind Summer Olympics and also repeat in a four-year cycle. From all over the world, the best athletes come to compete to establish the champion of champions. Everyone seems to have a wonderful time. Yet the Olympics are not without controversy.

1. In what country did the Olympic games begin?

2. How long have the modern Olympic games been going on, and how often are they held?

3. Why do you think many countries want to host these games? In your opinion, are they good or bad for the world community? Explain.

4. Should professional (paid) athletes be allowed to compete, or should the games be limited to amateurs?

Part 2 Reading Skills and Strategies

Outward Bound

Language Tip

Learning the specialized terms related to business can help you when you read or have discussions about business.

Before You Read

1 **Using the Context to Infer the Meanings of Words** Guess the meanings of the words in the sentences on pages 41–42 from their context or from clues within the words themselves. Choose the correct answer.

1. Kim Ssang Su is <u>CEO</u> of LG Electronics, Inc.
   - (A) the owner
   - (B) an outstanding employee
   - (C) the chief executive officer
   - (D) an assistant accountant

2. The managers seem happy that Kim has spent the day lecturing and <u>rallying</u> them.
   - (A) organizing and encouraging
   - (B) insulting and blaming
   - (C) boring
   - (D) complaining about

3. Kim Young Kee is a <u>V.P.</u> of LG Electronics.
   - (A) coordinator of prices
   - (B) Very important Person
   - (C) admirer
   - (D) Vice President

4. LG's <u>revenues</u> jumped 18% last year, to $17 billion, and net profits rose 33%, to $556 million.
   - (A) interest on their debts
   - (B) earnings before expenses and taxes are deducted
   - (C) earnings after expenses and taxes are deducted
   - (D) salaries for employees

5. LG's revenues jumped 18% last year, to $17 billion, and <u>net profits</u> rose 33%, to $556 million.
   - (A) interest on their debts
   - (B) earnings before expenses and taxes are deducted
   - (C) earnings after expenses and taxes are deducted
   - (D) salaries for employees

6. Kim wants to lift LG up to the level of the biggest companies that have <u>global brands.</u>
   - (A) huge buildings and equipment
   - (B) more than 10,000 employees on their payroll
   - (C) names and symbols known around the world
   - (D) giant computer networks

7. The advanced Korean market provides <u>a testing ground</u> for new technologies.
   - (A) a large amount of soil for planting
   - (B) a group of skilled scientists and technicians
   - (C) a laboratory for creating new inventions
   - (D) a place to try out the latest products

8. Kim grew up on a farm and admits to being more comfortable visiting <u>factories</u> than in his spacious office in Seoul.

    (A) manufacturing plants where products are built

    (B) places where products are stored

    (D) centers where ad campaigns are planned

    (D) administration offices

Strategy

Scanning

Scanning is reading quickly to find particular bits of information. When you read for business, numbers are important. You can pick up information about business by scanning for numbers and seeing what they mean.

To scan, follow these steps:

- Think of what you are looking for.
- Move your eyes quickly through the text until you find it. Do not pay attention to anything else.
- Stop and record the information.

2 Scanning for Numbers Scan the reading on pages 43–45 for the numbers needed to fill in the blanks below.

1. Kim Ssang Su is _____ years old.

2. He began his career _____ years ago.

3. LG Electronics' revenues for last year were _____ dollars, and its net profits were_____ dollars.

4. Samsung Electronics, LG's biggest competitor, had revenues of _____ dollars.

5. In Korea, _____% of households using the Internet have high-speed access.

6. Kim took over LG's appliance business in the year _____.

7. Under his guidance, sales in LG's appliance business reached _____ dollars last year.

8. Kim likes to hold breakfast meetings for top executives at _____ A.M. every morning.

Introduction

Just like sports, the world of business also runs on teamwork and competition. The following selection tells the story of a Korean businessman who uses some very unusual methods to inspire his team of workers and create a strongly competitive company. You may be surprised to find where he comes from and interested to learn how he and his company are moving outwards and expanding toward global success.

- What methods can you think of to inspire people to work together?
- For you, personally, what inspires you to work with others?

Outward Bound
Call Kim Ssang Su a Man of the People

A On a chilly night in the mountains south of Seoul, Kim, CEO of LG Electronics, Inc., holds a paper cup filled with *soju*, a clear, sweet Korean drink with a vicious bite. Surrounding him are a dozen of the 300 LG suppliers' managers whom Kim has spent the day lecturing and rallying. They have also been hiking up a snow-covered mountainside—necessary 5 training, he says, for the grand plans he has for South Korea's second largest electronics firm. At the end of the day, he treats a group of employees to an outdoor barbecue of grilled pork and bowls of fiery red kimchi. "Great people! Great company!" he barks. "Great company! Great company!" they chant back. 10

B When dancing girls in short skirts and blond wigs start jiggling to ear-numbing Korean pop music, the tireless Kim, 59, cavorts in a mosh pit* of workers near a stage. Later he ascends the stage himself, microphone in hand, to croon out a popular oldie called *Nui* (Sister). "We love our CEO," says Kim Young Kee, an LG executive V.P. "He shows us a good time." 15

---

*A mosh pit is an area right beside the stage where music is performed and where audience members "slamdance," a type of dancing where people bump into each other in time to the music.

C   CEOs rarely stoop to carouse with the common man in an Asia dominated by secretive business clans. But Kim is no ordinary Asian boss.

▲ Kim Ssang Su lecturing and inspiring his employees.

He began his career 35 years ago as a nondescript engineer at an LG refrigeration factory, climbed the ranks and claimed the CEO post in October. Now he aims to duplicate the same feat with LG—lifting a company little known outside Asia into the stratosphere of global brands with Sony, Panasonic, and Samsung. "I want to go down in LG history," says Kim. "After death, a tiger leaves its skin. A man leaves his name."

D   LG seems well on its way. Revenues jumped 18% last year, to $17 billion, and net profits rose 33%, to $556 million. Last year, LG was the world's largest seller of mobile phones operating on the CDMA standard, which allows more people to use a network at the same time. It makes dazzling flat-screen TVs and other leading-edge gadgets.

E   LG faces plenty of competition. Its biggest rival at home and abroad, Samsung Electronics, whose revenues of $36.4 billion are two times as large as LG's, has already hit the U.S.—and scored big successes. Samsung is also ahead of LG in developing a truly global brand.

F   In this new digital world, LG has a distinct advantage in its ultra-wired South Korean home base. The demanding Korean market, where an amazing 84% of households using the Internet have high-speed access, propels LG to develop more advanced products and provides a testing ground for new technologies. LG has outpaced Nokia and Motorola in cramming the hottest new features into its mobile phones. Its latest model, the SC8000, combines a PDA, an MP3 player, a digital camera, and a camcorder.

G   It may seem odd that LG has turned over its top job to a farm boy from a tiny village in eastern South Korea. Kim Ssang Su spent his childhood knee-deep in the family's rice paddies. He admits to being more comfortable visiting factory floors than in his spacious office overlooking Seoul's Han River.

H   It would be wrong, though, to underestimate Kim, who has become near legend in Seoul for the turnaround he engineered at LG's appliance business. When he took over in 1996, LG was making washing machines and refrigerators for low-cost Chinese companies. Kim sliced costs by moving production of low-end products to China. He proved there is room for innovation, introducing, for example, appliances like air conditioners that can be controlled from the Internet. The result: sales reached $4.7 billion last year, more than twice the number when Kim took control. 60

Kim is infusing LG's other businesses with the same vigor. Called a "commander in the field" by executives, he storms about LG's factories and offices poring over details, issuing commands and spurring on the staff by giving them what he terms "stretch goals." Awake at 5:30 each morning for 65 a brisk walk, he openly prefers "morning people" and holds 7 A.M. breakfast meetings with top executives. "I don't like the expression 'nice,'" Kim says, "I don't want LG to be perceived as nice. None of the great companies in the world are nice."

Source: "Outward Bound" *Time Magazine* (Michael Schuman)

Time, Inc. All rights reserved. Reprinted by permission. For the complete article, see pages 246-248.

After You Read

3 **Selecting the Main Idea** Circle the number of the statement below that you think best expresses the main idea of "Outward Bound." Why is it better than the other two?

Reading Tip
Main Idea Remember that the main idea of a piece of writing (a paragraph, an article, a book) brings together all or most of the different parts of that piece of writing. It does not express the idea of just one part.

1. LG Electronics is South Korea's second largest electronics firm and now seems to be increasing its revenues at a rate that is much faster than that of its competitors.

2. Kim Ssang Su rose from being a farm boy in a tiny village to CEO of LG Electronics, and his unique character and skills are mainly responsible for this company's growing success.

3. Kim Ssang Su provided a great inspiration for the managers of his 300 suppliers at the rally and party he organized for them, as well as giving them food, drink, entertainment and personal contact.

Strategy

Understanding Metaphors

Another aspect of readings that presents a challenge in a second language is the metaphor. A metaphor is an implied (suggested) comparison made by using a

▲ *Soju* is a Korean drink with a vicious bite.

word or phrase associated with one thing to describe something completely different. For example, in the reading, *soju* is described as a "Korean drink with a vicious bite." A drink does not bite, of course. But the taste of the drink is similar to the strength of a bite by a person or a wild animal. Personification, presenting a thing with the qualities of a person, is one type of metaphor. Metaphors add interest and sometimes humor to writing. <u>The taste of a drink</u> is being compared to <u>the bite of a wild animal.</u>

4 **Understanding Metaphors** Metaphors are often implied (suggested) through the verb in a sentence. Below are examples of sentences showing the common usage of certain verbs. These verbs are also used as metaphors in the reading selection. Work alone or with a partner and find the examples from the reading selection using this same verb as a metaphor. Look for the meaning in the surrounding sentences. Then explain what is being compared to what. The first one is done as an example.

1. common usage of *barks*: The dog <u>barks</u> as people pass the yard.

   Usage in the article :<u>"Great people! Great company!" he barks.</u> (see line 9)

   metaphor:<u>The way Kim shouts</u> is being compared to <u>the barking of a dog.</u>

2. common usage of *jumped*: The horse <u>jumped</u> over the fence.

   usage in the article: _____ . (see line 30)

   metaphor: _____ is being compared to _____ .

3. common usage of *chant*: The people in the temple <u>chant</u> religious songs.

   usage in the article: _____ . (see line 10)

   metaphor:_____ is being compared to _____ .

4. common usage of *cavorts*: The young calf <u>cavorts</u> in the field. [cavort = leap and prance around]

usage in the article: _____ . (see line 12)

metaphor: _____ is being compared to _____ .

5. common usage of *sliced*: The boy <u>sliced</u> (cut with a knife) some cheese for his sandwich.

usage in the article: _____ . (see line 57)

metaphor: _____ is being compared to _____ .

6. common usage of *to storm*: As it was <u>storming</u> outside, we stayed in the house, listening to the thunder and rain.

usage in the article: _____ . (see line 63)

metaphor: _____ is being compared to _____ .

USING COMPOUND ADJECTIVES

English has many compound adjectives: words made up of two smaller words connected by a hyphen. Usually you can guess the meaning by breaking the word into the two smaller words. The article about Kim uses several compound adjectives. For example, it talks about *leading-edge gadgets*. A *gadget* is a small device or object. This phrase is related to the idea of competition. Can you guess what kind of a gadget is a *leading-edge* gadget*?

---

5 **Using Compound Adjectives** Match each compound adjective on the left to the noun it is modifying on the right. You can scan the article to find each compound adjective and noun. Be prepared to explain the meaning if called upon.

1. _____ ear-numbing
2. _____ flat-screen
3. _____ high-speed
4. _____ knee-deep
5. _____ low-cost
6. _____ low-end
7. _____ snow-covered

a. access
b. Chinese companies
c. TVs
d. products
e. pop music
f. mountainside
g. in rice paddies

---

*The adjective *cutting-edge* is often used with the same meaning.

6 **Inferring Meaning: Same or Opposite?** Each of the following words in Column 1 is from the article on pages 43–45. Each is followed by a word or phrase in Column 2 that is a synonym (almost the same in meaning) or an antonym (almost the opposite). Check the box for either *Synonym* or *Antonym* in Column 3. For a word you are not sure about, scan the reading and use the context to infer its meaning.

Words from the Article	Other Words	Synonym or Antonym?	
1. ascend	move down	☐	☑
2. chilly	cold	☐	☐
3. croon	scream	☐	☐
4. duplicate	copy	☐	☐
5. goals	objectives	☐	☐
6. innovation	same old thing	☐	☐
7. nondescript	ordinary	☐	☐
8. oldie	new song	☐	☐
9. spur on	discourage	☐	☐
10. stoop	bend over	☐	☐
11. stratosphere	underground	☐	☐
12. tireless	lazy	☐	☐
13. turnaround	complete change	☐	☐
14. vicious	cruel and nasty	☐	☐
15. vigor	weakness	☐	☐

7 **Focusing on Words from the Academic Word List** Use the most appropriate word from the box to fill in each of the blanks below in the paragraph taken from Part 2. Do NOT look back at the reading right away; instead, first see if you can remember the vocabulary. Then check your answers on pages 44–45.

goals	innovation	odd	underestimate
job	issuing	perceived	

G   It may seem _____ that LG has turned over its top

_____ to a farm boy from a tiny village in eastern South
   2

Korea. Kim Ssang Su spent his childhood knee-deep in the family's rice

paddies. He admits to being more comfortable visiting factory floors than

in his spacious office overlooking Seoul's Han River.   5

H	It would be wrong, though, to _____ Kim, who has
3

become near legend in Seoul for the turnaround he engineered at LG's

appliance business. When he took over in 1996, LG was making washing

machines and refrigerators for low-cost Chinese companies. Kim sliced

costs by moving production of low-end products to China. He proved there	10

is room for _____, introducing, for example, appliances
4

like air conditioners that can be controlled from the Internet. The result:

sales reached $4.7 billion last year, more than twice the number when Kim

took control.

I	Kim is infusing LG's other businesses with the same vigor. Called a	15

"commander in the field" by executives, he storms about LG's factories and

offices poring over details, _____ commands and spurring
5

on the staff by giving them what he terms "stretch _____."
6

Awake at 5:30 each morning for a brisk walk, he openly prefers "morning

people" and holds 7 A.M. breakfast meetings with top executives. "I don't	20

like the expression 'nice,'" Kim says, "I don't want LG to be

_____ as nice. None of the great companies in the world
7

are nice."

8 **Guided Academic Conversation** In small groups, discuss three of the
following four topics. Write a group opinion statement about them.

1. Kim, the Man

What kind of a man is Kim? How is he different from the bosses at many firms?
Where did he grow up? How have his circumstances changed during his life?
What do we know about his tastes and preferences? What animals are
mentioned or suggested in the article in reference to his actions? What do
others call him or say about him?

2. Kim's Leadership Style

Would you describe Kim's style as strong or weak? Explain. Why does he make his
managers hike up a mountainside and call it "necessary training" for his plans for
the company? And why the party afterwards? What tactics does he use, according
to the article, that have helped him make LG Electronics more competitive?

3. Kim and his Company

Write down a list of all the different devices LG Electronics makes that you can find listed in this article. What is the function of each of these items? Which one of these would you most like to receive as a present and why? How does LG have a competitive edge with each of the devices you listed? How did he cause a turnaround in LG's appliance business?

4. Your Personal Reaction to Kim

Kim said in the article, "After death, a tiger leaves its skin. A man leaves his name." How do you think Kim wants people to think about his name? Is it important for people to leave a name for themselves in the world? How would you want people to remember you in the future? Why doesn't Kim like the word "nice"? Do you agree with him? What actions of his do you admire? Are there any of his actions that you dislike? Would you like to work in a company run by Kim? Why or why not? Explain.

Part 3   Tying It All Together

1 **End-of-Chapter Debate** Competition over teamwork? Teamwork over competition? Which of these is more important in the selection "Outward Bound"? Think about this for a couple of minutes. Your teacher will write *Competition* on one side of the board and *Teamwork* on the other side. Then you and your classmates will take a stand, literally. You will walk over and stand beside the word that you consider indicates the more important factor. Once there, your teacher may ask you why you chose the way you did. What will you say?

Now, think back to the first selection of the chapter, "Beckham: an Autobiography". If asked the same question, will you stay where you are or will you move? Why?

2 **Making Connections** Do some research on the Internet and take notes on one of the following topics and type in key words. Visit two or more sites. Share your results with the class or in a small group.

1. How has David Beckham's life changed since this autobiography was written in 2004? How is he doing now and how does the press view him?

2. Who is Zinedine Zidane, and what is his connection to the Real Madrid team? What was his role in the 1998 World Cup Championship? What was his role in the 2006 World Cup Championships? What is he doing now and how does the world press view him?

▲ Zinedine Zidane was instrumental in the outcome of the 1998 World
Cup and helped lead the French team to the finals in 2006.

3. What is new with Kim Ssang Su? Is he still the CEO of LG Electronics? What
   can you find out about him, his family, and his life in general?

4. Who are the CEOs of some of the other successful electronics companies? Are
   there any women among them? What is their average age? Do any of them have
   unusual or interesting styles of management?

Responding in Writing

WRITING TIP: DESCRIBING PEOPLE BY USING ADJECTIVES

You can describe a person with adjectives that represent his or her most outstanding
qualities. Then illustrate each of these with one or more concrete examples.

Example: *Ellen is a very generous person. She donates to several charities and
volunteers twice a week at a local hospital.*

---

3 **Writing and Using Adjectives** Write a paragraph that describes Kim Ssang
Su or David Beckham. This is like painting a portrait (a picture of a person) in words.
Follow these steps.

Step 1: Write down the name of the person you are going to describe. Look back at
the article about him and make a list of his most important qualities
(characteristics).

Step 2: Begin by writing *is* after his name and three or four adjectives that express
his main qualities or characteristics. (You may find these adjectives in the article or
you may have to think them up for yourself after you read about the actions and
words of the person you are describing.)

Step 3: Reread the article and find at least one detail that illustrates each of the
adjectives you mentioned.

Step 4: Scan the selection for the words and phrases that are in boldface and try to use them in your sentences.

Step 5: Check over what you have written to catch and correct any mistakes.

Step 6: Think of a clever, funny, or interesting title and write it at the top of the page.

Focus on Testing

General Testing Practice

Many standardized tests include multiple choice questions. There are strategies you can use when taking a multiple choice test.

1. Read the answers first.
2. Look for an answer that seems right and completes the question smoothly. If the question asks why something happened, then the answer must indicate a cause.
3. Try to eliminate any answers that are clearly wrong.
4. Notice the wording of questions. Look for qualifying phrases such as "which of the answers below is not true."
5. Statistically, the least likely correct answer on a multiple-choice question is the first choice.
6. When in doubt, pick the longer of two answers.
7. Always choose an answer, even if you're not sure which one is correct.

The following sample includes two sections from a test on reading comprehension. They are similar to sections on standardized exams given at many universities. You may find this test tricky. Most people can improve their scores on this kind of exam through practice.

After finishing, correct your work. Try to understand why you made the mistakes that you did.

Practice Section 1 (Questions 1–7) The questions in this part are based on two paragraphs about historical events. Choose the one best answer, and fill in the correct oval. Answer all questions according to what is stated directly or implied in the paragraph.

Paragraph 1:

An Augustinian monk named Gregor Mendel was the first person to make precise observations about the biological mechanism of inheritance. This happened a little over 100 years ago in an Austrian monastery, where Mendel spent his leisure hours performing experiments with pea plants of different types. He crossed them carefully and took notes about the appearance of various traits, or characteristics, in succeeding generations. From his observations, Mendel formed a set of rules, now known as the Mendelian Laws of Inheritance, which were found to apply not only to plants but to animals and human beings as well. This was the beginning of the modern science of *genetics*.

1. The importance of Gregor Mendel is that he was the first person to _____ .
   - (A) imagine that there existed a precise mechanism for inheritance
   - (B) approach the problem of inheritance scientifically
   - (C) think about why animals and plants inherit certain characteristics
   - (D) invent the word genetics

2. When did Mendel perform his experiments?
   - (A) in ancient times
   - (B) in the 1680s
   - (C) in the 1860s
   - (D) at the beginning of last century

3. Why did Mendel do this work?
   - (A) He formed a set of rules.
   - (B) He enjoyed it.
   - (C) He lived in Austria.
   - (D) He was paid for it.

4. The Mendelian Laws of Inheritance describe the transmission of biological traits in _____ .
   - (A) plants
   - (B) animals
   - (C) human beings
   - (D) all of the above

Paragraph 2:

The magnificent warship Wasa, which sank after a maiden "voyage" of some 1,500 yards, was salvaged and restored, after lying at the bottom of Stockholm's harbor for over 330 years. The ship now rests in the National Maritime Museum of that city.

5. The Wasa sank around the year _____ .
   - (A) 1330
   - (B) 1500
   - (C) 1650
   - (D) 1960

6. Which of the following statements about the Wasa is probably not true?
   - (A) It met with a catastrophe shortly after being built.
   - (B) It carried many soldiers and cannons.
   - (C) It was a veteran of many hard-fought battles.
   - (D) It was raised by modern salvaging techniques.

7. The Wasa ship appears to be _____ .
   - (A) Swedish
   - (B) Dutch
   - (C) American
   - (D) British

Practice Section 2 (Questions 8–10) In questions 8–10, choose the answer that is closest in meaning to the original sentence. Notice that several of the choices may be factually correct, but you should choose the one answer that is the closest restatement of the given sentence.

8. No hour is too early or too late to call Jenkins Plumbing Company.
   - (A) Jenkins Plumbing Company does not answer calls that are too early or too late.
   - (B) Jenkins Plumbing Company accepts calls at any hour of the day or night.
   - (C) Whether you call early or late, Jenkins Plumbing Company will come in one hour.
   - (D) If you call at an early hour, Jenkins Plumbing Company will never be late.

9. When TV first became available to large numbers of Americans in the 1950s and 1960s, most producers ignored its possibilities as a tool for education.
   - (A) In the 1950s and 1960s, there were not many educational programs on American TV.
   - (B) Until the 1950s and 1960s, most of the TV programs in the United States were tools for education.
   - (C) After the 1950s and 1960s, most American producers did not see the educational possibilities of TV.
   - (D) During the 1950s and 1960s, educational programs first became available to Americans.

10. In spite of the high interest rates on home loans, the couple did not change their plans to buy a new house.
    - (A) High interest rates caused the couple to change their plans about buying a house.
    - (B) The couple did not buy the house because of the high interest rates.
    - (C) Since interest rates were no longer high, the couple bought the house.
    - (D) Although the interest rates were high, the house was bought by the couple.

Self-Assessment Log

Read the lists below. Check (✓) the strategies and vocabulary that you learned in this chapter. Look through the chapter or ask your instructor about the strategies and words that you do not understand.

Reading and Vocabulary-Building Strategies

- ❏ Figuring out idiomatic expressions and specialized terms
- ❏ Using a graphic organizer to follow the sequence of events
- ❏ Using the context to infer the meanings of words
- ❏ Scanning
- ❏ Selecting the main idea
- ❏ Understanding metaphors
- ❏ Using compound adjectives
- ❏ Inferring meaning: same or opposite?

Target Vocabulary

Nouns
- ❏ CEO
- ❏ factories
- ❏ global brands
- ❏ goals*
- ❏ innovation*
- ❏ job*
- ❏ mountainside
- ❏ net profits
- ❏ oldie
- ❏ revenues*
- ❏ stratosphere
- ❏ testing ground
- ❏ turnaround
- ❏ vigor
- ❏ V.P.

Verbs
- ❏ ascends
- ❏ barks
- ❏ cavorts
- ❏ chant
- ❏ croon
- ❏ duplicate
- ❏ issuing*
- ❏ jumped
- ❏ perceived*
- ❏ rallying
- ❏ sliced
- ❏ stoop
- ❏ storms
- ❏ underestimate*

Adjectives
- ❏ chilly
- ❏ ear-numbing
- ❏ flat-screen
- ❏ high-speed
- ❏ knee-deep
- ❏ leading-edge
- ❏ low-cost
- ❏ low-end
- ❏ nondescript
- ❏ odd*
- ❏ snow-covered
- ❏ tireless
- ❏ vicious

Idioms and Expressions
- ❏ be our night
- ❏ bracing myself
- ❏ chested
- ❏ cross it
- ❏ cut in
- ❏ didn't (don't) really have a clue
- ❏ feel at home
- ❏ get the drift
- ❏ go for goal
- ❏ goalkeeper
- ❏ in a comfort zone
- ❏ kick-off
- ❏ left wing
- ❏ midfield
- ❏ miss out
- ❏ (the) near post
- ❏ spurring on
- ❏ took (take) a knock or two
- ❏ took (take) me off
- ❏ touch
- ❏ twist in the pit of my stomach
- ❏ whisked off

*These words are from the Academic Word List. For more information on this list, see www.vuw.ac.nz/lals/research/awl.

Gender and Relationships

In This Chapter

In many parts of the world, the last half of the 20th century led to dramatic changes in families and personal relationships in general. The consequences of these changes have spilled over into the new millennium. The first selection addresses one of the biggest social concerns of our times, the care of children in families with two working parents. It discusses how people are coping with the problem in the United States. This is followed by statistical charts with information on the changing makeup of what we call a family. The second selection talks about a Russian business which exports a surprising product: "mail-order" brides.

❝ A life without love is as bleak as a year without summertime. **❞**

—Swedish proverb

1. Look at the family in the photo. What do you think they are doing?

2. This chapter examines some of the changes in families since the middle of the 20th century. How have families changed in your culture during this time?

3. In your country, who typically takes care of the children? Do you know any men who stay at home to care for their children?

Who's Taking Care of the Children?

Before You Read

Strategy

Skimming for the General Idea

You can find the general idea of a reading selection by *skimming*. Follow these steps to find the general idea of a reading selection quickly.

1. Move your eyes rapidly over the whole piece, taking note of the title, headings, photos, and captions.

2. Read the first and last line of the long paragraphs. In the shorter ones, look at just a few key words in each line, the ones that seem to carry the message, then go on.

3. Try to summarize the general idea in two or three sentences.

1 **Skimming for the General Idea** Skim the following article, "Who's Taking Care of the Children?" Then circle the number of the summary below that best expresses what the whole reading is about. Why is it better than the other two?

1. In the United States, most women want to be professionals and work as doctors, lawyers, executives, engineers, or in sales or education. They depend on their families to help them with child care as they try to break through the "glass ceiling." The husband is no longer the only breadwinner.

2. In the United States, most mothers need day-care centers, or nannies to watch their children while they work outside of the home. Times have changed, and the definition of *family* has expanded. The increased role of fathers in child care and the option of working from home are new trends.

3. In the United States, most couples are influenced by monetary factors and are employed full time, part time, or in job-sharing positions. Many husbands and wives both work outside the home, do household chores, and stay at home with the children. Sometimes they care for children from former marriages.

Introduction

The following article discusses the big changes that have occurred in the family life and personal relationships of people in the United States in the last several decades. Today, young men and women work, socialize, and raise their children in ways that often seem surprising to their parents and grandparents.

- In your opinion, how is the life style of young people today in your culture different from that of your parents and grandparents?
- What changes have occurred in family life and personal relationships?
- What changes do you think will be described in the article?

Who's Taking Care of the Children?

A   Around the world, more and more women are working outside the home. In the United States, around 70 percent of women with children under 18 have another job besides that of mother and homemaker. Most are employed in traditional fields for females, such as clerical, sales, education, and service. However, a growing number choose a career that 5 necessitates spending many hours away from home. These women are engineers, politicians, doctors, lawyers, and scientists, and a few have begun to occupy executive positions in business, government, and banking, breaking through the so-called **glass ceiling**.

B   Monetary factors influence women to work. Some are employed full 10 time, some part time, and some seek creative solutions such as **flex-time** work schedules and **job sharing**. Many are single mothers raising children by themselves. But in most cases, one income in the household is simply not enough, so both parents must work to support the family.

C   A backward glance from this side of the new millennium reveals that the 15 role of married women in the U.S. has changed **radically** since the 1950s and 1960s, when it was taken for granted that they would stay home and raise the children. This is still the image so often **portrayed** in American movies and advertising. In fact, the traditional combination of the husband as exclusive **breadwinner** and the wife as a **stay-at-home** mom caring for 20 one or two children today accounts for only ten percent of the population in the United States.

D   Who, then, is taking care of the children?

E   When **extended families**—children, parents, grandparents, aunts, and uncles—lived in the same town and sometimes in the same house, a relative of the working parents took care of the children. But beginning with the Industrial Revolution, people moved away from farms and small towns to find better job opportunities in larger cities. Now, most often, the family is just the **immediate family**—mother, father, and children. Or, it could be a single-parent family, with either the mother or the father living with the children. Another variation is the **blended family**, the result of a marriage between a previously married man and woman who combine the children from their former marriages into a new family.

F   So who watches the children while the parents work? Answers to this question are varied.

- Some parents put children in day-care facilities.
- Some parents put children in informal day-care centers in private homes.
- Companies and hospitals are realizing that providing day care at the workplace makes for happier and more productive employees.
- Individuals or couples that are wealthy enough have a **nanny**, a woman who comes to care for the children in their own home. Many of these child-care workers are from other countries, e.g., South America, Eastern Europe, the Caribbean, and the Philippines.

G   A **trend** that has emerged recently is the sharing of child-care responsibilities between husband and wife. Young couples will try to arrange their work schedules so that they work opposite hours or shifts in order that one parent is always home with the children. Since child care is expensive, this saves money for the young couple trying to establish themselves and provide a secure environment for the family. Husband and wife may also share household chores. Some fathers are just as capable as mothers at cooking dinner, changing and bathing the baby, and doing the laundry.

H   In some cases, the woman's salary is for family expenses, and the father becomes the "**househusband**." These cases are still fairly rare. One positive trend, however, is that fathers seem to be spending more time with their children. In a recent survey, 41% of the children sampled said they spend equal time with their mothers and fathers. "This is one of our most significant cultural changes," says Dr. Leon Hoffman, who co-directs the Parent Child Center at the New York Psychoanalytic Society. In practice for over 30 years, Hoffman has found a "very dramatic difference in the involvement of the father—in everything from care taking to general decision making around kids' lives."

I   Another factor has recently been added to the child-care formula. The number of people who work from home nearly full time rose 23% from the

▲ A father working at home while caring for his child.

last decade. Some are **self-employed** and some work for companies. The accessibility of technology—computers, faxes, teleconferencing—has made it easier for at-home workers to be constantly **in** 70 **touch**. Of the 5.5 million "stay-at-home" parents in 2004, 5.4 million were moms and 98,000 were dads. Among these stay-at-home parents, 42 percent of mothers and 29 percent of fathers had their own children 75 under three living with them. Thirty-nine percent of mothers and 30% of fathers were under the age of 35. Will this new flexibility in the workforce bring a positive change for the well-being of children? Only time will tell. 80

Source: "Who's Taking Care of the Children?" (Miki Knezevic)

After You Read

2 **Matching Words to Their Definitions** Match each word on the left with the correct definition on the right. For a word you are not sure about, scan the reading for it, and use the context to infer its meaning.

1. __c__ glass ceiling
2. _____ flex-time
3. _____ job sharing
4. _____ radically
5. _____ in touch
6. _____ portrayed
7. _____ breadwinner
8. _____ extended family
9. _____ immediate family
10. _____ blended family
11. _____ trend
12. _____ "househusband"
13. _____ nanny
14. _____ self-employed

a. person who cares for children in their home
b. person who earns the money for a family
¢. invisible barrier to the promotion of women
d. man who stays at home and cares for his children
e. two people who each work part time at one job
f. tendency or movement in the course of events
g. to a great degree, completely
h. shown or represented in a pictorial way
i. varying arrival and departure times at work
j. children, parents, grandparents, and other relatives
k. children and parent(s)
l. parents and children from different marriages
m. working for yourself
n. able to contact each other

3 **Recalling Information** Underline the correct word or phrase in parentheses to complete the following sentences about the article.

1. About (30 / 50 / <u>70</u>) percent of American mothers with children under 18 work outside of the home.

2. In the 1950s and 1960s, it was taken for granted that a woman would be a (single mother / breadwinner / stay-at-home mom).

3. In the United States today, children most often live with their (immediate / blended / extended) family.

4. Beginning with the Industrial Revolution, many people moved to (farms / small towns / larger cities) far away from their relatives.

5. A recent trend is that American fathers seem to be spending (more / less) time with their children.

6. Another new factor is the number of people who work without leaving their homes rose approximately (10% / 20% / 30%).

7. Of the millions of "stay-at-home" parents in the U.S. in 2004, (most / many / some) were dads.

CLOSE TO HOME JOHN McPHERSON

"He's not much of a watchdog, but he's great with kids."

▲ Close to Home © 1995 John McPherson. Reprinted with permission of Universal Press Syndicate. All rights reserved.

Strategy

Reading a Chart for Information

A chart presents information to us in a clear and compact way. Often, it contains much more information than we need. This can make it hard to understand. When reading a chart for information, follow these three steps.

1. Skim for a general idea of what the chart shows.

2. Focus clearly on each question you want to answer.

3. Scan the chart for the specific information you want, moving your eyes quickly until you find it and then write it down. Ignore information that doesn't answer the question you're working on.

4 Reading a Chart for Information The chart below shows the living arrangements for children in the United States who do not live with their own parents. Work with a partner to follow the steps in the Strategy Box above and to find the answers to the questions on page 64.

Children in the United States Living with Nonparents

| Years of Age | | | | |
| Children under 18 years of age, March 2002. Numbers in thousands (000) | | | | |
Living Arrangement	Under 6	6–11	12–17	Under 18
with grandparent	635	462	476	1,573
with other relative	192	224	386	802
in foster home	62	81	92	235
with other nonrelative	137	171	268	576
with opposite-sex unmarried adults* (children under 15 only)	62	83	40	185

Source: U.S. Census Bureau, 2002

---

*"Opposite-sex unmarried adults" could be either relatives or nonrelatives. So these same children have been listed under other categories, too. This was probably done to help researchers who are comparing children raised by parental couples with those raised by non-parental couples.

1. With whom do most children live when they do not live with their parents?

2. Do more children live in foster homes or with "other nonrelatives"? (A foster home is a home where a child who is an orphan or whose parents cannot take care of them is placed by a government agency.)

3. In what age group are there the most children who live with their grandparents? Can you guess why this might be the case for this age group?

4. What age group has the largest number of children living with an "other relative" (a family member who is not the parent)? Which "other relatives" would you guess those children might be living with?

5. Why do you think that children in the U.S. are living with people who are not their parents? Make a list of as many reasons as you can think of.

6. How do you think the categories in the chart compare with children in a country you know well? Do you think the numbers living in different arrangements would be similar or different? Explain.

 5 **Guided Academic Conversation: Presenting Your Ideas** Read the *Rules for a Successful Marriage* in the box below, and discuss each of the five items with a partner, following these steps:

Step 1. Decide whether you agree or disagree with each rule, and give reasons.

Step 2. Find common ground with your partner, which means to come to an agreement about each rule. Mark the rules that you find common ground on and those that you don't find common ground on.

Step 3. Then join with another pair of students and compare your opinions.

Step 4. Have each set of partners in turn present their opinions. What do you think of the opinions of the other two? What do they think of your opinions? Are they exactly the same?

Rules for a Successful Marriage
a. A wife must be younger than her husband.
b. A husband needs to earn more money than his wife.
c. People say, "When you marry someone, you marry their whole family." So, if the families of the two people don't get along well with each other, there can be no marriage.
d. A couple should live together for at least a year before marrying.
e. Once there is a child, the mother should stay at home.

---

6 **What Do You Think?** Read the paragraph below and in small groups discuss the questions that follow.

International Adoption

"Thousands of children around the world need loving families," reads an advertisement on adoption in a North American newspaper. Wars, natural disasters, and abandonment leave many children parentless and destined to spend their early lives in orphanages. Adoption agencies offer children for adoption from countries such as China, Guatemala, the Ukraine, Korea, Colombia, and the Philippines to Westerners in North America, Europe, and Canada.

1. Should orphaned children stay in the country of their origin, perhaps in an orphanage, to remain a part of that culture?

2. Should children be allowed to be adopted to a more affluent situation in another country? Why or why not?

3. Who should be allowed to adopt these children? Only couples? Single people? Older people? People of a different race or religion than that of the child?

▲ A mother with her adopted daughter from another culture.

70 Brides for 7 Foreigners

Before You Read

1 **Scanning for Facts** Scan for the following information in the article "70 Brides for 7 Foreigners," and write the answers on the lines. (If needed, review the rules for scanning given on page 42.) Items are listed in order of their appearance. The first one is done as an example.

1. The percentage of Russian mothers wanting their daughters to marry foreigners: _23_____

2. The name of the Russian prince whose daughter became queen of France:

   _____

3. The number of phone calls an Australian man received within two days of placing his personal ad: _____

4. The number of Russian women who go each day to the Alliance dating agency in Moscow: _____

5. The percentage of Russian women from the agency's files who actually get married: _____

6. The three countries of origin of most of the foreign men applying for Russian wives: _____, _____,

   _____

7. The number of couples that get married at Wedding Palace Number 4 in Moscow each year: _____

Read

> ### Introduction
> Many years ago, there was a popular American musical called *Seven Brides for Seven Brothers*. The title of the following article contains an "echo" of that earlier title, but the numbers are different. The article is about Russian women who marry foreign men.
>
> - Why do you think they want to do that?
> - Why do you think some men from other countries want to marry Russian women?

70 Brides for 7 Foreigners

A   Russia seems to be turning into a major exporter of brides. Almost 1,500 marriages with foreigners are registered in Moscow every year. Another 10,000 women go to the international marriage agency Alliance each year, according to a poll, and 23 percent of Russian mothers would like their daughters to marry foreign citizens. Russian brides have 5 always been prized by foreigners—ever since the time of Yaroslav the Wise [an eleventh-century grand prince of Kiev], whose daughter became the queen of France. But during Joseph Stalin's time, the attitude toward marriages to foreigners was intolerant.

B   In the 1960s, the registration of foreign marriages was resumed, and 10 since then the trickle of Russian brides abroad has turned into a powerful torrent. Tens of thousands of Russian women dream of an advantageous marriage and look for foreign husbands. How? One way is through personal ads in newspapers. One ad read: "Man from Australia (37, 5 feet 5, 132 pounds) seeks short (5 feet 1 to 5 feet 5), slender 15 woman, 22–29 for marriage." The man is from Sydney. His mother advised him to marry a Russian woman because Australian women are very liberated, change men like gloves, and do not do housework. Russian women, in the opinion of the placer of the ad, love to clean, cook, stay home, and have children. In two days, he got 100 calls. 20

C   Many women are not shy about going to dating agencies. Alliance is one of the largest in Moscow, with branches in Russia's large cities and abroad. It has been flourishing for more than five years. The director, Tamara Alekseyevna Shkunova, is an academician and director of the Russian Institute of the Family at the International Academy of 25 Information Systems and editor in chief of *Moskovskaya Brachnaya Gazeta* (the *Moscow Marriage Gazette*).

D   Each day about ten women go to the agency, but only two to three of them are put in the files. There are criteria for selection. First, you must be successful in your professional milieu. Second, you must know a foreign 30 language. And third, you must meet a standard of "European looks": blond with blue eyes, slender with long legs. Of the 2,000 women a year who get into the files, only five percent get married. Of the 200 who have married recently, one was lucky enough to become the wife of a millionaire.

E   There are 700 foreign men in the files, mostly from the United 35 States, Germany, and Britain. Up to 300 men apply annually. They must meet only one requirement—that they be well-to-do. The information on the man's passport is checked, and a call is made to his place of work.

F

▲ This happy bride and groom start a new life together.

Once a husband is found, the next stop is Wedding Palace Number 4, the only place in Moscow that registers marriages to foreigners. Each year, 1,200 couples get married there. In 1992, the bridegrooms came from 96 countries. The greatest number came from the United States; in second place was Israel, followed by Turkey and Bulgaria.

G   Registration requires a passport and a guarantee from the groom's embassy that there are no obstacles to his getting married. The French embassy, for example, takes a very serious attitude toward marriages to foreign women. It requires that the French groom obtain certification of his "legal capacity for marriage." If an embassy official registers a couple that has not passed the requisite medical tests, the official is fined. Stiff requirements are also imposed by Germany.

H   The Wedding Palace requires confirmation that, in the given country, a marriage to a citizen of another state is valid. After all, in a number of countries a foreign wife and her children could find that they have no property rights. In Syria, for example, marriage to a foreigner is considered invalid without special permission.

I   Many countries are trying to erect barriers to the marital migration from Russia. For example, one Moscow woman tried for nine months to get permission to go to the United States, where her fiancé was waiting for her.

J   Another couple wanted to get registered in Canada. The fiancé was called to the Canadian embassy for an interview, but an entry visa was never granted. "Prove that this isn't a fictitious marriage," they said.

K   Many Russian women who marry foreigners quickly get divorced and come back. The reasons are well known: a sense of second-class status, a language barrier, financial difficulties. Deceptions are frequent: One "sweetheart" described his home as a palace with a fountain, but, in reality, it turned out that he lived in a small cottage without a bathtub.

Source: "70 Brides for 7 Foreigners" *World Press Review* tschure@worldpress.org (S. Kuzina)

After You Read

DISTINGUISHING BETWEEN GENERAL AND SPECIFIC STATEMENTS

A *general* statement describes or refers to a situation that is common and occurs in a number of different cases. For example, *Couples today often decide to have only one child.* A *specific* statement describes or refers to only one case or occurrence. For example, *My neighbors have only one child.*

2 **Distinguishing Between General and Specific Statements** Which one of the following two columns contains general statements related to the article and which contains specific statements? Write *General* or *Specific* in the blank above each column. Match each general statement to the specific statement that illustrates or supports it.

Column 1: _____ **Column 2:** _____

1. About 10,000 women go to the international marriage agency in Moscow every year.	**a.** Certain countries are trying to stop or slow down the influx of brides from Russia.
2. One husband described his home as a palace with a fountain, but it was really a cottage without even a bathtub.	**b.** Many Russian women are looking for foreign husbands.
3. The Canadian fiancé of a Russian woman was told at the Canadian embassy to "prove that this isn't a fictitious marriage."	**c.** It is not easy in Moscow for a woman to get in the files of a dating agency. **d.** Traditionally, Russian women have the reputation of being good wives.
4. An Australian man said that his mother advised him to marry a Russian woman because they love to clean, cook, stay home, and have children.	**e.** Many Russian women who marry foreigners get disappointed and come back to their homeland.
5. Each day, about ten women go to the agency, but only two or three of them are selected.	

3 **Selecting the Main Idea** The article uses both general and specific information to present one main idea. Circle the number of the statement that you think best expresses the main idea of the article. Why is it better than the other two?

1. Each year, 1,200 couples get married at Wedding Palace Number 4, the only place in Moscow that registers marriages to foreigners; in 1992, the bridegrooms came from 96 different countries.

2. Following an old tradition, a large number of Russian women are marrying foreign men, and, despite some obstacles and disappointments, this seems to be a trend that will continue.

3. Many foreign embassies take a very serious attitude toward the increasing number of brides who are leaving Russia to marry citizens from other nations.

IDENTIFYING ANTONYMS

Antonyms are words with the opposite meaning from another word; for example, *night* and *day*, or *good* and *bad*. Some people can remember a word better when they learn it with its antonym.

---

4 **Recalling Antonyms** Try to recall the word from the article that is an antonym for each of the words in italics. If you can't remember, scan the article for it.

1. People do not want to make a *disadvantageous* marriage, one that is bad for them; they want to make a good marriage, one that is _____. (**Hint:** Drop the prefix to change this word to its opposite.)

2. A person who brings products into a country is an *importer*; a person who sends products out of a country is an _____. (**Hint:** Here you need to change the prefix.)

3. Sometimes we hear a *true* story, but other times we hear one that is not true. We hear a _____ story. (**Hint:** One antonym of true is *false*, but there is a different one in the article, and it also begins with *f*.)

4. If a business is not having much success, we say it is *doing badly*. If a business is having a lot of success, we say it is _____. (**Hint:** Of course, one antonym is *doing well*, but there is a one-word antonym in the article, and it begins with *fl*.)

5. An activity that is not permitted by law is an *illegal* activity; an activity that is permitted by law is a _____ activity. (**Hint:** Drop the prefix.)

6. When Stalin was the head of state in Russia, the attitude toward marriage with a foreigner was not *tolerant*. It was _____. (**Hint:** Add the right prefix.)

7. A house that is large and splendid can be described as a *palace*. A house that is small and simple can be described as a _____. (**Hint:** This antonym begins with a *c*.)

8. When lots of water rushes into a container very fast, it is a *torrent*. When a little bit of water comes into a container slowly, it is a _____. (**Hint:** This antonym begins with a *t*.)

9. A document that is authentic and official is a *valid* document. One that is a fake or has expired is an _____ document. (**Hint:** Add the right prefix.)

10. A person who has very little money is *poor*. But a person who has a lot of money is _____. (**Hint:** This is a compound word made up of three parts connected by two hyphens.)

5 **Focusing on Words from the Academic Word List** Use the most appropriate word from the box to fill in each of the blanks on page 71 in the paragraph taken from the reading in Part 2. Do NOT look back at the reading right away; instead, first see if you can remember the vocabulary. Then check your answers on page 68. **Hint:** the word "requires" will be used twice.

attitude	legal	registers
couple	medical	requirements
guarantee	obtain	requires

G   Registration _____ a passport and a _____
                          1   2
from the groom's embassy that there are no obstacles to his getting

married. The French embassy, for example, takes a very serious

_____ toward marriages to foreign women. It
          3

_____ that the French groom _____   5
          4   5

certification of his "_____ capacity for marriage." If an
                            6

embassy official _____ a _____ that has
                        7   8

not passed the requisite _____ tests, the official is fined.
                                    9

Stiff _____ are also imposed by Germany.
          10

6 **Choosing Points for Discussion** In small groups, discuss three of the following questions. Be prepared to report on the opinions of your group after you finish.

1. What does the mother of the man from Sydney think about Australian women? Why do you think she feels this way? In your opinion, do women from some cultures make better wives than women from other cultures? Why or why not?

2. And what about the men? In your opinion, do men from some cultures make better husbands than men from other cultures? Why or why not?

3. What do you think about the *criteria* (standards) for selection of the dating agencies? Are they fair? Can they cause problems? Explain.

4. Would you consider marrying someone from a different culture? What advantages and disadvantages are there to such a marriage?

5. In some countries now it is legal for two people to marry, regardless of their gender. So a man can marry a man or a woman can marry a woman. What effects do you think this change will have on those societies? Do you think that in the future more countries will permit this? Why or why not?

7 **Reading Personal Ads** Find some ads from the personals section of a newspaper or magazine and bring them to class. In small groups, discuss the following questions.

1. What is your opinion of these personal ads as a way to find a marriage partner?
2. Would meeting people this way be safe and effective?

3. Would it be better to go to an agency that uses computers to match possible partners?

 8 **Looking Back at the Past** How much do things change from one generation to the next? There is a French saying that "The more things change, the more they stay the same." Work in a small group and look at the photos below. Then answer the questions on page 73.

▲ A wedding photo from the beginning of the 19th century in the U.S.

▲ A contemporary wedding photo in the U.S.

1. Look at the two wedding photos on page 72. What are some similarities between the two photos? What are some of the differences? Based on the similarities and differences you see, how do you think wedding traditions in the U.S. have changed? What things do you think have stayed the same?

2. Look at photo 1. How do you think the bride and groom feel? Why? Look at photo 2. How do you think the bride and groom feel? Why?

3. In the U.S. wedding traditions have changed over the past 100 years. For example, many people are getting married later in life. Also, many couples are choosing to get married in non-traditional places, such as on mountaintops or on beaches. How are wedding traditions changing in your culture? Do you know of anyone who has had a non-traditional wedding?

4. In your culture, is there anything that is considered lucky or unlucky on a wedding day?

5. What do you know about your parents' and/or grandparents' weddings? Are you married? If so, describe your wedding day. What did you wear? Where did you get married? How did you feel?

TOEFL® IBT

Focus on Testing

Answering Vocabulary Questions on Tests

Vocabulary questions in the reading section of the TOEFL® Internet-Based Test (iBT) are multiple-choice. You are given four possible answers and asked to choose the best one. The four possible answers often include:

- one item that is completely wrong and may even be the opposite of the target vocabulary item
- one item that is a "decoy"; it is similar in form to the target item but different in meaning
- one item that is close in meaning to the target item but not quite right
- one item that is correct

Vocabulary questions on the iBT come in two basic formats:

1. *Which of the following is closest in meaning to X, as it is used in Paragraph Y?*

2. *In Paragraph Y, X is closest in meaning to _____.*

("X" is a vocabulary item. "Y" is a paragraph number.)

Practice Look again at the reading "70 Brides for 7 Foreigners." Then answer the following questions.

1. Which of the following is closest in meaning to *registered*, as it is used in Paragraph A, line 2?

   Ⓐ officially recorded
   Ⓑ clearly shown
   Ⓒ happily celebrated
   Ⓓ absolutely forbidden

2. In Paragraph B, line 15, *seeks* is closest in meaning to

   Ⓐ marries

   Ⓑ has

   Ⓒ is interested in

   Ⓓ is looking for

3. Which of the following is closest in meaning to *shy about*, as it is used in Paragraph C, line 21?

   Ⓐ worried about

   Ⓑ afraid of

   Ⓒ angry about

   Ⓓ informed of

4. In Paragraph D, line 32–33, *get into* is closest in meaning to

   Ⓐ read

   Ⓑ change

   Ⓒ enter

   Ⓓ like

5. Which of the following is closest in meaning to *meet*, as it is used in Paragraph E, line 37?

   Ⓐ understand

   Ⓑ satisfy

   Ⓒ be introduced to

   Ⓓ gather

6. Which of the following is closest in meaning to *serious*, as it is used in Paragraph G, line 57?

   Ⓐ strict

   Ⓑ negative

   Ⓒ hopeful

   Ⓓ clear

7. In Paragraph G, line 60, *fined* is closest in meaning to

   Ⓐ rewarded by a boss

   Ⓑ removed from a job

   Ⓒ discovered at a workplace

   Ⓓ charged money as a penalty

8. Which of the following is closest in meaning to *barriers*, as it is used in Paragraph I, line 67?

   Ⓐ structures

   Ⓑ obstacles

   Ⓒ islands

   Ⓓ systems

1 Vocabulary Review Pantomime It is said that "actions speak louder than words." Actions can also help us to remember words.

Work with a group of two or three others to make a list of ten key words and phrases from the chapter that you think are especially interesting or important. Then practice ways to "pantomime" (show through actions) them. After you have finished, hide your list and work with another group. Take turns pantomiming a word or phrase that the other group must guess. Each time a team guesses correctly, it wins a point. Who is the best actor? Who is the best at guessing words and phrases?

 2 Making Connections Choose one of the topics below to research on the Internet.

1. **Mail Brides** Enter search terms on the Internet on the topic of Russian or "mail" brides and find information about what is happening now. Are there problems with this exporting business? Do you think the market has changed since the article in this chapter was written? What other countries export brides? Where are the customers who want to marry these brides from? Find and write down one interesting or surprising fact, idea, story, or statistic related to the topic and bring it to share with the class.

2. **International Adoption** Enter *international adoption* on a search engine and find new information about this topic. Write down one interesting or surprising fact, idea, story, or statistic that you learn and bring it to share with the class.

Responding in Writing

WRITING TIP: WRITING DOWN THE KEY
POINTS IN A SUMMARY
To do a *summary* of a reading, write down its *key* (most important) *ideas*. No opinion of your own is expressed in a summary.

3 **Writing a Summary** Look back over the chapter you have completed and write a *summary* of one of the two reading selections from this chapter, following these steps:

Step 1: Choose one of the selections from this chapter and skim it. Put down as your title:

My Summary of _____ (Write in the title of the article in this space.)

Step 2: Make a list of the key ideas from the article.

Step 3: Think about what the author is trying to say. Decide on what his or her main idea is and write this down *in your own words*. This is your first sentence.

Step 4: Then write a sentence for each of the other key ideas and put them in the order in which they occur.

Step 5: Read what you have written. Ask yourself: Is it in my own words or have I simply copied the sentences of the article? Of course, you can include words and short phrases taken from the article, but not complete sentences. (If you have copied long phrases or whole sentences from the article, then change what you have written so that it expresses the same ideas in a different way.)

Step 6: Is your summary clear? Is it short enough? A summary should be no longer than 20–30% of the original article. If your summary is too long, try to cut the parts that are not so important.

Step 7: Write a final sentence to conclude your summary. This should not be your opinion, but the author's. Try to think again of what the author wants to say, and express that in a different way from the first sentence with the main idea.

Step 8: It is not easy to write a good summary, but it is a useful skill for university, for business, and for almost any career. (More practice will be offered on summaries in the chapters ahead.) If you have time available in class, work in a group with two or three other students. Read all the summaries and talk about which one is the best (short, clear, complete, and interesting) and why. Then revise and improve your summary.

Self-Assessment Log

Read the lists below. Check (✓) the strategies and vocabulary that you learned in this chapter. Look through the chapter or ask your instructor about the strategies and words that you do not understand.

Reading and Vocabulary-Building Strategies

- ❏ Skimming for the general idea
- ❏ Matching words to their definitions
- ❏ Reading a chart for information
- ❏ Scanning for facts
- ❏ Distinguishing between general and specific statements
- ❏ Selecting the main idea
- ❏ Identifying antonyms

Target Vocabulary

Nouns

- ❏ attitude*
- ❏ blended family
- ❏ breadwinner
- ❏ cottage
- ❏ couple*
- ❏ criteria*
- ❏ exporter*
- ❏ extended families
- ❏ flex time
- ❏ glass ceiling
- ❏ guarantee*
- ❏ househusband

- ❏ immediate family
- ❏ job sharing
- ❏ nanny
- ❏ palace
- ❏ requirements*
- ❏ torrent
- ❏ trend*
- ❏ trickle

Verbs

- ❏ flourishing
- ❏ obtain*

- ❏ portrayed
- ❏ registered*
- ❏ requires*

Adjectives

- ❏ advantageous
- ❏ fictitious
- ❏ intolerant
- ❏ invalid
- ❏ legal*
- ❏ medical*
- ❏ self-employed

- ❏ stay-at-home (mom)
- ❏ valid*
- ❏ well-to-do

Adverb

- ❏ radically*

Idiom

- ❏ (be) in touch

*These words are from the Academic Word List. For more information on this list, see www.vuw.ac.nz/lals/research/awl.

Health and Leisure

People the world over are becoming increasingly interested in health and travel. Many spend their free time in gyms, on the tennis courts, in martial arts classes, and in health food stores in an effort to build up their bodies. Both young and old are journeying more and farther than ever before. The first reading selection in this chapter discusses the foods we eat and what effects they have on us. The second takes a look at some of the surprising effects that tourists have on the places they visit.

❝ A good laugh and a long sleep are the best cures in the doctor's book. ❞

—Irish proverb

Connecting to the Topic

1 Look at the photo. What are the man and the boy doing? What do you think their relationship is to each other?

2 People all over the world are becoming increasingly interested in health. What have you noticed people doing in order to improve their health?

3 This chapter also discusses travel and tourism. How do you think tourists can be helpful to the places they visit? How can they be harmful?

Eat Like a Peasant, *Feel* Like a King

Before You Read

Strategy

Using Headings to Preview
Picking out the headings in an article is one form of previewing. It improves comprehension by helping you see the organization and major ideas. Headings are usually of two kinds: they present or illustrate the main idea of a section, or they give a small detail to catch the reader's interest. The ones that tell the main idea are the most helpful.

1 **Using Headings to Preview** The article on pages 81–84 begins by introducing its subject. Answer the questions about headings.

1. After the introduction, there are two headings. List them below.

*Introduction*_____

_____

_____

2. In this story, which heading tells the main idea of the section?

3. Judging from the headings, what do you think you will read about in Sections 2 and 3?

2 **Getting Meaning from Context** Guess the meaning of words from their context by following these instructions.

1. The only uncommon word in the title is *peasant*. To infer its meaning, notice how it is in a parallel construction with the word *king*: "Eat Like a _____, Feel like a _____." A parallel construction is used either for comparison or for contrast. So *peasant* means either something very similar to *king* or something very different. With this clue in mind, read the sentence on lines 44 to 48, and tell what you think is meant by a *peasant diet*. How does this relate to the title?

_____

2. Notice the context: "Eat simple foods, not elite treats." The word *not* tells you that *elite treats* are the opposite of *simple foods*. *Elite* is also used in line 2 to describe a group of people. Look at this context too; then in your own words, explain the meaning of *elite*.

_____

3. Look at the second word of the second paragraph: *eclectic*. It describes the menu that makes up the entire first paragraph. Read that paragraph and think about what is special and unusual about the grouping of foods described here. Then explain the meaning of the word *eclectic*.

_____

4. Scan the first two sections of the essay for the noun *affluence* and its related adjective *affluent*, which are used four times. From the contexts, guess its meaning and write it here. Can you also find a synonym for affluence in the fifth paragraph, beginning with the letter *p*?

_____

5. The word *cuisine* is used three times in the essay. Scan for it and, using the contexts, explain what you think it means.

_____

Read

Introduction

"You are what you eat" is a popular American saying, and what you eat can contribute to improving or destroying your health. According to modern research, certain cultures have healthier diets than others. The following article from *American Health* magazine talks about the foods that can help to keep us healthy. Try to guess the answers to these questions which are discussed in the article:

- Which cultures have traditional diets that are good for our health?
- What foods should you choose in order to avoid cancer, hypertension, and heart disease?

Eat Like a Peasant, *Feel Like a King*

Research around the globe points to a recipe for well-being: Eat simple foods, not elite treats.

A   Start with miso soup, a classically simple Japanese recipe. For an appetizer, try a small plate of pasta al pesto. On to the main course: grilled chinook salmon, with steamed Chinese cabbage on the side. End 5 with a Greek salad, sprinkled with olive oil, and a New Zealand kiwi fruit for dessert.

B   An **eclectic** menu, to be sure. But it could contain some of the world's healthiest dishes. Miso soup, according to recent Japanese research, may help **prevent cancer**, as may cabbage. Salmon, olive oil, and the garlic in pesto can all help fight **heart disease**. Even kiwi is rich in **fiber**, potassium, and vitamin C. In the last few years, nutritionists have been studying such international superfoods—dishes from around the globe that may hold the key to healthy eating. They're building on research that began in the '40s and '50s, when researchers first realized that a country's **diet** is intimately connected to the health of its people.

▲ A healthy meal has lots of vegetables

C   Since then, an explosion of medical studies has produced a flood of information on diverse human diets—from the Inuit of the Arctic to the Bushmen of Africa's Kalahari Desert. But the globe-trotting researchers have done more than discover the best features of each country's **cuisine**. They've also demonstrated broad nutritional principles that apply to people all over the world. And their clearest finding is a sobering one.

D   In many countries, they've found, the healthiest diet is simple, inexpensive, traditional fare—precisely the diet that people abandon as they move into **affluence**. Japanese immigrating from the high-carbohydrate Pacific to high-fat America have a greater risk of heart disease the more westernized their diet becomes. The same pattern holds for developing nations that emerge from poverty into **prosperity**. Poor people who can't get enough to eat are at risk, of course, whatever their diet. But as a country's food becomes richer, the scourges of poverty (infectious disease and malnutrition) are replaced by the "diseases of civilization" (arteriosclerosis, certain cancers, obesity).

▲ A "fast food" meal is often unhealthy.

E   The simple, ideal diet—often called the "**peasant** diet"—is the traditional cuisine of the relatively poor, agrarian countries. It's usually based on a **grain** (rice, wheat, corn), fruits and vegetables, small amounts of meat, fish, eggs or dairy products, and a legume.

F   The advantages are obvious: low fat and high fiber, with most calories coming in the grains and **legumes**. "A low-fat, high-fiber diet is a preventive diet for heart disease, certain cancers, hypertension, adult-onset diabetes, obesity," says Dr. Wayne Peters, director of the Lipid Consultation Service of Massachusetts General Hospital.

Early Diets: Nuts and Plants

G   According to Peters, "We evolved eating a low-fat diet, and that's what our genetic composition is really designed to handle." Studies of one of the world's most primitive diets—and one of the healthiest ones—back him up. In southern Africa's Kalahari Desert, some tribes still eat as early humans did, hunting and gathering.

▲ The !Kung people eat mongono, an abundant nut.

H   "Hunting and gathering may not have been such a bad way of life," says Richard Lee, an anthropologist at the University of Toronto who has studied the !Kung tribe since the 1960s. "The main element of the !Kung diet is the mongongo, an abundant nut eaten in large quantities. They routinely collect and eat more than 105 edible plant species. Meat is secondary."

I   Another student of the !Kung, Steward Truswell, a professor of human nutrition at Australia's University of Sydney, says their eating schedule is really continual "snacking" (the gathering) punctuated by occasional feasts after a successful hunt. They are nutritionally healthy, the only shortfall being fairly low caloric intake.

J   Few people, though, would choose a !Kung diet—or even a simple peasant diet from western Europe (which is now much less common there). In an **affluent** society, it takes willpower to keep fat intake down to the recommended maximum: 30% of total calories. (The average American gets more than 40% of his or her calories from fat.) When a country reaches a certain level of affluence, as the U.S. and Japan, grain and beans give way to beef and butter.

K   In India, for example, many middle-income people are now gaining weight on a rich diet—even though the poor half of the population still can't afford enough to eat. As the middle class has become more affluent, they've been able to indulge, and Indian doctors are reportedly seeing more obesity, hypertension, and heart disease. Very recently, though, Indians have gone for the diets and aerobics classes that are popular among the rest of the world's elite.

L   If it's just too difficult to stay with a really low-fat "peasant" diet, the alternative is to rehabilitate high-calorie dishes. Cut down on overall fat intake and substitute, in the words of one researcher, "nice fats for nasty fats." Americans have already been following this advice. In the past 20 years, the consumption of "nasty" saturated fats has declined, while we've taken in more of the polyunsaturated fats, such as corn and safflower oils, that can help lower blood cholesterol. This change may help explain the simultaneous 20% to 30% drop in heart disease in the U.S.

Why Socrates* Loved Olive Oil

M   An even better strategy for changing our fat intake may come from studying diets in the Mediterranean—Spain, Greece, and southern Italy.

▲ Olive oil is healthy for you.

With some regional variation, people in these cultures eat small amounts of meat and dairy products and get almost all of their fat in the form of olive oil, says physiologist Ancel Keys, professor emeritus at the University of Minnesota School of Public Health and leader in international dietary studies.

N   Keys has noted that farmers sometimes quaff a wineglass of oil before leaving for the fields in the morning. Elsewhere in the Mediterranean, bread is dipped in olive oil. Salads are tossed with it. Everything's cooked in it.

O   Though people in some of these countries eat nearly as much total fat as Americans, they are singularly healthy, with very little heart disease. Now laboratory studies of olive oil help explain why. Unlike most other vegetable oils common in the West, olive oil consists mainly of "monounsaturated" fats. Recent research indicates that **monounsaturates** do a better job of preventing heart disease than the more widely touted polyunsaturates.

P   As Americans become ever more concerned with healthy eating, we're likely to pay more and more attention to world cuisines. The polyglot among nations, we've started to seek out ethnic flavors from everywhere. "Foreign" ingredients, from seaweed and bean curd to tortillas and salsa, are now readily available in large supermarkets. And Mexican and Asian restaurants have become more widespread than any other eateries except ice cream parlors, hamburger stands, and pizzerias, according to the National Restaurant Association.

Q   But the trick to finding healthy food, wherever it comes from, is to look carefully at each dish. No single cuisine is all good or all bad. Each has something to teach us.

Source: "Eat Like a Peasant, *Feel* Like a King" *American Health Magazine* (Andrew Revkin)

*Socrates was an ancient Greek philosopher. He is often used to represent a wise man.

After You Read

3 **Recalling Information** Based on what you have read, match the food on the left to its description on the right.

Food

1. a grain, a legume, fruits, vegetables and a bit of meat, eggs or fish

2. garlic and salmon

3. olive oil

4. miso soup and cabbage

5. kiwi fruit

Description

a. a monounsaturate that seems to prevent heart disease

b. rich in fiber, potassium, and vitamin C

c. may help prevent cancer

d. the simple "peasant diet" that is good for you

e. can help fight heart disease

Strategy

Paraphrasing Main Ideas
Learn to express the main ideas from readings in your own words, simply and clearly. This is sometimes called *paraphrasing.* You can use words or short phrases taken directly from the author but not long phrases or sentences.

4 **Paraphrasing Main Ideas** Read and respond to the items below. Use your own words.

1. The main idea of the article is given in simple terms in the title and the italicized sentence that follows it. In your own words, what is the main idea?

_____

_____

2. Another key idea is the relationship between affluence, diet, and health. The article illustrates this by referring to several different societies. Explain how affluence changes diet and health, and refer to at least two cultures that illustrate it.

_____

_____

_____

_____

_____

_____

Strategy

Recognizing Synonyms
Synonyms are words with similar meanings like *fast* and *quick*. You can enrich your vocabulary by learning and using synonyms. This will also add variety and interest to your speech and writing.

5 **Recognizing Synonyms** Match each vocabulary word from the reading to its *synonym* or definition in the right column. Can you use these words in a good English sentence?

Vocabulary Word

1. _____ affluent

2. _____ cuisine

3. _____ eclectic

4. _____ elite

5. _____ peasant (adjective)

6. _____ prosperity

Synonym

a. combining different influences

b. simple, from a farm

c. rich

d. wealth

e. upper class

f. style of cooking

Strategy

Organizing Information Using a Continuum
As you learned in Chapter 1, one way of organizing information is to rank it by showing the relationship of different items on a continuum.

6 **Ranking Foods on a Continuum** Work with a partner to rank the food items below from most healthy to least healthy. Write them on the continuum. Then compare your work with that of the rest of the class.

beans (legumes)	crackers	kim chee
beef	eggs	noodles
butter	fish	olive oil
cheese	fruit	pizza
chicken	guacamole	rice

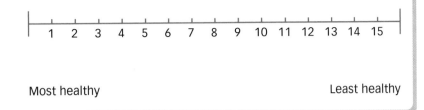

1	2	3	4	5	6	7	8	9	10	11	12	13	14	15

Most healthy   Least healthy

7 **Taking a Stand: Agree or Disagree?** Work in a small group. Read the following statements and choose two that you all agree upon (either *for* or *against*). With your group, write a list of reasons that support your stand on each of the two questions. Be prepared to defend your position to the class.

1. Tea is better for you than coffee.

2. Exercise is essential for mind and body, and the best exercise is running.

3. Fast food is junk food: no exceptions.

4. You can never be too thin.

5. It is more important to sleep well than to exercise.

6. Smoking four or five cigarettes a day does not harm your health.

7. It is always better to eat at home than at a restaurant.

8 **Guided Academic Conversation** Gain confidence and improve your speaking ability by doing one of the following tasks with one or more of your classmates.

1. **Become a Salesperson!** Choose a food mentioned in the article and make up a TV ad for it. First think of a *catchy phrase*—one that catches people's attention. For example, "Olive oil will make you live longer!" Then present it in a surprising or humorous way. For example, a group of people singing while they make a salad with olive oil. Finally, talk about the good qualities of your product. For example, "It's healthy, tasty, easy to use." Write out a script and perform your ad for the class or a small group.

2. **Create a Menu for a Healthy Restaurant.** Pretend that you have just opened a restaurant and want to attract health-conscious customers. Invent a catchy name for your restaurant and make up a menu of three courses (appetizers, main dishes, and desserts) and a list of beverages. Then show the menu to the class, tell them about each course, and explain why it is good for their health.

Analyzing Compound Words

As we saw in Chapter 1 (page 11), many English words are made up of two shorter words. These are called compound words, and they are usually adjectives or nouns. Some compound words are written with a hyphen between them, such as *low-fat*; others such as *wineglass*, are written as one word. Breaking apart compound words can help you understand their meaning. For example, look at the word *well-being* in the introductory quote in the reading selection "Eat Like a Peasant, *Feel* Like a King." What do you think it means?

When taking vocabulary tests, try breaking apart the compound words to help understand their meaning.

Practice Choose the word or phrase that best explains the meaning of the underlined word or phrase. Refer back to the selection "Eat Like a Peasant, *Feel* Like a King" if necessary.

1. globe-trotting researchers (line 25)
   - Ⓐ professors and students of geography
   - Ⓑ investigators who travel around the world
   - Ⓒ people who study the movement of the Earth
   - Ⓓ experts in the benefits of exercise

2. shortfall (line 73)
   - Ⓐ unusual action
   - Ⓒ shift from bad to good
   - Ⓑ change in the way of thinking
   - Ⓓ absence of something needed

3. intake (lines 74, 90)
   - Ⓐ interference
   - Ⓒ entering into (the body)
   - Ⓑ planning for (the future)
   - Ⓓ disease

4. middle-income (line 82)
   - Ⓐ rich
   - Ⓒ arriving early
   - Ⓑ overweight
   - Ⓓ average salary

5. seaweed (line 121)
   - Ⓐ plants that need sun
   - Ⓒ plants in the ocean
   - Ⓑ ethnic food
   - Ⓓ plants in the desert

6. widespread (line 123)
   - Ⓐ large in size
   - Ⓒ present in many locations
   - Ⓑ open to the public
   - Ⓓ complicated by different rules

9 **What Do You Think?** Read the paragraph below and then discuss the questions that follow.

Smoking

Medical evidence proves that smoking is a health risk. Smokers have a greater chance of developing cancer, emphysema, and heart problems. Second-hand smoke, which exposes nonsmokers to smokers' fumes, also increases the chances for nonsmokers of developing serious diseases. Yet, many smokers feel they have a right to smoke and that it is no worse than certain other practices, such as overeating or drinking too much alcohol.

1. Are the people you know who smoke smoking more or less nowadays?

2. What do you think about restrictions against smoking inside public buildings? Should it also be restricted outside? Explain.

3. Do you smoke? Why or why not?

10 **Discussing information from a chart**   Look at the chart and the list of benefits below. Then answer the questions on page 90.

Some Benefits of Quitting Smoking

Source: American Cancer Society, Inc., 1599 Clifton Road, Atlanta, GA 30329: Phone (800)227-2345

Within 20 Minutes
- Blood pressure drops to a level close to that before the last cigarette
- Temperature to hands and feet increases to normal

Within 8 Hours
- Carbon monoxide level in the blood drops to normal

Within 24 Hours
- Chance of heart attack decreases

Within 2 Weeks to 3 Months
- Circulation improves
- Lung function increases up to 30%

Within 1 to 9 Months
- Cough, sinus congestion, fatigue, and shortness of breath decrease
- Cilia regain normal function in the lungs, increasing the ability to handle mucus, clean the lungs, reduce infection

Within 1 Year
- Excess risk of coronary heart disease is half that of a smoker's

Within 5 Years
- Stroke risk is reduced to that of a nonsmoker 5–15 years after quitting

Within 10 Years
- Lung cancer death rate about half that of a continuing smoker's
- Risk of cancer of the mouth, throat, esophagus, bladder, kidney, and pancreas decreases

Within 15 Years
- Risk of coronary heart disease is that of a nonsmoker's

1. What, according to this chart, are the benefits of quitting smoking? Can you think of other benefits that are not in the chart?

2. In your opinion, which three of the benefits from quitting smoking are the most important? Why?

3. Which benefits might be most likely to motivate people to stop smoking?

Part 2 Reading Skills and Strategies

Here Come the Tourists!

Before You Read

Strategy

Understanding Point of View
A piece of writing presents ideas about a certain subject. It may also present a certain attitude or point of view about the subject. The point of view may be positive, in favor of the person, place, or thing being talked about. On the other hand, it may be negative, against it. The third possibility is a point of view that is somewhere in between and shows both positive and negative aspects of the subject.

1 Skimming for the Point of View It is obvious from the title that the following reading deals with tourism. But what point of view does it express about it? Skim the reading to identify its point of view. Then put a check in front of the statement below that best expresses the point of view of the article.

1. _____ Tourism has a good effect on the places visited.

2. _____ Tourism has a bad effect on the places visited.

3. _____ Tourism has both good and bad effects on the places visited.

2 Analyzing the Point of View Answer the questions about the point of view in the reading with a partner.

1. What do you think of this point of view?

2. Is it similar to your own attitude toward tourism?

3. Does the photo on page 93 illustrate the point of view of the selection? Explain.

3 Getting the Meaning of Words from Context Read the analysis following each of these sentences from the reading to learn some new words and methods of figuring out meanings. Then fill in the the best response.

1. It was hard to believe that the community began its ecotourism project in 1992 in order to protect natural resources. (lines 2–4)

The word *ecotourism* has only been in use for about the last 25 years. The first part, *eco-*, is taken from the word *ecology*, which means "the relationship between people and their natural surroundings or environment." In recent years, concern for a healthy ecology has become an important theme.

Judging from this, what kind of tourism do you think *ecotourism* is?

- (A) tourism that does not cost much
- (B) tourism for the very rich
- (C) tourism that does not harm the environment
- (D) tourism that uses the environment for adventure

2. Their repeated "requests" annoyed tourists. (lines 7–8)

Quotation marks are sometimes used to show that a word does not have its usual meaning. Usually, a *request* is the action of asking for something politely. Here, an example of a typical "request" made to tourists is given in the first sentence. This gives you a clue about the meaning of *annoyed*.

What does it mean to *annoy* someone?

- (A) to make someone happy
- (B) to make someone sad
- (C) to make someone confused
- (D) to make someone angry

3. Some locals were more skilled and playful in their requests, others up-front and demanding. (lines 8–10)

Adjectives in English can often be used as nouns if a word like *the* or *some* is put in front of them. The word *local* is used that way here, and then made plural with an *s*. Scan the second paragraph and you will see it used in three other sentences.

What does the word *locals* mean?

- (A) people from nearby
- (C) beggars
- (B) people from far away
- (D) workers

The adjective *up-front* is a compound word, so the two short words that make it up can give you some clue to its meaning. Also, it is paired with *demanding* and both words are put in contrast with *skilled* and *playful*. That means they mean something very different from *skilled* and *playful*.

What does *up-front* mean?

- (A) tall
- (C) smart
- (B) direct
- (D) funny

4. Indigenous people in the Andes demand compensation for having their photographs taken. . . . (lines 28–29)

The word *indigenous* is followed by the word *peoples*. This gives you a clue about its meaning. These people live in the Andes mountains, and that gives you another clue.

What does *indigenous* mean?

- (A) rude
- (C) foreign
- (B) courteous
- (D) native

5. These young vacationers like to distinguish themselves as "travelers" not "tourists." (lines 53–54)

In this sentence, two words are put in quotation marks because they are direct quotes of what people say and also because they are used in a special way. The first is said to distinguish people from the second.

What does *distinguish* mean?

- (A) make similar
- (B) make different
- (C) go far away
- (D) come closer

6. But in "frontiers" like Kathmandu, Goa, and Bangkok, where a backpacking subculture has existed since it became part of the "hippie" routes in the 1960s . . . (lines 55–57)

Once again, we have a word in quotation marks because it is used with a special meaning that is not the usual one. The word *frontier* has two usual meanings: a place near the border of another country, or a new, unexplored area of the world or of knowledge.

What do you think the word *frontiers* means here?

- (A) very popular places for tourists
- (B) places where no tourists ever go
- (C) places where only adventurous tourists go
- (D) places where tourists may go in the future

The prefix *sub-* means "under" as in the word *submarine* (a vehicle that goes under the water) or "lesser in importance."

What does *subculture* mean in the phrase "a backpacking subculture"?

- (A) a group of people who are all very different
- (B) a group of people with similar customs
- (C) a group of people who are very wealthy
- (D) a small group of people with an excellent education

7. . . . such travelers have a reputation for *stinginess* and rude, hard *bargaining*. (lines 57–58)

The suffix *-ness* tells us this is a noun, the quality of being stingy. For clues to the meaning of *stingy* and *stinginess*, look at the examples of how the young vacationers and backpackers act in the sentences before and after this one.

What does *stinginess* mean?

- (A) practice of insulting people for no reason
- (B) attitude of kindness and humility
- (C) custom of not spending or giving money
- (D) habit of spending and giving money freely

Related to the word *stinginess* is the word *bargaining*. This is the gerund (-*ing* form) of the verb *to bargain*, which is used in line 58.

What do you think the verb *to bargain* means?

- (A) to look at something carefully before buying it
- (B) to try to make the price of something lower
- (C) to give away one thing in exchange for another
- (D) to sell something for very little money

Introduction

This selection is an excerpt taken from a book by Deborah McLaren called *Rethinking Tourism and Ecotravel*. The author is a journalist and director of the Rethinking Tourism Project, a nonprofit group that supports networking and indigenous self-development. She has lived and worked in various parts of Asia and the Americas and has her residence in Washington, D.C.

- What do you think tourists bring to the places they visit?
- What do they take away?
- Do you expect to learn something new about travel in this article? Why or why not?

Here Come the Tourists!

A   "Give me the t-shirt," the woman said to the tourist. The small village in the Amazon was almost filled with beggars. It was hard to believe that the community began its ecotourism project in 1992 in order to protect natural resources. The villagers had lost interest in the land ⁵ and became enchanted by the things the tourists had. Their repeated "requests" annoyed tourists. Some locals were more skilled and playful in their requests, others up-front and demanding. "They have money ¹⁰ and many things," said the woman asking for the t-shirt. "It's no problem for tourists."

B   It is easy for the locals to perceive tourists as incredibly wealthy. The entire tourist experience revolves around money ¹⁵ and purchases. The community itself is being purchased. Tourists are superconsumers who bring their foreign languages and communications, strange and inappropriate clothing, and cameras into the community. In the context of a brief visit, sometimes an overnight, few real friendships are formed between tourists ²⁰ and locals. Tourists are eager for adventure, or at least the perfect photo opportunity. If the tourist becomes upset in the midst of the excitement, the local usually pays the price. But these strange people sometimes give away token gifts to locals, even money. This results in begging, which becomes

▲ Tourists visiting the Amazon

increasingly widespread as locals begin to see themselves as "poor" and tourists as "rich." The psychological pressure of viewing oneself as poor or backward can manifest itself in crimes not previously common in a community.

C   Indigenous people in the Andes demand compensation for having their photographs taken, saying it's intrusive. A woman in Otavalo, Ecuador, explained to me, "We see ourselves and our children on postcards and in books. We do not benefit from having our photos taken. A foreigner does. We demand part of the profits." In some indigenous communities, photography is taboo because it is believed to cause physical and spiritual harm to the person who is photographed. In India, young children have had limbs torn from their bodies to make them more pathetic and hence "better" beggars. Adults who commit this violence often have several children who work for them. Other forms of begging, sometimes found amusing by tourists, offend many locals. An indigenous leader from Panama told me, "It breaks my heart to see the young boys swimming after the coins the tourists throw in the water. We spent years acquiring our rights to these lands. Now with tourism, the people here do not care about the land anymore. They just want tourist dollars."

▲ Children in the Amazon endanger wild animals by capturing them to show to tourists.

D   While tourists believe they can contribute to destination communities, locals don't always agree. Money spent by budget travelers—especially backpackers—may go into the local economy. They tend to stay in cheaper hotels and eat in cheaper restaurants owned by locals and so get closer to the local culture. These young vacationers like to distinguish themselves as "travelers" not "tourists." They live by budget travel guides and often flock to the same inexpensive areas of villages and cities. But in "frontiers" like Kathmandu, Goa, and Bangkok, where a backpacking subculture has existed since it became part of the "hippie" routes in the 1960s, such travelers have a reputation for stinginess and rude, hard bargaining. In Indonesia, I met a British bicyclist who was cycling around the world. He was proud that he had spent virtually no money on his trip. He lived with families that took him in every night from the road and ate what was offered to him by people he met along his way. He had not worked in any of the places he had visited. He was extremely happy that he had just bargained a local merchant down from the equivalent of ten cents to a penny for four pieces of bread. I thought it was rather odd that he was taking advantage of everyone he met and wouldn't even pay a fair price to a poor baker.

Source: "Here Come the Tourists!" Excerpt from *Rethinking Tourism and Ecotravel* (Deborah McLaren)

Strategy

Distinguishing Between Fact and Opinion

The distinction between fact and opinion often is not clear. Events taken to be common knowledge (the Earth revolves around the sun), statements supported by scientific evidence (many studies show that vitamin C is good for our health), or statements about something that can be confirmed (Bangkok is the capital of Thailand) are generally taken to be facts. Beliefs expressed by only one person are usually considered opinions, unless the person is judged to be an expert or authority on the matter. (Hamburgers are delicious.)

4 **Distinguishing Between Fact and Opinion** Which of the following statements from the reading do you think are facts and which ones are opinions? Why? Write *F* in front of the facts and *O* in front of the opinions. Compare your answers with those of your classmates. Line numbers are given so you can examine the contexts.

1. _____ The community began its ecotourism project in 1992. (lines 2–4)

2. _____ The villagers lost interest in the land. (line 5)

3. _____ The entire tourist experience revolves around money and purchases. (lines 14–16)

4. _____ Few real friendships are formed between tourists and locals. (lines 20–21)

5. _____ If the tourist becomes upset, the local usually pays the price. (lines 22–23)

6. _____ Indigenous people in the Andes demand compensation for having their photographs taken. (lines 28–29)

7. _____ In some communities, photography is taboo because it is believed to cause harm. (lines 33–35)

8. _____ Tourists believe they can contribute to destination communities. (line 49)

9. _____ Budget travelers tend to stay in cheaper hotels and eat in cheaper restaurants. (lines 51–53)

10. _____ In Kathmandu, Goa, and Bangkok, a backpacking subculture has existed since the 1960s. (lines 55–57)

5 **Scanning for Vocabulary** Find the following words in the article, using your scanning skills and the clues given here. Words are asked for in order of their appearance in the selection. (If necessary, review instructions for scanning, page 42).

1. A two-word phrase meaning *things that a country has and can use to its benefit, such as coal and petroleum:* n_____ r_____

2. An adjective that starts with *e* and means *delighted, pleased as if by magic:*

e _____

3. An adjective starting with the prefix *in-* and meaning *not correct for the occasion:* in_____

4. An adjective that came into English from the islands of Tonga and means *considered not acceptable and so forbidden:* t_____

5. A synonym for *getting* or *obtaining:* a_____

6. A verb that means *to move together in a group* (like birds): f_____

7. An adjective starting with the prefix *in-* and meaning *not costing very much:* in_____

8. A word in quotation marks that refers to the group of young people in the late 1960s who wore flowers and strange clothes, reacted against traditional values, and took mind-altering drugs: h_____

9. An adverb that means *almost completely, for the most part:* v_____

10. A verb starting with *b* that means *to negotiate and come to an agreement about something, particularly the price of something:* b_____

6 **Focusing on Words from the Academic Word List** Use the most appropriate word from the box to fill in each of the blanks below in the paragraph taken from Part 2. Do NOT look back at the reading right away; instead, first see if you can now remember the vocabulary. Check your answers on page 94.

acquiring	communities	found	physical
benefit	compensation	hence	

c   Indigenous peoples in the Andes demand _____ for

having their photographs taken, saying it's intrusive. A woman in Otavalo,

Ecuador, explained to me, "We see ourselves and our children on postcards

and in books. "We do not _____ from having our photos

taken. A foreigner does. We demand part of the profits." In some indigenous   5

_____, photography is taboo because it is believed

to cause _____ and spiritual harm to the person who is

photographed. In India, young children have had limbs torn from their bodies to make them more pathetic and _____ "better" ⁵

beggars. Adults who commit this violence often have several children who ¹⁰

work for them. Other forms of begging, sometimes _____ ⁶

amusing by tourists, offend many locals. An indigenous leader from

Panama told me, "It breaks my heart to see the young boys swimming after

the coins the tourists throw in the water. We spent years

_____ our rights to these lands. Now with tourism, the ¹⁵ ⁷

people here do not care about the land anymore. They just want tourist

dollars."

Strategy

Using a Venn Diagram to Compare and Contrast
Comparing (finding similar points) and contrasting (finding different points) two
items (people, places, things, or groups) can aid your understanding of them and
help you to remember the main ideas and important details.

You can use a Venn diagram to compare, contrast, and evaluate items or ideas. A
Venn diagram is made up of two or more overlapping circles as seen below.

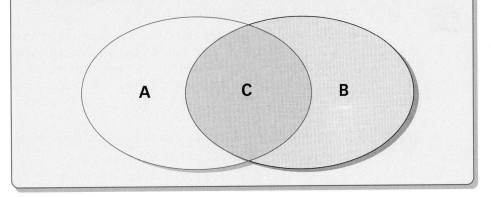

7 **Comparing and Contrasting with a Venn Diagram** Scan the article to
find examples of the actions and attitudes of tourists. Write them in circle A. Then do the
same for the actions and attitudes of the locals and write them in circle B. If there are
actions and attitudes that you think both groups share, put those in the middle part C,
where the two circles intersect. Compare your diagram with the diagrams of others in
the class and be prepared to explain your choices.

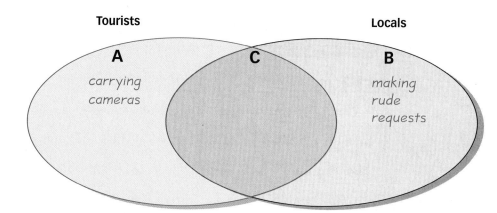

Tourists

Locals

A

*carrying
cameras*

C

B

*making
rude
requests*

8 **Guided Academic Conversations** In small groups, discuss the first topic below. Then choose two others to discuss. Reach a group consensus (agreement by everyone) and write up a group opinion statement for each topic you discuss.

1. **Jobs and tourism** Is tourism good or bad for the economy of a region? What kinds of jobs does tourism bring? Are these good or bad jobs? Who benefits from them? What places have you visited as a tourist and what did you observe about the people who lived and worked there?

2. **Begging** Does giving to beggars help or hurt the local people? Where is begging a problem? Is it wrong to pass by a beggar and not give anything, or is that the correct thing to do? Should you sometimes give to women and children who beg in the street, but not to men? Is there anything that you can give to beggars besides money?

3. **Taboos** Are taboos important cultural norms or just silly superstitions? Why is photography taboo in some communities? Do you ask permission before taking photos of strangers? Why or why not? Are there any actions that are taboo in your culture but are done by tourists?

4. **Different kinds of travelers** Which ones are good and which ones are bad? What is a "budget traveler" and why do such travelers sometimes bring money into the local economy? What do you think of the attitude of the British tourist who was cycling around the world? What actions and attitudes do you dislike in certain travelers?

9 **Reading Charts** Look at the three charts that follow and work together with a group to answer the questions about them.

1.

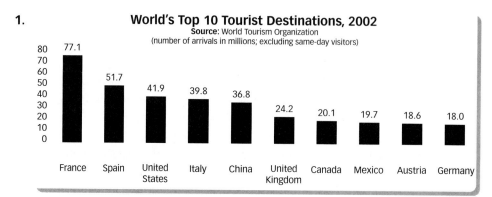

World's Top 10 Tourist Destinations, 2002
Source: World Tourism Organization
(number of arrivals in millions; excluding same-day visitors)

France	77.1
Spain	51.7
United States	41.9
Italy	39.8
China	36.8
United Kingdom	24.2
Canada	20.1
Mexico	19.7
Austria	18.6
Germany	18.0

2.

Top Countries in Tourism Earnings, 2002
Source: World Tourism Organization
International tourism receipts (excluding transportation): in billions of dollars

Rank	Country	Receipts 2001	Receipts 2002	% change	Rank	Country	Receipts 2001	Receipts 2002	% change
1.	United States ...	$72.3	$66.5	−7.4	8.	Hong Kong, China	$8.2	$10.1	22.2
2.	Spain	32.9	33.6	2.2	9.	Greece	9.1	9.7	3.1
3.	France	29.6	32.3	7.8	10.	Mexico	8.4	8.9	5.4
4.	Italy	25.9	26.9	4.3	11.	Canada	10.8	8.7	−19.3
5.	China[1]	17.8	20.4	14.6	12.	Turkey	8.9	8.5	4.8
6.	United Kingdom .	15.9	17.8	9.5	13.	Australia	7.6	8.1	6.1
7.	Austria	12.0	11.2	11.1	14.	Thailand	7.0	7.9	11.7

(1) Excluding Hong Kong

3.

Average Number of Vacation Days per Year, Selected Countries
Source: World Tourism Organization

Country	Days	Country	Days	Country	Days
1. Italy	42	4. Brazil	34	7. Korea	25
2. France	37	5. United Kingdom	28	8. Japan	25
3. Germany	35	6. Canada	26	9. United States	13

1. On Chart 1, what is meant by the "World's Top 10 Tourist Destinations"? On what basis are these countries *ranked* (put in order)? Which continent has the largest number of top countries? Do you think that this is due to its location or to other factors? Explain.

2. How is Chart 2 different from Chart 1? Which countries are on this chart that were not in the top ten on the first one? In your opinion, what qualities do these 14 countries have in common that make them attractive to tourists?

3. What information do we learn from Chart 3? How much difference is there between the country ranked as number 1 and the country ranked as number 9? What effects do you think this has on production, on the health of workers, and on the general happiness of the populations? What do you consider the ideal number of vacation days per year? Why?

Part 3   Tying It All Together

1 **End-of-Chapter Game Show** Supplies: small pieces of paper on which to write questions, two bags, small prizes (candies or fancy pencils, etc.)

The class should divide into two equal-sized groups. Each group chooses a team name, and then works together to write ten questions on ten pieces of paper, covering material from Chapter 4. (These questions can cover vocabulary or content, such as, What does the word *indigenous* mean? or Which foods may prevent heart disease?) Each team puts their pieces of paper into a bag.

Teams line up on different sides of the classroom in pairs. The instructor takes a question from team 2 and asks it to the first pair from team 1. If they answer the question correctly, team 1 gets a point. Then the instructor asks a question from team 1 to the first pair from team 2, and so on until all the questions have been asked. If a team's question doesn't ask about information from Chapter 4, the other team gets a point. When the game ends, the team with the higher number of points wins the prizes.

 2 Making Connections Choose one of the topics about health below. Answer the questions about that topic by finding facts and opinions on the Internet. Report your findings to the class.

1. **Diets to lose weight** Which diet is more popular for losing weight: the low fat or the low carb? Which is more effective?

2. **Herbal teas** Are they really good for your health? Can they be dangerous?

3. **Exercise classes** What kinds are in fashion now? What types of people take them? Why?

4. **Vitamins** Why do many people take them every day? Can they help you to feel good or to live longer?

5. **Meditation** What is it? Can it really improve your health? Why or why not?

6. **Reiki** What is it? Does it help you or is it a fraud?

7. **Bathing at a spa** A spa is a place that usually has a hot tub, sauna, or steam room. Why do so many people do it? What are the different styles of enjoying water as a method of cleaning and relaxation? Which do you prefer?

8. **Acupuncture or Chiropractic** What is it? Can it cure illness? Explain.

9. **Junk food** Is it a big business? How is it affecting people's health around the world?

Responding in Writing

WRITING TIP: STRUCTURING AN ARGUMENT TO SUPPORT YOUR OPINION

First, think about a topic and form your opinion. Then structure an argument in favor of it by presenting your main point, listing details that support it, and finishing with a concluding statement.

3 Writing a Paragraph that Expresses Your Opinion Write a paragraph expressing your opinion on one of the following topics: 1) The Best Way to Improve Your Health; or 2) The Best Way to Travel. Follow these steps:

Step 1: Work with a partner and brainstorm to find all the ideas you can on the topic you have chosen and make a list of them, in any order.

Step 2: Choose the idea you like best, the main idea that expresses your opinion on the topic.

Step 3: Write one sentence that states this idea clearly.

Step 4: Look through your list and back through the chapter. Think of at least three examples that support or illustrate your main idea. Make up sentences about these in your own words.

Step 5: Write a final sentence that either repeats your idea in different words or makes a new personal comment about it.

Step 6: Invent a good title for your paragraph. Try to think of something that will catch people's interest and make them want to read it.

Self-Assessment Log

Read the lists below. Check (✓) the strategies and vocabulary that you learned in this chapter. Look through the chapter or ask your instructor about the strategies and words that you do not understand.

Reading and Vocabulary-Building Strategies

- ❑ Using headings to preview
- ❑ Getting meaning from context
- ❑ Paraphrasing main ideas
- ❑ Recognizing synonyms
- ❑ Organizing information using a continuum
- ❑ Understanding points of view
- ❑ Skimming for the point of view
- ❑ Distinguishing between fact and opinion
- ❑ Scanning for vocabulary
- ❑ Using a Venn diagram to compare and contrast
- ❑ Reading charts

Target Vocabulary

Nouns

- ❑ affluence
- ❑ bargaining
- ❑ begging
- ❑ benefit*
- ❑ cancer
- ❑ communities*
- ❑ compensation*
- ❑ cuisine
- ❑ diet
- ❑ ecotourism
- ❑ fiber
- ❑ frontiers
- ❑ grain
- ❑ heart disease
- ❑ hippies

- ❑ legumes
- ❑ locals
- ❑ monounsaturates
- ❑ natural resources
- ❑ peasant
- ❑ prosperity
- ❑ requests
- ❑ stinginess
- ❑ subculture
- ❑ tourists
- ❑ treats

Verbs

- ❑ acquiring*
- ❑ bargained

- ❑ distinguish
- ❑ flock
- ❑ found* (find)
- ❑ prevent

Adjectives

- ❑ affluent
- ❑ annoyed
- ❑ demanding
- ❑ eclectic
- ❑ elite
- ❑ enchanted
- ❑ inappropriate*
- ❑ indigenous
- ❑ inexpensive

- ❑ peasant
- ❑ physical*
- ❑ taboo
- ❑ up-front

Adverbs

- ❑ hence*
- ❑ virtually*

*These words are from the Academic Word List. For more information on this list, see www.vuw.ac.nz/lals/research/awl.

5

High Tech, Low Tech

In This Chapter

Technology keeps transforming our world, providing important solutions to global problems. The first article presents the benefits of the hybrid car as a compromise in a world with pollution problems that needs to slowly move away from dependence on gasoline. The second describes recent advancements in information and communication technology in developing countries and the great changes that technology can bring.

❝ Men [and women] have become tools of their tools. ❞

—Henry David Thoreau,
U.S. philosopher and writer (1817–1862)

Connecting to the Topic

1 Look at the photo below. Where is this man? What is he doing?

2 Today's technology allows people to be in contact from almost anywhere all of the time. What are the advantages and disadvantages of this?

3 In your opinion, what are our biggest global problems? How do you think technology is solving, or could help solve these problems?

How Hybrid Cars Work

Reading Tip

Use what you learned about skimming in Chapter 3, page 58 to find the general idea of the reading. This will give you a context to help you understand the new vocabulary.

Before You Read

1 **Skimming for the General Idea** Skim the article on pages 108–110 (without looking up any words) by quickly reading the title, the first two paragraphs, the headings, the picture captions, and the first sentence of each of the remaining paragraphs. Then circle the letter of the most appropriate ending to the following statement:

This article focuses on _____.

  a. the new types of cars on the market, including gasoline-powered, electric, and hybrid cars by different car companies.

  b. the hybrid car itself, how it combines features of gasoline-powered and electric cars, and the reasons for it being produced.

  c. the various ways to get better mileage from your car and how fuel tanks and batteries can be used to store energy.

Strategy

Scanning for Definitions of Key Terms
When you see a word near the beginning of an article or in its title and you're not completely sure of the definition, scan the article to see if the definition is included. Then when you read, you will understand the meaning better.

2 **Scanning for Definitions of Key Terms** Scan this article to find the following definitions.

  1. What makes a vehicle a *hybrid*? Any vehicle is a hybrid when _____ _____.

  2. What is a *gasoline-electric hybrid car*? _____ _____.

Inferring Meaning

In Chapters 1 and 2, you practiced the skill of inferring the meaning of words from their context. Now, extend that skill by inferring the meaning of expressions, groups of words that have a special meaning when used together. Remember that an inference can also be called an "educated guess." You guess what something means based on what you know about the general idea or context behind it.

3 **Inferring the Meaning of Expressions from Context and Vocabulary** Now that you know the general idea of the article, read the statements below and try to infer (make an inference about) the meaning of the phrases or expressions in these questions. Use the hints to help you.

1. Have you pulled your car up to the gas pump lately and been *shocked* by the high price of gasoline?
   (**Hint:** Literally, a *shock* is what you might get if you put a metal object into an electrical socket, but the word can also mean any reaction a person has that would be similar to receiving this type of electrical current jolt.) In this sentence, *being shocked* means _____.
   - Ⓐ injuring oneself seriously
   - Ⓑ being forced to pay more money than you expected
   - Ⓒ feeling completely surprised and upset

2. Have you pulled your car up to the *gas pump* lately?
   (**Hint:** *Gas* is short for "gasoline" and a *pump* is what is used to move liquid from one area to another.) So *gas pump* here means _____.
   - Ⓐ the device used to put gasoline in your car at the gas station
   - Ⓑ part of the car's engine, not on an electric car
   - Ⓒ the place where they remove the gasoline from the ground

3. Maybe you thought about trading in that SUV (short for *sport utility vehicle*— any small multi-use truck that is not a pickup or minivan) for something that gets *better mileage.*
   (**Hint:** *Mileage* comes from the word "mile," the unit of measure still used in some countries instead of kilometers.) *Better mileage* here means

   _____.
   - Ⓐ it can move more quickly or for many miles
   - Ⓑ more attention from consumers
   - Ⓒ more distance for each liter or gallon of gasoline

4. Or maybe you're worried that your car is contributing to *the greenhouse effect.*
   (**Hint:** A *greenhouse* is a warm building that traps the heat of the sun where plants are kept.) So the *greenhouse effect* is _____.
   - Ⓐ an increase in the earth's temperature due to pollution that traps the sun's rays
   - Ⓑ the process of growing more plants to replace those used for food
   - Ⓒ the negative effect of too much traffic on people's minds

5. Or maybe you just want to have *the coolest car on the block*.
   (**Hint:** While *cool* can mean "not too warm," the common expression *that person is so cool!* does not mean that she or he is feeling cold.) As in the case of the *cool* person, instead, *the coolest car on the block* means _____.

   - (A) a car that is cold and never overheats
   - (B) the car everyone admires
   - (C) the car with the best air-conditioning system

6. The gasoline engine turns a generator, and the generator can *charge* the batteries.
   (**Hint:** The word *charge* can have many meanings, such as *to accuse—or charge someone with murder; to pay with credit or to charge it to a credit card; or to supply, fill, or load something.*) In this sentence, *charge* means _____.

   - (A) to fill with energy
   - (B) to accuse
   - (C) to pay for the batteries with credit

7. The reason behind making an electric car is *twofold*: to reduce tailpipe emissions and to improve mileage.
   (**Hint:** *Twofold* is a compound word.) Here *twofold* means _____.

   - (A) a tailpipe is folded in two parts
   - (B) there are two reasons
   - (C) it's two times more important

8. The reason behind making an electric car is twofold: to reduce *tailpipe emissions* and to improve mileage.
   (**Hint:** *Tailpipe* is a compound word that describes well the part of the car it represents, and *emissions* comes from the verb "emit," which means "to give off" or "to release.") In this sentence, *to reduce tailpipe emissions* means _____.

   - (A) to increase the size of the pipe in back of the car
   - (B) to decrease the pollution given off by the car
   - (C) to send out a more pleasant mixture of chemicals

9. These goals are actually tightly *interwoven*.
   (**Hint:** *Interwoven* is a compound word combining *woven* (the past participle of the verb "to weave," meaning to "knit or sew") with *inter,* meaning "together" or "with each other." *These goals are tightly interwoven* means that they _____.
   - (A) are closely related to each other, as though sewn together
   - (B) involve an activity that resembles knitting or sewing
   - (C) need to use a system that is tightly closed so pollution does not escape

Introduction

Air pollution (air contaminated by smoke, waste, or chemicals) has become a growing concern in the global community, with agreements such as the Kyoto Protocol[1] aimed at reducing its devastating effect on the world. With more and more people driving all the time, the automotive industry has become one of the big targets of measures to reduce pollution.

The following selection presents one result of this effort to revolutionize the automotive industry: the hybrid car. In this selection, you will learn terminology in English relating to the technology of automobiles, and you will also get to practice discussing the important issue of climate control.

- What do you think about air pollution? Is it a problem in the place where you live?

- In your opinion, what would the perfect car be like?

▲ A hybrid car is more fuel efficient. Although most hybrid cars use diesel or gas, alternative fuels such as ethanol are also used sometimes. In the U.S. corn is the primary stock used for making ethanol. Source: wikipedia.org

---

[1]The Kyoto Protocol is an agreement of over 150 countries to reduce emissions of greenhouse gases between the years 2008 and 2012 by at least 5% from 1990 levels. It was adopted by the United Nations Framework Convention on Climate Change in 1997.

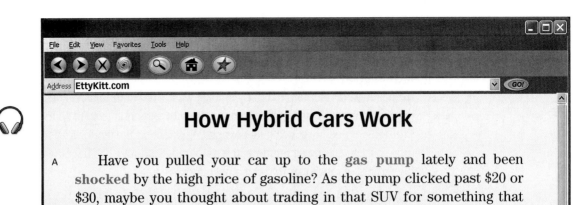

Address EttyKitt.com

How Hybrid Cars Work

A   Have you pulled your car up to the **gas pump** lately and been **shocked** by the high price of gasoline? As the pump clicked past $20 or $30, maybe you thought about trading in that SUV for something that gets better **mileage**. Or maybe you're worried that your car is contributing to the **greenhouse effec**t. Or maybe you just want to have the coolest car **on the block**. 5

B   The auto industry now has the technology that might answer all of these needs. It's the *hybrid car*. 10

What Makes it a "Hybrid"?

C   Any vehicle is a hybrid when it combines two or more sources of power. For example, a *moped* (a motorized pedal bike) is a type of hybrid because it combines the power of a gasoline engine with the pedal power of its rider. 15 20

    Hybrid vehicles are all around us. Most of the **locomotives** we see pulling trains are *diesel-electric hybrids*. Cities like Seattle have diesel-electric *buses*—these can draw electric power from overhead wires or run on diesel when they are away 25 30 35

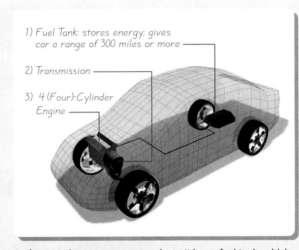

1) *Fuel Tank: stores energy; gives car a range of 300 miles or more*

2) *Transmission*

3) *4 (Four)-Cylinder Engine*

▲ **Figure 1** shows a gas-powered car. It has a fuel tank, which supplies gasoline to its **four-cylinder engine**. Gas car engines can operate at **speeds** of up to 8,000 **rpm**.

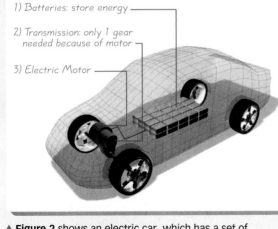

1) *Batteries: store energy*

2) *Transmission: only 1 gear needed because of motor*

3) *Electric Motor*

▲ **Figure 2** shows an electric car, which has a set of batteries that provides electricity to an electric motor. Batteries give the car a range of about 50–100 miles.

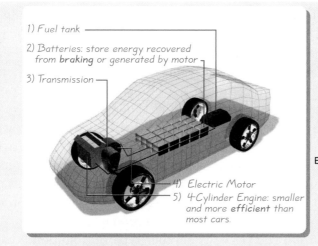

1) Fuel tank

2) Batteries: store energy recovered from *braking* or generated by motor

3) Transmission

4) Electric Motor

5) 4-Cylinder Engine: smaller and more *efficient* than most cars.

▲ **Figure 3** shows a typical parallel hybrid. You'll notice that the fuel tank and gas engine connect to the transmission. Its engine is smaller than that of most cars, but it is **efficient**. The batteries and electric motor also connect to the transmission independently. As a result, in a parallel hybrid, both the electric motor and the gas engine can provide propulsion power.

from the wires. Any vehicle that combines two or more sources of power that can directly or indirectly provide **propulsion power** is a hybrid. 40

E The *gasoline-electric hybrid car* is just that— a cross between a gasoline-powered car and an electric car. Let's start with a few diagrams to explain the differences. 45 50

Hybrid Structure

F You can combine the two power sources found in a hybrid car in different ways. One way, known as a *parallel hybrid*, has a **fuel tank**, which supplies gasoline to the engine. But it also has a set of **batteries** that supplies power to an electric motor. Both the 55 engine and the electric motor can turn the **transmission** at the same time, and the transmission then turns the wheels.

G By contrast, in a *series hybrid* (Figure 4 below), the gasoline engine turns a **generator**, and the generator can either **charge** the batteries or power an electric motor that drives the transmission. Thus, the gasoline 60 engine never directly powers the vehicle. Take a look at the diagram of the series hybrid, starting with the fuel tank, and you'll see that all of the **components** form a line that eventually connects with the transmission. 65

Why Build Such a Complex Car?

H You might wonder why anyone would build 70 such a complicated machine when most people are perfectly happy with their gasoline-powered cars. 75

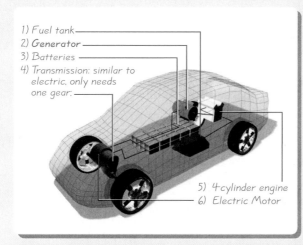

1) Fuel tank
2) Generator
3) Batteries
4) Transmission: similar to electric, only needs one gear.
5) 4-cylinder engine
6) Electric Motor

▲ **Figure 4** Shows a series hybrid car that works with a generator. The generator can either charge the batteries or power the electric motor that drives the transmission. The batteries store the energy recovered from **braking**.

The reason is **twofold**: to *reduce tailpipe emissions* and to *improve mileage*. These goals are actually tightly **interwoven**.

I   California emissions standards dictate how much of each type of pollution a car is allowed to emit in California. The amount is usually specified in grams per mile (g/mi). For example, the low emissions vehicle *(LEV)* standard allows 3.4 g/mi of carbon monoxide.

J   The key thing here is that the amount of pollution allowed does not depend on the mileage your car gets. But a car that burns twice as much gas to go a mile will generate approximately twice as much pollution. That pollution will have to be removed by the emissions control equipment on the car. So decreasing the fuel consumption of the car is one of the surest ways to decrease emissions.

K   Carbon dioxide (CO_2) is another type of pollution a car produces. The U.S. government does not regulate it, but scientists suspect that it contributes to *global warming*. Since it is not regulated, a car has no devices for removing CO_2 from the **exhaust**, so a car that burns twice as much gas adds twice as much CO_2 to the atmosphere.

L   Automakers in the U.S. have another strong incentive to improve mileage. They are required by law to meet *Corporate Average Fuel Economy* (CAFE) standards. The current standards require that the average mileage of all the new cars sold by an automaker should be 27.5 mpg (8.55 liters per 100 km). This means that if an automaker sells one hybrid car that gets 60 mpg (3.92 liters per 100 km), it can then sell four big, expensive luxury cars that only get 20 mpg (11.76 liters per 100 km)!

Source: "How Hybrid Cars Work" (Karim Nice) as appeared on HowStuffWorks.com website. Courtesy of HowStuffWorks.com

After You Read

Strategy

Learning Specialized Terms
Learning specialized terms about a topic can help you understand the reading. Specialized terms in the article "How Hybrids Work" are words that you might use when talking about automobiles.

4 **Inferring the Meaning of Specialized Terms** Match each term on the left to the correct synonym or definition on the right. For a term you are not sure about, scan the article or diagrams for it, and use the context to infer its meaning.

Definitions

1. _____ locomotives [line 27]

2. _____ transmission [line 56]

3. _____ fuel tank [line 54]

4. _____ four-cylinder engine [Figure 1]

5. _____ parallel [line 53]

6. _____ components [line 65]

7. _____ propulsion power [line 41]

8. _____ braking [Figure 4]

9. _____ efficient [Figure 3]

10. _____ generator [line 59]

11. _____ rpm [Figure 1]

12. _____ global warming [line 90]

13. _____ exhaust [line 91]

14. _____ speeds [Figure 1]

a. rotations per minute (how fast something turns)

b. the slowing down of the car

c. the greenhouse effect causes it

d. engine cars that pull trains

e. a machine that converts mechanical into electrical energy

f. how fast something moves

g. storage place in car for gasoline

h. two parts having a similar function or functioning interchangeably

i. a motor with four chambers in which pistons move

j. producing results with minimum effort

k. waste gases released from an engine

l. parts that make up a whole

m. the force to move something

n. vehicle part transmitting power from the engine to the wheels

Strategy

Using a Graphic Organizer Chart for Comparison
Creating a chart can often help you clearly see the similarities and differences between different objects or concepts. First, make a list of important factors or qualities on the left. Then put columns across the top with the name of the different objects or concepts, and fill in the specific numbers or descriptions for each. See the chart in Activity 5 for an example.

5 **Filling Out a Chart for Comparison** Look at the diagrams for the gasoline-powered car, the electric car, the parallel hybrid, and the series hybrid to try to understand the similarities and differences between these types of cars. Work together to fill in the chart on page 112, putting a check mark (✓) to indicate the cars that have the qualities described in the column on the left.

Quality	Gasoline Car	Electric Car	Parallel Hybrid	Series Hybrid
1. Has a fuel tank				
2. Has batteries to store energy				
3. Can operate at speeds of up to 8,000 rpm.				
4. Has a range of 50–100 miles				
5. Runs only on electricity				
6. Has a generator				
7. Has a four-cylinder engine				
8. Has both a four-cylinder engine and an electric motor				
9. Has a four-cylinder engine in the trunk (back) area				

6 **Talking It Over** Discuss the following questions with a partner. Afterwards, compare your opinions with those of two other classmates.

1. Do you know anyone who owns a hybrid car? What is your opinion of hybrid cars?

2. Would it be better for society if more people owned one? Or should we all be encouraged to move to purely electric cars? Why or why not?

3. What do you think of the CAFE standard for automakers in the U.S.? Explain why automakers can sell four big expensive luxury cars if they sell one hybrid. Should there be more laws and regulations like this to push forward the manufacturing of hybrids? Why or why not?

4. How are the series and parallel types of hybrid cars different? Which is better, in your opinion, and why?

5. Can you think of possible ways to get consumers to buy hybrid or electric cars? Write down three persuasive things you could tell consumers that would get them to buy hybrid cars.

7 **Researching a Gadget** New technology is coming out all the time to provide us with new products that propose to make our lives easier or more enjoyable. Some of these products are large, like cars, but others are gadgets, small mechanical devices that we can carry around and use in our homes and at work. Look at the list below, and choose a gadget you'd like to research.

1. An MP3 player or iPod®

2. A PlayStation®

3. A cellular phone with camera, PDA, email capacity, and/or other capabilities

4. Other: _____

Find out everything you can about this gadget. What can it do? Why is it fun (or not fun) to have? How much does it cost? Where can you get it? You can talk about your own experience with the gadget, look it up on the Internet, or go to a store where the gadget is sold.

Take notes on your findings and come to class prepared to talk about it either to the whole class or in a small group. You may even want to bring your gadget if you already own one!

Leapfrogging the Technology Gap

Before You Read

Strategy

Identifying the Pattern of Organization in a Reading
All professional writing has some set structure. Professional writers are careful in where they put their main points and how they organize their specific details. Understanding the logic behind this structure helps you understand better what is being communicated and also helps you improve your own ability to write well.

1 Identifying the Pattern of Organization Look at the title, illustrations, and instructions of the article on pages 117–118. What problem is being discussed? What solution is being offered?

Now that you know the topic, try to identify the way the article is organized. This can help you to read it more easily. First, look quickly at the following three common patterns. Then take a couple of minutes to skim the article. After you finish, read the three patterns with more care and tell which pattern best describes the article's organization.

Pattern 1: From General to Specific

- Description of a problem
- Description of the solution(s)
- History of why the problem exists
- Examples to illustrate the problem and solution

Pattern 2: From Specific to General

- Description of a number of specific examples of a larger problem
- Explanation of the problem and its history
- Solution(s)

Pattern 3: From Specific to General to Specific

- One specific example to attract readers' interest and introduce the topic
- Description of the problem
- Description of the solution(s)
- Further examples to develop and illustrate the problem and solution

2 **Outlining the Specific Details** The article uses detailed examples of the types of technology that can play an important role in underdeveloped countries, but these details come out most clearly in the specific locations used to illustrate them. Scan the article to identify which areas (cities and/or countries) the author uses to present examples and write the areas below:

I. _____

II. _____

III. _____

IV. _____

V. _____

3 **Analyzing the Main Point (Thesis) of an Article** Before reading the article, answer the questions below.

1. The following quotation presents the main point of the article:
"Villages like Robib have been described as leapfroggers: communities or even whole countries in the developing world that are using information and communication technologies to leapfrog directly from being an agricultural to an information economy."

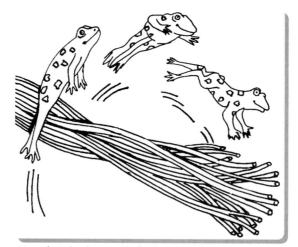

▲ Leapfrogging is not only for frogs.

From the quotation above, what does the term *leapfrog* mean? What two words make up this compound word? What metaphor (image of one thing representing another) do you get from this term? The image of a _____

represents _____. Explain how one thing could represent the other.

2. What do you think an *agricultural economy* is? What is an *information economy?*

3. Even before you read the article, do you know (or can you guess) what type of economy usually comes between an agricultural and an information economy that is being skipped over in these "leapfrogging" countries?

UNDERSTANDING COMPOUND WORDS

A number of words in this article, like the words *leapfrog* or *schoolchildren* in the second sentence are actually compound words. (See Chapter 1 page 11 to review what compound words are and how to guess their meaning.)

4 **Understanding Compound Words** Figure out the meaning of the compound words in the following sentences by breaking them up into parts or by looking at the context. Circle the letter of the phrase that best expresses the meaning of each underlined compound word.

1. Schoolchildren are seeing their country's most famous landmarks for the first time.
- (A) a monument, building, or other object that serves as a typical marker on the land
- (B) a plot of land marked out for a house to be put up
- (C) an important person, like a politician or police officer

2. The village economy is taking off, fueled by the sale of its handmade silk scarves on the global market.
- (A) kept close at hand
- (B) made with a pattern of handprints
- (C) made by hand, not by a machine

3. Each motorcycle has a transmitter that allows it to upload and download email and data.
- (A) to move the computer mouse up and down while riding in a vehicle
- (B) to move information up [from vehicle to computer or server] and to move information back down [from server to vehicle]
- (C) to package and unpackage the computer before and after loading it in a vehicle that carries information to places that need it

4. Farm economies made room for craftsmen and artisans, who gave way to industrial production.
- (A) people who are sneaky and crafty
- (B) people who make crafts with their hands
- (C) workers in large industrialized factories

5. Widespread industrial development would still leave much of Africa, Asia, or Latin America a generation behind Europe and North America.
- (A) extending all over the globe
- (B) circulation in limited areas
- (C) widely recognized by many people

6. The Internet kiosks [booths or stands] that access a global <u>marketplace</u> can also be used to access political information or organize grassroots campaigns in emerging democracies.

    (A) a covered building used for trading food and clothing

    (B) meeting of representatives from different countries for the purpose of providing aid.

    (C) place where ideas, as well as goods, are bought and sold

7. The Internet kiosks [booths or stands] . . . can also be used to access political information or organize <u>grassroots</u> campaigns in emerging democracies.

    (A) based on (rooted in) the needs of ordinary people.

    (B) natural and friendly to the environment

    (C) occurring in areas that are full of grass, like fields

8. Pondicherry, India's information and communications technology development strategy traces back to a 1998 project that brought Internet-linked <u>telecentres</u> to the region's villages. (Note: Also spelled *telecenters*)

    (A) televisions for viewing programs and movies

    (B) meeting places for community activities, like team sports, shows, or political rallies

    (C) locations for long-distance communication by computer, telephone, telegraph, television, etc.

Read

Introduction

In the world today, there are many countries whose development and quality of life still lag behind that of the countries traditionally known as "first world." Moving from an agrarian economy to an industrialized economy and then to an information economy took many decades in Europe, Japan, the United States, and Canada. However, at the present time, some developing countries are bypassing the long route to development. They are "leapfrogging" into the information age by using combinations of high-tech and low-tech technology in creative ways. Read the following article to find out more about this new path to development.

- Have you ever seen a frog leap? What does it look like?
- Why are some developing countries now called "leapfroggers"?
- What technologies do you think you will read about in this article?

Leapfrogging the Technology Gap

A   In Robib, Cambodia, villagers are getting medical advice from the world's best doctors. Schoolchildren are seeing their country's most famous landmarks for the first time. And the village economy is taking off, fueled by the sale of its handmade silk scarves on the global market.

B   All these benefits are coming via motorcycle—Internet-enabled 5 motorcycles. A wireless network links computers in the village to computer chips on each of the five motorcycles. Each vehicle has a transmitter that allows it to upload and download email and data as it passes by village computers. At the end of the day, the bikes return to a hub where they upload the information received. The next morning, they download email 10 and data from the hub and take it out to the villages for transmission.

C   Villages like Robib have been described as "leapfroggers:" communities or even whole countries in the developing world that are using information and communication technologies to leapfrog directly from being an agricultural to an information economy. It's a phenomenon that combines technology high 15 and low in innovative ways, and is generating not only economic benefits but a new world of education, social, and political opportunities.

D   In highly developed countries, the information economy has emerged from a long evolution—farm economies made room for craftsmen and artisans, who gave way to industrial production, and manufacturing has 20 yielded to the rise of an information and service-based economy.

E   Economists and development experts wonder whether the developing world can—or should—follow the same path. Widespread industrial development would still leave much of Africa, Asia, or Latin America a generation behind Europe and North America. 25

F   Of greater concern is the potential environmental impact of widespread industrialization: large-scale factory production in the developing world could greatly increase global energy consumption and pollution levels, particularly if factories use cheaper and dirtier production methods.

G   Information and communication technologies provide an alternative to 30 this environmental and economic nightmare. The hardware, software, and networks that have propelled developed economies out of the industrial era and into the information age are now promising to take the developing world directly from agrarian to post-industrial development.

H   The same satellite networks that link remote villages to urban markets can 35 bring classroom education to communities too small or poor to support secondary schools. The cell phone systems that power community businesses can connect patients or doctors, or disparate family members. The Internet kiosks that access a global marketplace can also be used to access political information or organize grassroots campaigns in emerging democracies. 40

Societies that place a high value on education, like Vietnam, are at an advantage, because a highly educated population is ready for work in a knowledge-based economy. Bangalore, India, is the best-case scenario. Recognized as the Silicon Valley of the developing world, Bangalore has parlayed India's wealth of well-educated, tech-savvy, English-speaking 45 programmers into a massive hive of interlocking programming shops, call centres, and tech companies.

▲ Students using technology in the classroom.

While Bangalore's technological, education, and linguistic advantages have 50 given it a head start on leapfrogging, regions that lack those advantages stand to gain even more from the creative use of technology. Indeed, the countries that stand to benefit most from a leapfrogging strategy are those 55 with limited infrastructure, limited education access, and limited literacy rates.

In Bolivia, a rural radio station uses the Internet to answer questions from listeners—like the farmer who wanted help dealing with 60 a worm that was devouring his crops. Working online, the station found a Swedish expert who identified the worm and broadcast the information on pest control to the entire community.

"The development community has placed a great emphasis on being able to meet basic development objectives," says Richard Simpson, the 65 Director of E-Commerce for Industry Canada. "It is not about rich countries getting richer. It's not even about emerging economies. It's about countries at every stage of development using technology in a way that is appropriate to their needs." Needs like those of Nallavadu, a village in Pondicherry, India. A region in which many people live on incomes of less than one dollar a day, 70 Pondicherry's information and communications technology development strategy traces back to a 1998 project that brought Internet-linked telecentres to the region's villages. Today, villagers routinely use the Internet to access information that helps them sell their crops at the latest commodity prices, obtain medical advice, and track regional weather and transport. 75

How does that kind of technology affect daily life? Just look at what happened in the village of Nallavadu. Vijayakumar Gunasekaran, the son of a Nallavadu fisherman, learned of December's earthquake and tsunami [2004] from his current home in Singapore. When Gunasekaran called home to warn his family, they passed along the warning to fellow 80 villagers—who used the village's telecentre to broadcast a community alarm. Thanks to that alarm, the village was evacuated, ensuring that all 3,600 villagers survived.

Source: "Leapfrogging the Technology Gap" from pipermail.org (Alexandra Samuel)

After You Read

Strategy

Creating a Study Outline
To help you review an article or prepare for a test on it, you can create an informal outline. Write out a list of main points you want to remember, using roman numerals (I, II, III, IV, V, VI, VII, etc.); then put examples under each, using regular numbers (1, 2, 3, etc.). Use your outline when filling in exercises, preparing for class discussion, or reviewing for an exam.

5 **Creating a Study Outline** Complete the study outline below for the article "Leapfrogging the Technology Gap." In this case, it will be an outline of places that can be called "leapfroggers" with examples of the development in those places. First, fill in the locations, I–V, that you outlined in Activity 2 on page 114. Then write the main example (or examples) of the types of development occurring there. You can look back through the article to complete the outline.

I. Location: _Rohib, Cambodia_

　　1. _Motorcycles are Internet-enabled. They carry information between remote villages and central computer hubs._

II. Location: _____

　　1. _educated population can work in a_ _____ _economy_

III. Location: _____

　　1. _shops_ _____

　　2. _centers_ _____

　　3. _____

IV. Location: _____

　　1. _a rural_ _____ _uses the_ _____ _to research information_

V. Location: _____

　　1. _____ _telecentres_

　　2. _used as a community_ _____ _during the_ _____ _of 2004_

UNDERSTANDING COMPOUND ADJECTIVES

Often when two or more words come before a noun and function together as an adjective (word that describes something), they are linked together by a hyphen (-).

6 **Analyzing Compound Adjectives with Hyphens** Analyze the meanings of the words in italics by looking at the shorter words that are connected by the hyphen and at the context. Write explanations in the blanks.

1. All these benefits are coming via motorcycle—*Internet-enabled motorcycles*
   motorcycles that can access the Internet

2. Farm economies made room for craftsmen and artisans, who gave way to industrial production, and manufacturing has yielded to the rise of an information and *service-based economy*. [**Hint:** *service* here relates to jobs in which employees provide something nontangible rather than producing goods.]

   _____

3. *Large-scale factory production* in the developing world could greatly increase global energy consumption and pollution levels.

   _____

4. Societies that place a high value on education, like Vietnam, are at an advantage, because a highly educated population is ready for work in *a knowledge-based economy*.

   _____

5. Bangalore, India, is the *best-case scenario*. [**Hint:** *scenario* here means a course of action that could happen]

   _____

6. Recognized as the Silicon Valley of the developing world, Bangalore has successfully parlayed India's wealth of *well-educated, tech-savvy, English-speaking* programmers into a massive hive of interlocking programming shops, call centers, and tech companies.
   a. *well-educated programmers* are _____
   b. *tech-savvy programmers* are [**Hint:** "savvy" comes from the Spanish word *sabe* which means "know."] _____

7. Therefore, *well-educated, tech-savvy, English-speaking programmers* are

   _____

8. Pondicherry's information and communications technology development strategy traces back to a 1998 project that brought *Internet-linked telecentres* to the region's villages.

   _____

7 **Focusing on Words from the Academic Word List** Use the most appropriate word from the box to fill in each of the blanks on page 121 in the paragraph taken from Part 2. Do NOT look back at the reading right away; instead, first see if you can remember the vocabulary. One word will be used twice. Check your answers on page 117.

> benefits   data   global   network   vehicle
>
> computers   economy   medical   transmission   via

A   In Robib, Cambodia, villagers are getting _____ advice

1

from the world's best doctors. Schoolchildren are seeing their country's most famous landmarks for the first time. And the village

_____ is taking off, fueled by the sale of its

2

handmade silk scarves on the _____ market.   5

3

B   All these _____ are coming _____

4   5

motorcycle—Internet-enabled motorcycles. A wireless _____

6

links _____ in the village to computer chips on each of

7

the five motorcycles. Each _____ has a transmitter that

8

allows it to upload and download email and _____, as it   10

9

passes by village computers. At the end of the day, the bikes return to a hub where they upload the information received. The next morning, they

download email and _____ from the hub and take it out

10

to the villages for _____.

11

Talking It Over

8 **Discussing Information Technology** Discuss the following questions. Then compare your answers with those of another group.

1. The article mentions various solutions for getting information technology into developing communities. What solutions are mentioned? Which solution do you consider the most creative and/or effective? Why?

2. Do you think that companies could make money providing this type of service or would it be purely charity work on their part? Is it possible to fulfill both of these goals at once?

3. Can you think of other countries where this type of revolution in technology is happening or should happen? Explain.

4. Besides the advantages (educational programs, medical and crop advice, warning systems, etc.) of communications technology offered here, what other advantages can you think of? In your opinion, will there be disadvantages, too? Explain.

 9 **What Do You Think?** Read the paragraph below and discuss the questions that follow.

Using Cellular Phones

An estimated 30% of the world's population owns a cellular phone. This means that any time of day or night, these people can call or be called if the phone is on. Their phones can ring at the theater, in the coffee shop, in the classroom, in the car, in the bedroom.

1. Do you think it's a good idea that a person can be reached at anytime? Why or why not?

2. Where and when do you think that sending or receiving calls should not be allowed? In restaurants? At the movies? At a concert? In the classroom? Explain your point of view.

3. What kind of restrictions should be put on phone calls while a person is driving?

4. Look at the cartoon below. What do you think the artist is trying to say?

Pepper . . . and Salt

THE WALL STREET JOURNAL

▲ "I was addicted to my cell phone, but now I have a patch for it."

Part 3 Tying It All Together

 1 **Guided Academic Conversation** Follow the directions on page 123 to conduct an interview and compare answers.

Step 1: Interview Interview a classmate on the following questions. Then have that classmate interview you. Take notes on what your classmate says and use those notes in Step 2.

1. How often do you use email? Explain how often and why to your classmate.
   a. more than five times a day
   b. one to four times a day
   c. every few days
   d. once a week or less

2. Do you prefer talking with friends on the telephone, exchanging email, or communicating in a chat room? Why?

3. In your opinion, does email make life easier or harder for people? Explain.

4. What do you use the Internet for? Explain your answer to your classmate. Some possible answers:
   a. I don't ever or almost never use it.
   b. I use it for research for my work or studies.
   c. I use it for socializing or personal interest research.
   d. I use it for work, personal interest, and just about everything in my life.

5. Would you use the Internet for romance? Explain why or why not. Some possible answers:
   a. No. This is dangerous or foolish.
   b. Yes. This is a safer way of meeting an appropriate friend or potential life partner with similar interests and beliefs.
   c. Only under certain circumstances.

6. Have you ever read or written a blog? If so, what kind of blog?

7. Write your own interview question that you want to ask people:

_____

Culture Note

A **blog** is an informal journal that a person writes on the Web. It tells the story of a trip (a travel blog), news (recent elections), personal or family updates for friends (a baby's development), or it can be on a particular topic like studying abroad. Often blogs include references and links to other websites, making them more interactive and interesting.

Step 2: Comparing Answers After you have finished with the interviews, create a Venn diagram similar to the one below to compare your answers. Put the name of your classmate above one circle and your own name above the other circle. Then write the items you agreed on in the space where the two circles cross over and items you had different answers for in each of the two separate circles. What is your conclusion? Is yours and your classmate's usage of the Internet similar or different?

Example   **My classmate:**   *Kim*   *Me*

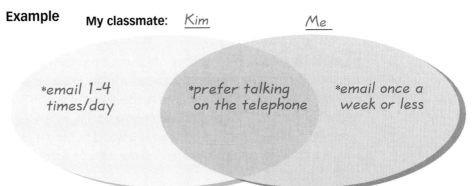

*email 1–4 times/day   *prefer talking on the telephone   *email once a week or less

2 Making Connections Choose one of the following three topics to do extra research on, using the Internet or other sources, and report back to the class. Be sure to copy down the websites that give you the information.

1. **Hybrid cars** Play detective and bring to class the answer to one of these three questions: 1) Which car in the world today uses the least amount of gasoline per kilometer (or mile)? How much does it use? 2) What manufacturer sells the most popular cars? How many does it sell each year? 3) What manufacturer sells the highest number of electric or hybrid cars? How many is that? Then find an interesting current fact or statistic related to hybrid or electric cars and write it down to share with the class.

2. **Jordan Education Initiative** One important example of a program enabling countries to become connected with information and communication technologies is the Jordan Education Initiative (JEI), launched in 2003 by the company Cisco in conjunction with His Majesty King Abdulla II of Jordan and a couple dozen other World Economic Forum members. The idea is that Jordan will serve as a model and that other countries, like Bahrain, Oman, and the United Arab Emirates, will follow with similar initiatives. Search on the web and find out how this initiative is progressing and bring some facts or stories about it to share with the class.

3. **Kyoto Protocol** What is happening with the Kyoto Protocol? (See page 107.) Which countries have complied with the guidelines? Which ones haven't? When was the most recent meeting about this? Where was it held and who attended it? On the basis of what you find, make your own personal prediction regarding this plan and present it to your classmates, along with your reasons for believing as you do.

Responding in Writing

WRITING TIP: SELECTING STRONG EXAMPLES TO SUPPORT YOUR POINT OF VIEW

To express your point of view on a subject, start by examining how you feel about this topic and why. If you have decided that you are in favor of it, choose examples that illustrate its good effects. If you have decided that you are against it, choose examples that show the bad effects it causes. Review your list and if there are too many examples, cut out the ones that seem the weakest. Choose only the examples that are convincing and develop them with details.

3 Writing About Technology Think about your own life and the society you live in. Do you think modern technology has had a more positive impact or a more negative one? Are you basically a high-tech or a low-tech kind of person? Choose one piece of technology that has made a big impact on your society or on your life for better or for worse. Then write a paragraph about what it would be like if it would suddenly be taken away and could no longer be used. Follow the steps on page 125.

Step 1: Decide if you want to discuss this in the general context of society or on a personal level, referring to your own life. Choose one of the following topics, filling in the blank with the piece of technology you're writing about, and choosing one of the adjectives (either *Sad* or *Happy*).

Our (Sad / Happy) Society Without _____

My (Sad / Happy) Life Without _____

Step 2: Look back over this chapter at the ideas and vocabulary presented. Select items that can be used to develop your theme and write them down.

Step 3: Imagine what things would be like without the technology you have chosen. Make a list of examples to show how society or your life would be either worse or better without it.

Step 4: Write a good beginning sentence that expresses your feelings about this technology and its impact.

Step 5: Select three to five examples from the list you made in Step 3 and express each one in a good sentence or two.

Step 6: Write a final sentence to conclude. Two common ways of concluding are 1) to repeat the main idea (given in the first sentence) in different words, or 2) to express a personal reaction, such as a wish or a rhetorical question (one that is asked in a general way with no expectation of an answer).

Step 7: Title your paragraph. Use either the theme you chose and adapted from Step 1 or another original title.

TOEFL® iBT

Focus on Testing

Using a Computer on Tests

The TOEFL® Internet-Based Test (iBT) is given by means of a computer. None of the test is on paper. In the reading section, you will see each reading passage on the computer screen for up to 20 minutes. You select most of your answers by clicking on them with a mouse. After each reading passage, one question will require you to drag items with a mouse and drop them into a summary box or a table.

An earlier version of the test, the "Computer-based TOEFL® test " (CBT), also used computers. The CBT was "adaptive," meaning that the computer chose which questions you should get, depending on your performance. The TOEFL® iBT, however, is not adaptive but "linear." Everyone taking the test at any one time will get the same questions.

During the 20 minutes for each reading, you can go back and forth between the reading and any of its questions. You can skip hard questions and answer the easy ones first. If you need to change any of your reading answers, you can. The computer provides a table of all the questions for a given reading and shows which questions you have already answered. Finally, the computer gives you a limited glossary during the test. For a few vocabulary items, shown in blue on the screen, a short definition is available if you click on the blue item.

Here are some helpful tips to remember when taking the iBT.

1. Read the directions for each question. Is it multiple choice? Should you select only one answer or two? Are you supposed to click with your mouse on an answer or drag and drop an answer?

2. A small timer appears in a corner of the screen and shows you how much time you have left. Use this on-screen timer to pace yourself.

3. You may take notes on a sheet of notepaper provided by the test supervisor. You may not take notes on the computer.

4. Make sure you understand how to use the mouse. Practice taking computerized tests in your school's language lab or library.

5. If you have any questions, don't be afraid to ask before the test starts. The supervisor is there to make sure everyone understands what to do before beginning the test.

Practice Based on the information in the box above, write a correct word or phrase in each blank. A correct answer can replace the word in italics. Review the information above as often as necessary. The first one is done for you as an example.

1. Test questions appear on the screen, and the test-taker clicks on the correct answer with *a pointing device*. _mouse_

2. The CBT is *programmed to select questions depending on the test taker's performance*. _____

3. The iBT is *programmed to give the same questions to all test-takers at a given time*. _____

4. The iBT reading section provides a *kind of chart* listing all the questions and showing whether you have answered them or not. _____

5. Always carefully read the *set of instructions that tell you how to answer each question*. _____

6. In addition to clicking on multiple-choice items, you may have to *move some answers with your mouse and put them in the correct place*. _____

7. The iBT reading section provides a *definition feature* which can help you understand certain words that are printed in blue. _____

8. A small *clock-like display* on the iBT screen shows you how much time you have left. _____

9. Although you cannot takes notes on the computer, you can take them *on sheets of paper* that the supervisor gives you. _____

Self-Assessment Log

Read the lists below. Check (✓) the strategies and vocabulary that you learned in this chapter. Look through the chapter or ask your instructor about the strategies and words that you do not understand.

Reading and Vocabulary-Building Strategies

- ❑ Skimming for the general idea
- ❑ Scanning for definitions of key terms
- ❑ Inferring the meaning of expressions from context and vocabulary
- ❑ Inferring the meaning of specialized terms
- ❑ Filling out a chart for comparison
- ❑ Identifying the pattern of organization in a reading
- ❑ Analyzing the main point (thesis) of an article
- ❑ Understanding compound words
- ❑ Creating a study outline
- ❑ Analyzing compound adjectives with hyphens

Target Vocabulary

Nouns

- ❑ benefits*
- ❑ best-case scenario
- ❑ braking
- ❑ components*
- ❑ computers*
- ❑ craftsmen
- ❑ data*
- ❑ economy*
- ❑ exhaust (from a car)
- ❑ four-cylinder engine
- ❑ fuel tank
- ❑ gas pump
- ❑ generator
- ❑ global warming
- ❑ greenhouse effect
- ❑ hybrid car
- ❑ landmarks
- ❑ leapfroggers
- ❑ locomotives
- ❑ marketplace
- ❑ mileage
- ❑ network*
- ❑ propulsion power
- ❑ rpm (rotations per minute)
- ❑ scenario*
- ❑ speeds
- ❑ tailpipe emissions
- ❑ telecenters (also spelled telecentres)
- ❑ transmission*
- ❑ vehicle*

Verbs

- ❑ charge (batteries)
- ❑ download
- ❑ upload

Preposition

- ❑ via*

Adjectives

- ❑ efficient
- ❑ English-speaking
- ❑ global*
- ❑ grassroots
- ❑ handmade
- ❑ Internet-enabled
- ❑ Internet-linked
- ❑ interwoven
- ❑ knowledge-based
- ❑ large-scale
- ❑ medical*
- ❑ parallel*
- ❑ service-based
- ❑ shocked
- ❑ tech-savvy
- ❑ twofold
- ❑ well-educated
- ❑ widespread*

Expression

- ❑ on the block

---

*These words are from the Academic Word List. For more information on this list, see www.vuw.ac.nz/lals/research/awl.

6

Money Matters

In This Chapter

"Money makes the world go 'round," according to an old English saying, and being able to talk about money matters is important in all cultures. The first selection describes the success story of a business that started in Spain with a small idea and grew to make money and create jobs across many borders. The second selection, written by one of the greatest short story writers of the English language, William Somerset Maugham, focuses on a more personal aspect of the financial question: the embarrassment and difficulties that a lack of money can cause in a social situation.

❝ One coin in an empty moneybox makes more noise than when it is full. **❞**

—Arabic proverb

Connecting to the Topic

1. Look at the photo. How would you describe this woman? Do you think she is careful with money? Why or why not?

2. What things do you consider to be a waste of money? What things do you like to splurge (spend a lot of money) on, i.e. nice clothes, eating in fancy restaurants, travel, the latest technology?

3. What difficulties can money cause among friends?

Executive Takes Chance on Pizza, Transforms Spain

Before You Read

Strategy

Previewing a Reading
Get a general idea of what an article is about before fully reading it. Often, the title presents key points that can help your comprehension.

1 **Scanning for Specific Information** Look at the title of the article on page 132. Then read the questions below about the title and take one minute to scan the article for the information needed to answer the questions. Compare your answers with those of your classmates.

1. Who is the *executive (business manager)* mentioned in the title?

2. What does it mean to say he "takes a chance on pizza"?

3. To *transform* something means to change it, and not just in a small way. How does this man "transform Spain"? Do you think this title uses exaggeration?

Strategy

Recognizing Word Families
A good way to expand vocabulary is through recognizing word families—groups of words related in form and meaning, such as *combine, combined,* and *combination*.

2 **Recognizing Word Families** Scan the reading selection for words related to the given words in column one and write them in the second column. Read the meaning in the third column. The words are in the order of their appearance in the article.

	Related Word in Reading	Meaning of Related Word
1. global	*globalization*	A noun meaning *the growth of something worldwide*
2. pizza		A noun meaning *a place that produces or sells pizza*
3. convenient		A noun meaning *quality of being convenient, easy, or suitable*
4. modern		A verb meaning *becoming modern*
5. manage		A noun meaning *the act or manner of managing*
6. prosperous		A verb meaning *did well or became prosperous (wealthy)*
7. special		A noun meaning *types of food, or other products that are special*
8. afford		An adjective meaning *can be afforded by a person's financial means, not too expensive*
9. mental		A noun meaning *mental outlook, way of thinking*
10. mature		A present participle (-*ing* word) meaning *growing older and wiser, becoming more mature*

Read

Introduction

The following article gives us some examples of **globalization**: a term used to describe how business, travel, communications, and other institutions spread quickly throughout the globe, without being stopped by borders, distance, language, and regulations the way they were in the past. Leopoldo Fernandez was born in one country, grew up in another, and then went to work in a third country. The article discusses how he starts a business that has an impact on many other countries.

- Why do people move from one country to another? Is this always their choice?

- Have you ever lived in a different country? Would you like to do that some day?

Executive Takes Chance on Pizza, Transforms Spain

A   MADRID, Spain—Leopoldo Fernandez was earning $150,000 a year as an **executive** in Spain with Johnson & Johnson when he decided to open a **pizzeria** on the side.

B   "Keep in mind, I knew nothing about pizza. My job was about selling heart valves, heart monitors, surgical instruments," said the 47-year-old Cuban American, a former **marketing** director for the U.S. medical supply company.

C   Six years later, Fernandez is the president of TelePizza, a **multinational** company with **projected sales** of $120 million this year. By year's end, the Madrid-based pizza businessman's name will adorn more than 200 **outlets** in ten countries. The company, one of the first to answer a need for **convenience** goods in **modernizing** Spain, may even be the world's fastest growing pizza **chain**, according to a recent issue of the trade magazine *Pizza Today* and research by TelePizza.

D   "I thought I'd just open five little stores and keep my job at Johnson & Johnson," recalled Fernandez in an interview as he puffed a $5 Cuban cigar. Two small Cuban flags are placed on his desk top.

E   Success came "so quickly my biggest problem has been keeping on top of the growth-money management, people **management**, training. Most new businesses grow at 10–20 percent yearly. We've grown at 10 percent a month since we opened," Fernandez said.

F   After his first shop **prospered** in Madrid, Fernandez left his job, sold his house and stocks, and cobbled together $300,000 to put into the business. From then on, new pizzerias opened rapidly, first in Spain and then abroad.

G   At the time TelePizza began in the late 1980s, pizzas were available in Spain only in Italian restaurants, and home delivery of any food was rare. But with more women in the workplace and Spain still modernizing, there was a growing need for convenience foods. TelePizza's success is widely credited with setting off a **boom** in home-delivered fast food in Spain.

H   Hundreds of motorbikes now ply Madrid's streets delivering everything from pizza to traditional **specialties** like Spanish tortillas (egg and potato omelettes) and paella.

I   Like the Domino's chain of U.S. fame, TelePizza's pies come fast—the company guarantees that pizzas will arrive in under 30 minutes, depending on where customers live. They are fairly **affordable**, with a pie for up to four people costing $13, compared with $6 for a McDonald's quarter pounder, fries, and Coke, undelivered.

J   Some say Spain's growing appetite for fast food is undermining the country's healthy Mediterranean diet. "There's a saying, when we were poor we made better eating choices than we do now," said Consuelo Lopez

Nomdedeu, a nutritionist with the government-run National College of Health. But Fernandez dismissed such complaints. "The key is variety in the diet," he said. "I wouldn't eat pizza daily or hamburgers (nor would I eat) Spanish dishes like lentils or garbanzos." 40

K   Along with crediting the untapped Spanish market for his success, Fernandez noted that growing up as an immigrant in the United States probably also helped. Like many other refugees fleeing the Castro revolution, Fernandez moved to Florida from Cuba in 1960 with his parents. 45

▲ Making a delivery on two wheels

L   "An immigrant has to find ways to succeed because he's on the bottom," said Fernandez, who also has worked for Procter & Gamble Co., the leading U.S. consumer products company. 50

M   "Here, my advantage is that I understand Spanish mentality better than Americans do, and I understand Americans better than Spaniards do," Fernandez said. 55

N   So far, his recipe for success is working. Fernandez said TelePizza outsells its three biggest rivals in Spain—Domino's, Pizza Hut, and Pizza World—combined. The company has a fleet of more than 2,000 motorbikes in Spain and sells 25,000 pizzas daily in the Spanish market. 60 65

CLOSE TO HOME JOHN McPHERSON

"Didn't that pizza delivery kid used to be our paperboy?"

▲ Close to Home © John McPherson, Reprinted with permission of *Universal Press Syndicate*. All rights reserved.

O   About two-thirds of TelePizza outlets in Spain are franchises while 90 percent of the 40 stores abroad are company-owned. In addition to Spain, there are TelePizza outlets located in Mexico, Colombia, Chile, Portugal, Belgium, Greece, and Poland—with stores in France and Brazil set to open before year's end. 70

"We plan to go into the U.S. in due time," Fernandez said. "For now we are maturing and learning from growth markets." 75

P

Source: "Executive Takes Chance on Pizza, Transforms Spain" *Wisconsin State Journal* (Stephen Wade)

After You Read

3 **Getting the Meaning of Words from Context** Use the context and the clues to explain the following business terms.

1. *marketing* (line 6) A market is a place where products are bought and sold. So, *marketing* is _promoting the buying and selling of products_ .

2. *multinational* (line 8) Break the word apart to find its meaning.

   _____

3. *projected sales* (line 8) Think about projecting something such as fireworks into the sky. Then think about the time frame it refers to.

   _____

4. *outlets* (line 10) Break the word apart and remember we are talking about a product that is being marketed. _____

5. *chain* (line 12) Imagine a picture of a chain, made up of separate parts called links. _____

6. *boom* (line 28) The meaning can be inferred partly from the sound of this word (which is used to describe the sound of an explosion).

   _____

7. *untapped market* (line 44) *To tap* something means "to open or start," as in tapping an oil well. Then consider how the prefix *un-* affects the meaning.

   _____

8. *franchises* (line 67) Notice these stores are contrasted with others that are company owned. _____

9. *growth markets* (line 75) Take a guess from the words themselves.

   _____

4 **Checking Your Comprehension** Choose the most appropriate answer related to the reading.

1. Before starting a pizza business, Fernandez worked for a company that sold _____.
   - (A) Cuban cigars
   - (B) surgical instruments
   - (C) restaurant supplies

2. Telepizza grew very fast in the 1980s because at that time in Spain _____ was very rare.
   - (A) Italian food
   - (B) good restaurants
   - (C) home delivery

3. Another factor that helped the business is that there were more _____ in the workplace than before.

- Ⓐ women
- Ⓑ engineers
- Ⓒ young people

4. According to Consuelo Lopez Nomdedeu, fast food like pizza is not good for Spain because it is _____.

- Ⓐ very expensive
- Ⓑ too foreign
- Ⓒ not healthy

5. Fernandez feels that being an immigrant in the U.S. _____.

- Ⓐ caused many problems for him and his family
- Ⓑ was an advantage to him in business
- Ⓒ did not affect him in any way

6. Telepizza has many outlets in Spain and in different countries and these are _____.

- Ⓐ franchises
- Ⓑ company owned
- Ⓒ both franchises and company owned

5 **Guided Academic Conversation: Globalization and How It Affects Us**
In small groups, discuss the following issues. Then compare your answers with those of another group. After Leopoldo Fernandez opened his first TelePizza, the company quickly expanded to hundreds of outlets in many countries, including Spain, Germany, Sweden, Chile, Mexico, Morocco, Poland, and Portugal. Obviously, globalization was good for Mr. Fernandez, but is it good for everyone?

1. Chain Stores Make a list of the chain stores, restaurants, or businesses that are popular in the place where you live. Note if they are nationally owned or foreign. Do you know the difference? What is more important: the product or the ownership, or both? Do foreign-owned businesses hurt or help the local economy? What is your group's favorite chain? Why?

2. Owning Your Own Business Would you like to have your own business some day, or do you prefer to work for someone else? Explain your choice. What chain stores, restaurants, or businesses from your country have outlets in other countries? Would you consider working for one of them? Would you work for a chain from a different nation? Why or why not?

3. Fast Food: a Curse or a Blessing? Does fast food mean bad food? What are its advantages? There must be a reason that it is so much in demand. Pretend that your group has been given money to set up a new international fast-food chain in foreign markets. What foods would you choose to export from your culture? How would you set up the atmosphere of the outlets? What name would you give to your business?

6 **Making Connections** Look up TelePizza on the Internet or in a library and look for information on one of the following topics to share with the class. (You may find that much of the information is in languages other than English. If you can't find enough, look for information on home delivery of pizza in general to find out what other businesses exist that are similar and how they are doing.)

1. What has happened to the business ownership after so many years? Is it still in the hands of the original owner or his family? Or have there been new owners?

2. What conflicts have occurred between management and employees? Have these been resolved? Does the business still exist in many countries or has it succeeded more in some than in others?

3. How successful is this business now? Has it gone up or down since its early amazing period of fast growth?

Focus on Testing

Reading Between the Lines

In many reading comprehension tests, you are asked to read a passage and choose the best answer to some questions about it. Often these questions ask you to make an inference about the reading. Remember that an inference is a true idea that is not stated directly but can be inferred (concluded or deduced) from what is stated. In English, this is often called "reading between the lines."

In order to choose the correct inference, you must decide why three of the answers are not correct. Tests can fool you, so be careful! In many tests, as in the practice test below, one of the choices is false. Another is probably true, but we don't have enough information to decide for sure. Another of the choices may be true but is already directly stated in the passage in different words; therefore, it is not an inference. Now, through the process of elimination, we have cut out three choices and are left with the one correct answer. So, choose that answer.

Practice Following are three passages from the article on pages 132–133, "Executive Takes Chance on Pizza, Transforms Spain." Each passage is followed by a question about it. Choose the best answer to each question.

Passage 1

Leopoldo Fernandez was earning $150,000 a year as an executive in Spain with Johnson & Johnson when he decided to open a pizzeria on the side. "Keep in mind, I knew nothing about pizza. My job was about selling heart valves, heart monitors, surgical instruments," said the 47-year-old Cuban-American, a former marketing director for the U.S. medical supply company.

What can be inferred from the passage about Leopoldo Fernandez?

- Ⓐ He is middle-aged.
- Ⓑ He was born in Cuba.
- Ⓒ He is a risk taker.
- Ⓓ He was poor before starting a business.

Passage 2

At the time TelePizza began in the late 1980s, pizzas were available in Spain only in Italian restaurants, and home delivery of any food was rare. But with more women in the workplace and Spain still modernizing, there was a growing need for convenience foods. TelePizza's success is widely credited with setting off a boom in home-delivered fast food in Spain.

What can be inferred from the passage about TelePizza's customers?

- Ⓐ They like to buy on credit.
- Ⓑ They do not like Italian restaurants.
- Ⓒ Many are very traditional.
- Ⓓ Many are working women.

Passage 3

Along with crediting the untapped Spanish market for his success, Fernandez noted that growing up as an immigrant in the United States probably also helped. Like many other refugees fleeing the Castro revolution, Fernandez moved to Florida from Cuba in 1960 with his parents.

"An immigrant has to find ways to succeed because he's on the bottom," said Fernandez, who also has worked for Procter & Gamble Co., the leading U.S. consumer products company.

What can be inferred from the passage about Fernandez's opinion of immigrants?

- Ⓐ Immigrants usually don't work as hard as others.
- Ⓑ Immigrants usually work harder than others.
- Ⓒ Immigrants are employed by big companies.
- Ⓓ Immigrants receive support from their families.

Buying on the Internet

People love to shop, and more and more of them are shopping on the Internet. Some are pleased with the variety of goods offered and the ease of shopping in the comfort of their own homes. Yet some are worried about the quality of goods they'll receive or the safety of their credit card numbers.

▲ Do you like to shop on the Internet?

1. Have you ever shopped on the Internet? If so, what products have you bought?

2. Do you prefer to shop online, use a catalog, or go to a store in person? Why?

3. Some consumers think it's not safe to shop on the Internet. Do you agree or not? What precautions would you take before completing a transaction on the Internet?

4. Have you ever heard of "identity theft"? What is it? Do you think it could happen if you buy products on the Internet? Explain.

The Luncheon

Before You Read

Strategy

Identifying the Setting, Characters, and Conflict in a Narrative
Reading a story is easier if you first identify the key elements that every story must have. These are called the *narrative elements.*

- **setting**: the time and place
- **characters**: the main people who are in the story
- **plot**: the action that starts with a **conflict**, develops into a complication, and ends with a resolution (a solution of the conflict)

1 **Identifying the Setting, Characters, and Conflict** Find the setting by looking at the illustration and skimming the first few paragraphs.

1. When does the story take place (more or less)? _____ Where?
_____

2. Who are the main characters? There is of course the *narrator* (the one speaking) since the story is written in the first person (using *I* and *me*). The other character is a woman whose name we are never told. What do we know about this woman?

Characters: _____

About the woman: _____

3. We cannot identify in advance the whole plot, but we can find out where it begins. The action always starts with a conflict (a problem or difficulty) because if everything were fine, there would be no story. Read quickly up to line 24 and find the conflict. Explain it here.

_____

_____

You will have to read the story to see how this conflict gets complicated, rises to a climax (the most difficult and intense moment of the action), and then ends in the resolution.

2 **Getting the Meaning of Words from Context** The author uses exact adjectives and adverbs to describe the feelings of the characters and the appearance of their surroundings. Look for clues in the context and choose the word or phrase closest to the meaning of the word in italics.

1. But I was *flattered* and I was too young to have learned to say no to a woman. (lines 19–20)

- Ⓐ worried about the future
- **Ⓑ pleased by the praise**
- Ⓒ confused about what to do

Notice the clue in line 19

2. She was not so young as I expected and in appearance *imposing* rather than attractive. (lines 26–27)

- Ⓐ notable
- Ⓑ good looking
- Ⓒ unattractive

3. I was *startled* when the bill of fare was brought, for the prices were a great deal higher than I had anticipated. (lines 33–34)

- Ⓐ depressed by sad memories
- Ⓑ scared by a sudden surprise
- Ⓒ filled with hope

4. "What would you like?" I asked, hospitable still, but not exactly *effusive*. (lines 56–57)

- Ⓐ enthusiastic
- Ⓑ silent
- Ⓒ timid

5. She gave me a bright and *amicable* flash of her white teeth. (line 58)

- Ⓐ angry
- Ⓑ false
- Ⓒ friendly

6. It would be *mortifying* to find myself ten francs short and be obliged to borrow from my guest. (lines 92–93)

- Ⓐ embarrassing
- Ⓑ boring
- Ⓒ tiring

7. The asparagus appeared. They were enormous, *succulent*, and appetizing. (lines 99–100)

- Ⓐ too ripe
- Ⓑ dry
- Ⓒ juicy

8. I knew too—a little later, for my guest, going on with her conversation, *absentmindedly* took one. (lines 126–127)

- Ⓐ with a cruel intention
- Ⓑ without thinking
- Ⓒ in a careful way

9. The bill came and when I paid it I found that I had only enough for a quite *inadequate* tip. (lines 131–132)

- Ⓐ generous
- Ⓑ small
- Ⓒ exact

10. But I have had my revenge at last. I do not believe that I am a *vindictive* man, but. . . (lines 141–142)

    Ⓐ forgiving and peaceful

    Ⓑ filled with contentment

    Ⓒ set on getting revenge

Read

Strategy

Predicting Events in a Narrative

It is helpful while reading a narrative to think ahead of the action. You don't have to understand every word, just try to follow the action, understand what is happening, and think about what might happen next.

3 **Predicting Events in a Narrative** As you read the next selection, try to predict what is going to happen next. The story will be interrupted at a few points and you will be asked some questions to guide you. Do not worry about understanding every word. Just try to follow the action and understand what is happening.

Introduction

▲ William Somerset Maugham

The following selection is a narrative (a story) by one of the master short story writers of the English language, William Somerset Maugham (1874–1965). Born in Paris and educated in England, he worked as a secret agent for the British government in World War I and then spent the rest of his life writing and traveling throughout many parts of the world. In "The Luncheon," the narrator starts out by describing how he went to the theater and met a woman he had not seen in 20 years. This brings to his mind the memory of that time long ago, and so he tells the story of that earlier meeting.

Have you ever had the experience of meeting someone you once knew and had not seen in years? How did the experience turn out?

■ In what ways do people change over the years?

The Luncheon

I caught sight of her at the play and in answer to her beckoning I went over during the interval and sat down beside her. It was long since I had last seen her and if someone had not mentioned her name I hardly think I would have recognized her. She addressed me brightly.

"Well, it's many years since we first met. How time does fly! We're none of us getting any younger. Do you remember the first time I saw you? You asked me to luncheon."

Did I remember?

It was twenty years ago and I was living in Paris. I had a tiny apartment in the Latin Quarter overlooking a cemetery and I was earning barely enough money to keep body and soul together. She had read a book of mine and had written to me about it. I answered, thanking her, and presently I received from her another letter saying that she was passing through Paris and would like to have a chat with me; but her time was limited and the only free moment she had was on the following Thursday: she was spending the morning at the Luxembourg and would I give her a little luncheon at Foyot's afterwards? Foyot's is a restaurant at which the French senators eat and it was so far beyond my means that I had never even thought of going there. But I was flattered and I was too young to have learned to say no to a woman. (Few men, I may add, learn this until they are too old to make it of any consequence to a woman what they say.) I had eighty francs (gold francs) to last me the rest of the month and a modest luncheon should not cost more than fifteen. If I cut out coffee for the next two weeks I could manage well enough.

What do you think of the request that the woman has made of the main character? Why do you think that he accepted it? Do you think he is going to get into trouble? Why or why not?

I answered that I would meet my friend-by-correspondence at Foyot's on Thursday at half past twelve. She was not so young as I expected and in appearance imposing rather than attractive. She was in fact a woman of forty (a charming age, but not one that excites a sudden and devastating passion at first sight), and she gave me the impression of having more teeth, white and large and even, than were necessary for any practical purpose. She was talkative, but since she seemed inclined to talk about me I was prepared to be an attentive listener.

I was startled when the bill of fare was brought, for the prices were a great deal higher than I had anticipated. But she reassured me.

"I never eat anything for luncheon," she said. 35

"Oh, don't say that!" I answered generously.

"I never eat more than one thing. I think people eat far too much nowadays. A little fish, perhaps. I wonder if they have any salmon."

Well, it was early in the year for salmon and it was not on the bill of fare, but I asked the waiter if there was any. Yes, a beautiful salmon had just 40 come in—it was the first they had had. I ordered it for my guest. The waiter asked her if she would have something while it was being cooked.

What did the man notice about the woman's appearance? Does it perhaps give a clue to her character? From what she has said so far, do you expect her to order any more food? Why?

"No," she answered. "I never eat more than one thing. Unless you had a little caviar. I never mind caviar."

My heart sank a little. I knew I could not afford caviar, but I could not 45 very well tell her that. I told the waiter by all means to bring caviar. For myself I chose the cheapest dish on the menu and that was a mutton chop.

"I think you're unwise to eat meat," she said. "I don't know how you can expect to work after eating heavy things like chops. I don't believe in overloading my stomach." 50

Then came the question of drink.

What do you think the woman is going to say about the question of drink? What do you think she is going to do? And the man? Why?

"I never drink anything for luncheon," she said.

"Neither do I," I answered promptly.

"Except white wine," she proceeded as though I had not spoken. "These French white wines are so light. They're wonderful for the digestion." 55

"What would you like?" I asked, hospitable still, but not exactly effusive.

She gave me a bright and amicable flash of her white teeth.

"My doctor won't let me drink anything but champagne."

I fancy I turned a trifle pale. I ordered half a bottle. I mentioned 60 casually that my doctor had absolutely forbidden me to drink champagne.

"What are you going to drink, then?"

"Water."

She ate the caviar and she ate the salmon. She talked gaily of art and literature and music. But I wondered what the bill would come to. When 65 my mutton chop arrived she took me quite seriously to task.

"I see that you're in the habit of eating a heavy luncheon. I'm sure it's a mistake. Why don't you follow my example and eat just one thing? I'm sure you'd feel ever so much better for it."

"I *am* only going to eat one thing," I said, as the waiter came again with the bill of fare. 70

The waiter has come once again. What will happen next?

She waved him aside with an airy gesture.

"No, no, I never eat anything for luncheon. Just a bite, I never want more than that, and I eat that more as an excuse for conversation than anything else. I couldn't possibly eat anything more—unless they had some 75 of those giant asparagus. I should be sorry to leave Paris without having some of them."

"Madame wants to know if you have any of those giant asparagus," I asked the waiter.

I tried with all my might to will him to say no. A happy smile spread 80 over his broad, priest-like face, and he assured me that they had some so large, so splendid, so tender, that it was a marvel.

"I'm not in the least hungry," my guest sighed, "but if you insist, I don't mind having some asparagus."

I ordered them. 85

"Aren't you going to have any?"

"No, I never eat asparagus."

"I know there are people who don't like them. The fact is, you ruin your palate by all the meat you eat."

Something is ironic *when it is the opposite of what is true or expected. What is ironic about what the woman keeps saying? How do you think the man feels about this? Do you think the man or the woman will order more food?*

We waited for the asparagus to be cooked. Panic seized me. It was not a 90 question now of how much money I should have left over for the rest of the month, but whether I had enough to pay the bill. It would be mortifying to find myself ten francs short and be obliged to borrow from my guest. I could not bring myself to do that. I knew exactly how much I had and if the bill came to more I had made up my mind that I would put my hand in my pocket and with 95 a dramatic cry start up and say it had been picked. Of course it would be awkward if she had not money enough either to pay the bill. Then the only thing would be to leave my watch and say I would come back and pay later.

A fancy restaurant in Paris in the 1930s.

The asparagus appeared. They were enormous, succulent, and appetizing. The smell of the melted butter tickled my nostrils as the nostrils of Jehovah were tickled by the burned offerings of the virtuous Semites. I watched the abandoned woman thrust them down her throat in large voluptuous mouthfuls and in my polite way I discoursed on the condition of the drama in the Balkans. At last, she finished.

"Coffee?" I asked.

"Yes, just an ice cream and coffee," she answered.

I was past caring now, so I ordered coffee for myself and an ice cream and coffee for her.

"You know, there's one thing I thoroughly believe in," she said, as she ate the ice cream. "One should always get up from a meal feeling one could eat a little more."

"Are you still hungry?" I asked faintly.

"Oh, no. I'm not hungry; you see, I don't eat luncheon. I have a cup of coffee in the morning and then dinner, but I never eat more than one thing for luncheon. I was speaking for you."

"Oh, I see!"

Then a terrible thing happened. While we were waiting for the coffee, the head waiter, with an ingratiating smile on his false face, came up to us bearing a large basket full of peaches. They had the blush of an innocent girl; they had the rich tone of an Italian landscape. But surely peaches were not in season then? Lord knew what they cost. I knew too—a little later, for my guest, going on with her conversation, absentmindedly took one.

"You see, you've filled your stomach with a lot of meat"—my one miserable little chop—"and you can't eat any more. But I've just had a snack and I shall enjoy a peach."

The bill came and when I paid it I found that I had only enough for a quite inadequate tip. Her eyes rested for an instant on the three francs I left for the waiter and I knew that she thought me mean. But when I walked out of the restaurant I had the whole month before me and not a penny in my pocket.

So far the luncheon has gone badly for the man. Somerset Maugham is known for his irony and surprise endings. Can you think of some way he might turn the situation around? Will the man somehow get his revenge?

"Follow my example," she said as we shook hands, "and never eat more than one thing for luncheon."

"I'll do better than that," I retorted. "I'll eat nothing for dinner tonight."

"Humorist!" she cried gaily, jumping into a cab. "You're quite a humorist!"

But I have had my revenge at last. I do not believe that I am a vindictive man, but when the immortal gods take a hand in the matter it is pardonable to observe the result with complacency. Today she weighs twenty-one stone.*

Source: "The Luncheon" *Cosmopolitans* (W. Somerset Maugham)

*The stone is a British unit of measurement. One stone equals fourteen pounds, or 6.35 kilos.

After You Read

UNDERSTANDING THE PLOT: RECALLING THE SERIES OF EVENTS

Besides setting, character, and conflict, another narrative element is the plot. The *plot* is the series of events as they occur in a narrative; they make up the action of the story.

This story, like many others, is a *framework tale.* That means that it contains "a story within a story." The narrator begins by telling us about himself in the present time as a kind of framework to a shorter story, or memory from the past, that he then tells us. (When this technique is used in a movie, it is called a *flashback,* because the picture *flashes back* to an earlier time.)

Reading Tip

Recall that you can use a **chain of events diagram** to take notes on a series of events.

4 **Understanding the Plot: Recalling the Series of Events** Read through the events A through H on page 147 and decide in which are told they occur *in the story.* Write the letter of each statement in a box on the timeline to represent the order of occurrence.

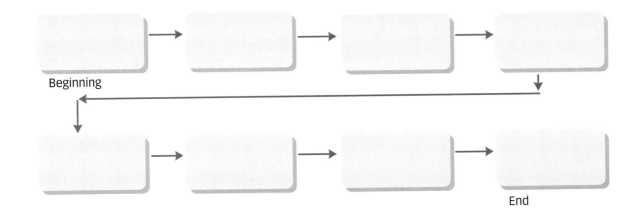

Beginning

End

A. The man remembers that he had no money for expenses for one month.

B. The man remembers that the woman ate a lot of expensive food for lunch.

C. The man mentions that the woman is very much overweight.

D. The man remembers the woman writing him a letter about his book.

E. The man meets the woman at a play, after not seeing her for many years.

F. The man remembers that he is barely able to pay the bill.

G. The man remembers the woman asking him to take her to lunch.

H. The man remembers that the woman insists she doesn't eat lunch.

5 **Focusing on Words from the Academic Word List** Use the most appropriate word from the box to fill in each of the blanks below in the section taken from the reading. Do NOT look back at the reading right away; instead, first see if you can remember the vocabulary. Check your answers on pages 142–145.

anticipated	found	inadequate
drama	imposing	inclined
enormous		

She was not so young as I expected and in appearance _____ rather than attractive. . . . She was talkative, but

                                 1

since she seemed _____ to talk about me I was prepared

                                 2

to be an attentive listener.

I was startled when the bill of fare was brought, for the prices   5

were a great deal higher than I had _____. . . .

                                 3

The asparagus appeared. They were _____, succulent,

                                 4

and appetizing. . . . I watched the abandoned woman thrust them down her

throat in large voluptuous mouthfuls and in my polite way I discoursed

on the condition of the _____ in the Balkans. At last,   10

                                 5

she finished. . . . The bill came and when I paid it I _____

                                 6

that I had only enough for a quite _____ tip.

                                 7

Guided Academic Conversation

6 Creating a Skit With a partner, discuss the question below. Then make up a short skit (where one person is the man and one is the woman) to illustrate what the man might have done to get out of the situation. Present this skit to another pair of students and see if they agree with your solution to the man's problem. Then watch their skit and see if you agree with their solution.

Question: What should the young man have done to get out of this difficult situation? Do you think that he was trapped by the rules of courtesy and good manners? What would you have done in similar circumstances?

7 Solving Problems Discuss the following questions in a group of four.

1. Why do you think the woman behaved as she did? Did she want to take advantage of the young man, or was she simply ignorant of his money problems? Or didn't she care if he had problems?

2. How has the author used irony in this story to create humor?

3. Have you ever been in an embarrassing situation because of money? If so, how did you get out of it?

4. Why do you think some people continually have money problems? Is it the fault of credit cards? Is it the lack of experience or training?

5. Working with your whole group, write out what you all think is the best rule for

    managing your money: _____

    _____

Be prepared to read this to the class. Then take a vote to see which group came up with the best rule.

Part 3 Tying It All Together

1 Making Connections

> While globalization is pushing some countries in the European Union to move towards having one common currency (form of money)—the Euro—other countries take pride in their individual national currencies. Some of these currency names even have an interesting history.

Use the Internet or library to find information about one of the following items and present it to the class.

1. The Venezuelan currency is named after a revolutionary hero who led wars of independence in what is now five other countries beside Venezuela. Which countries were these? Who was this hero?

What was his name and what is the name of the unit of money in Venezuela today? What dream did he have for Latin America that was never fulfilled?

2. In Peru, the name of the currency reflects the ancient Inca culture's worship of the Sun. What was the currency called until 1985? What new name was given to it then? Then how was that name changed again in 1991? How do you explain these changes?

3. In Canada, the one-dollar coin is named after a water bird. What is it called and why? Why is this term also somewhat of a Canadian joke? What does the dollar coin look like? What color is it and how many sides does it have? What is the two-dollar coin called and what does it look like?

4. Go to a currency exchange website and look up the names of the currencies of some other countries. Try searching some of these names and come up with an interesting fact or history of the name of a currency from some country that interests you. You could also try to find information by going to an international chat room and chatting with people from other countries about what they know about their currency's name. Be prepared to share your findings with the class.

Responding in Writing

WRITING TIP: MAKING A CLUSTER DIAGRAM

Using a cluster (see page 151) diagram is a good way to get your ideas flowing and to organize your ideas. When you brainstorm, put the main idea in the center circle of the diagram. Write other ideas related to the main idea around the main idea. Circle your ideas and connect them to the main idea. Then write more ideas related to your first ideas in circles and connect them to your primary ideas.

2 Using a Cluster Diagram to Organize Ideas and Write a Paragraph

Successful entrepreneurs (people who start new businesses) from around the world offer advice about how to succeed in business in the following quotes. Write a paragraph about one of the quotes telling what you think it means and why you like it or dislike it. Read the quotes; then follow the steps outlined below:

1. "Lead, follow, or get out of the way."

   —Thomas Paine

2. "Never get discouraged and quit. Because if you never quit, you're never broken."

   —Ted Turner, founder of CNN and TNT

3. "Develop a product where there is no market, then create one."

   —Akio Morita, Sony Electronic

4. "Success is the one percent of your work that results from the 99 percent that is called failure."

   —Soichiro Honda, Honda cars and motorcycles

5. "Build 'em strong and sell 'em cheap."

   "Concentrate on one product used by everyone, every day."

   —Baron Marcel Bich, Bic pens, razors

6. "A computer on every desk and in every home."

   —Bill Gates, Microsoft Corporation

▲ Bill Gates, CEO of Microsoft, is a successful international businessman.

Step 1: Choose the quotation that is most interesting to you and write it down, with the name of its author, at the beginning of your composition.

Step 2: Brainstorm your ideas (by yourself, or with someone who has chosen the same quotation.) on what this quotation means and why you like or dislike it by using a cluster diagram like the example on page 151. In a circle in the center of your paper, put the quotation you chose, then write any ideas that come to you that relate to the quotation, circle them, and connect them to the quotation. Then write ideas related to the first ideas in circles and connect them to the primary ideas. (A cluster diagram is a good way to get your ideas flowing and to begin to organize them.)

Step 3: Considering just the points you want to make from your cluster diagram, make up a good beginning sentence to introduce the main point of your paragraph.

Step 4: Write each of the points you want to use from the cluster diagram into sentences to support your main point.

Step 5: Write a final sentence to conclude. Remember, two common ways of concluding are: 1) to repeat the main idea (given in the first sentence) in different words; or 2) to express a personal reaction, such as a wish or a rhetorical question (one that is asked in a general way with no expectation of an answer).

Step 6: Check over your paragraph for spelling and punctuation. Read it through to make sure that it makes sense.

Step 7: Write a title for your paragraph that describes it. The title should not be too broad ("Computers" for the example above), but should describe exactly what your main point is ("Gates's Philosophy of Marketing"). You could even try to make it creative with alliteration (using words that begin with a similar letter) or by saying something funny. Most important is that your title makes sense and relates to your main point. Hand in your cluster diagram along with your paragraph.

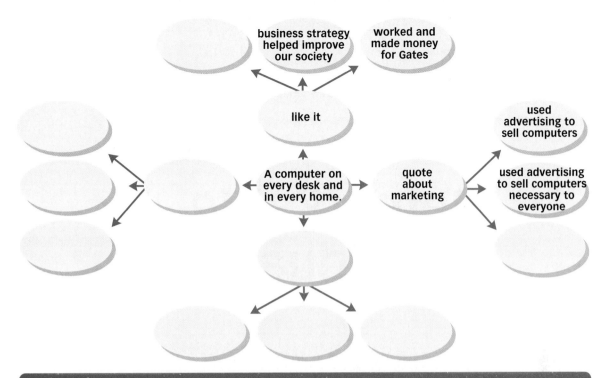

Bubbles in the diagram contain:
- business strategy helped improve our society
- worked and made money for Gates
- like it
- used advertising to sell computers
- A computer on every desk and in every home.
- quote about marketing
- used advertising to sell computers necessary to everyone

Self-Assessment Log

Read the lists below. Check (✓) the strategies and vocabulary that you learned in this chapter. Look through the chapter or ask your instructor about the strategies and words that you do not understand.

Reading and Vocabulary-Building Strategies
- ❑ Scanning for specific information
- ❑ Recognizing word families
- ❑ Identifying the setting, characters, and conflict in a narrative
- ❑ Getting the meaning of words from context
- ❑ Predicting events in a narrative
- ❑ Understanding the plot: recalling the series of events

Target Vocabulary

Nouns
- ❑ boom
- ❑ chain (as in a group of similar businesses
- ❑ convenience
- ❑ drama*
- ❑ executive
- ❑ franchises
- ❑ globalization*
- ❑ growth markets
- ❑ management
- ❑ mentality*
- ❑ outlets (as in individual businesses in a chain)
- ❑ pizzeria
- ❑ projected sales
- ❑ specialties
- ❑ untapped market

Verbs
- ❑ anticipated*
- ❑ flattered
- ❑ found* (find)
- ❑ maturing*
- ❑ modernizing
- ❑ prospered
- ❑ startled
- ❑ transform*

Adjectives
- ❑ affordable
- ❑ amicable
- ❑ effusive
- ❑ enormous*
- ❑ imposing*
- ❑ inadequate*
- ❑ inclined*
- ❑ marketing
- ❑ mortifying
- ❑ multinational
- ❑ succulent
- ❑ vindictive

Adverb
- ❑ absentmindedly

_____
*These words are from the Academic Word List.

Remarkable Individuals

In This Chapter

People can be remarkable in many ways. The first reading in this chapter is about a man who has had a profound influence on society through the greatness of his intellect for over 2,500 years. The second is about five present-day heroes of extraordinary courage who have fought ardently on four different continents for the rights and dignity of the oppressed.

❝ A good reputation sits still; a bad one runs about. **❞**

—Russian proverb

1. Look at the photo? What are the man and girl doing? What do you think their relationship is to each other?

2. This chapter is about remarkable people. What makes a person remarkable? Does someone need to be famous in order to be remarkable? Why or why not?

3. What three people past or present do you consider to be remarkable? What makes them remarkable in your opinion?

Confucius, 551 B.C.E. – 479 B.C.E.*

Before You Read

1 **Skimming for the General Idea** Who was Confucius? Skim the article on pages 156–157 for the answer to this question. (To refresh your memory about how to skim for the general idea of a reading, see page 58.) After you skim, fill in the letter of the statement that best expresses the overall idea of the reading. Why is it better than the other two?

(A) Confucius is a historical figure famous for his brilliant invention of a new philosophy that transformed the society of his times and has remained popular in China continuously until the present day.

(B) Confucius was a powerful leader of ancient China whose ideas about mathematics, science, and human behavior formed the basis for traditional values and later inspired the communist government.

(C) Confucius was the learned teacher responsible for a book of ethical and moral principles that has influenced Chinese society for many centuries, surviving attacks by different groups opposed to these principles.

Strategy

Figuring Out Words from Structure Clues
Structure, as well as context, can help you figure out the meaning of words. Deconstruct (break apart) a word into its smaller parts, such as prefixes, suffixes, or smaller words to help figure it out.

Compound Words: Some words in English are compound words, which are made up of two or more smaller words.
supermarket: The smaller words, *super* and *market*, indicate a big market.
taxpayer: The smaller words, *tax* and *payer*, indicate someone who pays taxes.

Prefixes and Suffixes: Some words contain a smaller word and a prefix or a suffix. An example is *adulthood*: The suffix *-hood* shows a shared quality or condition, so *adulthood* is the shared condition of being adults (people who have grown older and are not children).

2 **Figuring Out Words from Structure Clues** Separate the following words into smaller words, prefixes, or suffixes. Then use the clues (and your creativity) to make up a working definition.

*B.C.E. means "Before the Common Era," which begins with the year 1, assumed to be approximately the year of the birth of Jesus Christ.

Word	Clue and Definition
1. childhood	The suffix -*hood* shows a shared quality or condition. So *neighborhood* is the shared condition of neighbors (who all live in the same place), and *childhood* is ＿＿＿＿＿＿＿ ＿＿＿＿＿＿＿＿＿＿＿＿ .
2. background	The *ground* is the place where things are done, and *back* can refer to going back in space or time, so a person's *background* refers to ＿＿＿＿＿＿＿＿＿＿＿＿＿＿＿＿＿＿＿ .
3. principality	A *kingdom* is a territory ruled by a king, and a *principality* is a ＿＿＿＿＿＿＿＿＿＿＿＿＿＿ .
4. cornerstones	The stones in the corners give the main support for a building. So the *cornerstones* of a philosophy are ＿＿＿＿＿＿＿＿＿＿ .
5. benevolent	The root *bene-* means "good" (as in *benefit*, a good thing), and the root *vol* means "wishing" or "willing" (as in *volunteer*, one willing to do something), so *benevolent* means ＿＿＿＿＿＿＿＿＿＿＿ ＿＿＿＿＿＿＿＿ .
6. defender	The suffix -*er* means "one who . . . ," so a *defender* is ＿＿＿＿＿＿ ＿＿＿＿＿＿＿＿ .
7. outlook	Breaking the word into two smaller words, your *outlook* is the way you ＿＿＿＿＿＿＿＿＿＿＿＿＿＿＿ .
8. innovator	*To innovate* means "to start something new" and the suffix -*or* means the same as -*er*, so an *innovator* is ＿＿＿＿＿＿＿＿＿ ＿＿＿＿＿＿＿＿＿＿＿＿＿＿＿＿＿ .
9. commoners	Commoners are people who ＿＿＿＿＿＿＿＿＿＿＿＿ .

Read

Introduction

The following selection describes the background and philosophy of the great ancient Chinese philosopher Confucius, whose ideas continue to impact people all over the world right up to the present day.

- Have you heard about Confucius before? If so, what ideas do you associate with this name?
- Can you think of any other great men or women whose ideas have lasted for hundreds or thousands of years?

Confucius, 551 B.C.E. – 479 B.C.E.

A   No other philosopher in the world has had more **enduring** influence than Confucius. For over two thousand years his concept of government, and his ideas about personal conduct and morality, **permeated** Chinese life and culture. Even today, his thoughts remain **influential**.   5

▲ Confucius

B   There was little in his **childhood background** that predicted the remarkable **prestige** that Confucius eventually achieved. He was born in a small **principality** in northeastern China, was **reared** in poverty, and had no formal   10 education. Through **diligent** study, however, he educated himself and became a learned man. For a while he held a minor government post; but he soon **resigned** that position and spent most of his life as a teacher. Eventually, his most important   15 teachings were gathered together into a book, the *Analects*, which was compiled by his disciples.

C   The two **cornerstones** of his system of personal conduct were *jen* and *li*. *Jen* might be defined as "**benevolent** concern for one's fellow men." *Li* is a term less **easily** translated: it   20 combines the **notions** of **etiquette**, good manners, and due concern for rituals and customs. Confucius believed that a man should **strive** after truth and virtue rather than wealth (and in his personal life he seems to have acted on that principle). In addition, he was the first major philosopher to state **the Golden Rule**, which he phrased as "Do not do unto others that   25 which you would not have them do unto you."

D   Confucius believed that respect and obedience are owed by children to their parents, by wives to their husbands, and by subjects to their rulers. But he was never a **defender** of **tyranny**. On the contrary, the starting point of his political **outlook** is that the state exists for the benefit of the   30 people, not the rulers. Another of his key **political** ideas is that a leader should govern **primarily** by moral example, rather than by force.

E   Confucius did not claim to be an **innovator**, but always said that he was merely urging a return to the moral standards of former times. In fact, however, the reforms which he urged represented a change from—and a   35 great improvement over—the **governmental** practices of earlier days.

F   At the time of his death, Confucius was a respected, but not yet greatly influential, teacher and philosopher. Gradually, though, his ideas became widely accepted throughout China. Then in the third century B.C.E., Shih

Huang Ti united all of China under his rule and decided to reform the country entirely and make a complete break with the past. Shih Huang Ti therefore decided to **suppress Confucian** teachings, and he ordered the burning of all copies of Confucius' works. (He also ordered the destruction of most other **philosophical** works.) 40

G   Most Confucian books were indeed destroyed; but some copies survived the **holocaust**, and a few years later, after the **dynasty** founded by the "First Emperor" had fallen, Confucianism re-emerged. Under the next dynasty, the Han, Confucianism became the official state philosophy, a position it maintained throughout most of the next two millennia. 45

H   Indeed, for much of that period, the civil service examinations in China were based primarily on knowledge of Confucian classics. Since those examinations were the main route by which **commoners** could enter the administration and achieve political power, the governing class of the largest nation on Earth was largely composed of men who had carefully studied the works of Confucius and absorbed his principles. 50 55

I   This enormous influence persisted until the 19th century, when the impact of the West created revolutionary changes in China. Then in the 20th century, the Communist party **seized** power in China. It was their belief that, in order both to **modernize** China and to eliminate economic injustice, it was necessary to make radical changes in society. As the ideas of Confucius were highly conservative, the communists made a major effort to **eradicate** his influence, the first such effort since Shih Huang Ti, 22 centuries earlier. 60

Source: "Confucius" *The 100: A Ranking of the Most Influential Persons In History* (Michael H. Hart)

After You Read

3 **Identifying Key Terms** The terms in the column on the left are from the reading. Choose the best explanation for each of them from the column on the right. One item on the right will be left over.

_____ **1.** *The Analects*

_____ **2.** a Confucian teaching

_____ **3.** the Golden Rule

_____ **4.** *jen*

_____ **5.** *li*

_____ **6.** Shi Huang Ti

a. A leader must sometimes use tyranny to achieve benefits for the state.

b. benevolent concern for other people

c. collection of the teachings of Confucius, made by his disciples

d. Don't do to others what you don't want them to do to you.

e. emperor of China in the third century who suppressed Confucianism

f. etiquette, good manners, and concern for rituals and customs

g. The state exists for the people, and leaders should govern by example, not force.

4 Forming New Words from the Same Word Family Fill in the blanks with the word from the reading that is related to each word in italics (from the same word family).

1. the adjective related to *endure*   more *enduring* influence
2. the adjective related to *influence*   his thoughts remain _____
3. the adverb related to *easy*   a term less _____ translated
4. the adjective related to *politics*   his key _____ ideas
5. the adverb related to *primary*   _____ by moral example
6. the adjective related to *government*   the _____ practices
7. the adjective related to *Confucius*   to suppress _____ teachings
8. the adjective related to *philosophy*   other _____ works
9. the verb related to *modern*   to _____ China

5 Matching Words to Their Definitions Match each word on the left with the correct synonym or definition on the right. For a word you are not sure about, scan the reading for it, and use the context to infer its meaning.

1. _____ enduring
2. _____ permeated
3. _____ reared
4. _____ prestige
5. _____ diligent
6. _____ resigned
7. _____ notions
8. _____ etiquette
9. _____ strive
10. _____ tyranny
11. _____ suppress
12. _____ holocaust
13. _____ dynasty
14. _____ seized
15. _____ eradicate

a. fame, good reputation
b. the attempt to completely erase or do away with a group of people or an idea.
c. try hard, make an effort, attempt
d. get rid of completely, erase, do away
e. filled, were present in all parts of
f. abuse of power, cruel treatment of people under you
g. rule, government
h. hardworking, industrious, persistent, reliable
i. took control of, grabbed
j. lasting, continuing
k. ideas, concepts
l. gave up, quit
m. push down, stop something from having an influence
n. raised, brought up
o. good manners, correct way of acting

Strategy

Finding Facts to Support or Disprove General Statements
Look for specific facts in your reading to support or disprove general statements about a subject. This will help give you a clearer idea about that subject.

6 **Finding Facts to Support or Disprove General Statements** Working with a small group, read the following four statements about Confucius aloud and decide whether they are true or false. Then find specific facts in the reading to support or disprove them. Compare your ideas with those of another group.

1. Confucius was a commoner, from a humble background.

2. He was a brilliant man who achieved greatness through the help of rich and influential friends.

3. The philosophy of Confucius has always been admired and respected in China.

4. A society that follows Confucian teachings would be orderly and peaceful.

7 **Guided Academic Conversation** In small groups, discuss the following questions.

1. In your opinion, why has Confucianism had such an enduring influence?

2. How do you think that governments should exert control over their citizens? Should some ideas be prohibited? Can ideas really be prohibited? Explain.

3. What do you think of the Golden Rule? Is it a universal rule for human behavior? Why or why not?

4. Some people believe that even in the world of today, *jen* and *li* are still the two most important principles for human social behavior. On two large pieces of paper, work in your group to draw representations of what *jen* and *li* mean to you, *jen* on one paper and *li* on the other. These can be elaborate drawings, stick figures, simple objects representing the concept, or even words that represent it well. (**Hint:** for *li* you might think particularly of etiquette or rituals particular to a culture or society that your group thinks are good.) Then each group in turn explains their drawing in front of the class.

What Do You Think?

8 **Rating Leaders** Remarkable leaders—history makers—can be either good or bad. Brainstorm some examples of those leaders who most people would consider good and those who most people would consider bad. Do a search on the Internet to identify a leader you think of as particularly good or bad, and bring in some information on this leader to share with the class. Each student should write the name of the leader he or she chose on the board, and tell what is good or bad about that leader.

9 **Rating Leaders Using a Continuum Graph** In groups, try to place all the leaders chosen by the class on a continuum graph to show which ones you think did the most harm and the most good for their communities and the world. Then discuss the questions below.

The Most Harm   The Most Good

1. What makes the difference between a good leader and a bad leader?

2. Do both types have some of the same characteristics? What are they?

3. Can a leader be both good and bad? Give some examples.

Part 2 Reading Skills and Strategies

Courage Begins with One Voice

Before You Read

1 **Previewing to Determine Organization** Look at the following three patterns of organization. Then skim the article and decide which pattern is used. Circle the number of the pattern used in the article.

> **Reading Tip**
>
> You can see from the title and illustrations that the following article is about people who show great courage in working for human rights. An article like this usually includes a general description of the subject and specific examples, but these can be organized in various ways.

1. Two or more specific examples / General description

2. General description / Two or more specific examples

3. One lively specific example / General description / Other specific examples

2 **Using Expressive Synonyms** Find synonyms: (words or phrases) from the reading to replace the common words and phrases in italics.

1. There is a common _____ (*complaint*) that there are no more heroes . . .

2. . . . these women and men spoke to me with compelling _____ (*speaking ability*) . . .

3. Their determination, _____ (*bravery*), and commitment . . .

4. . . . in the face of _____ (*very great*) danger . . .

5. . . . challenge each of us to _____
   (*work*) for a more decent society. (Look for a four-word expression.)

6. The crisis of authority is one of the causes for all the _____
   (*cruel acts*) . . .

7. . . . and a writer of _____ (*strong*) essays on
   repression and dissent.

8. . . . they are still ready to _____ (*give up*) their lives . . .

9. Today, she _____ (*keeps track of*) rights violations . . .

10. . . . the two greatest _____ (*barriers*) to human progress . . .

11. The decisions we make about how to _____ (*lead*) our lives . . .

12. . . . to _____ (*pay*) for the alleged crimes of their relatives.

Read

Introduction
Kerry Kennedy has interviewed impressive people who are doing great things for their fellow human beings in countries as diverse as India, the Czech Republic, Cambodia, Costa Rica, and Ghana. Read the following selection to learn more about courage and five heroes who possess this quality.

- Can you guess what kinds of humanitarian work these "heroes" are doing?
- If you were to choose one person to add to a list of courageous individuals who help society, whom would you choose?

"Courage Begins with One Voice"

A There is a common lament that there are no more heroes. . . . That perception is wrong. I have spent the last two years interviewing 51 people from 40 countries about the nature of courage. Imprisoned, tortured, threatened with death, these women and men spoke to me with compelling eloquence on the subjects to which they have devoted their lives and for which they are willing to sacrifice them—from free expression to women's rights, from environmental defense to eradicating slavery.

B Among them are the internationally celebrated, including Nobel Prize laureates. But most of them are unknown and (as yet) unsung beyond their national boundaries. . . . Their determination, valor, and commitment in the face of overwhelming danger challenge each of us to take up the torch for a more decent society.

Kailash Satyarthi, India

C   "Small children of six, seven years and older are forced to work 14 hours a day without a break or a day for rest," says Kailash Satyarthi of the more than six million children in India who work in bonded labor—a form of slavery where a desperate family is forced to hand over a child as guaranty for a debt. "If they cry for their parents, they are beaten and tortured. They are often kept half-fed and are not permitted to talk or laugh out loud." Since 1990, Satyarthi has helped to free more than 40,000 people, including 28,000 children, from overcrowded, filthy, and isolated factories, particularly in the massive carpet industry. "I have faced threats, and two of my colleagues have been killed," says Satyarthi, who heads the South Asian Coalition on Child Servitude. "But I think of it all as a test. If you decide to stand up against such social evils, you have to be fully prepared—physically, mentally and spiritually."

▲ Kailash Satyarthi, India

Vaclav Havel, Czech Republic

D   "The crisis of authority is one of the causes for all the atrocities we are seeing in the world today," says Vaclav Havel, 63, Czechoslovakia's leading playwright and a writer of compelling essays on repression and dissent. "The post-communist world presented a chance for new moral leaders. But gradually people were repressed, and much of that opportunity was lost." In 1989, he was elected president of the newly formed Czech Republic, the first non-communist leader in more than 40 years. Havel remains one of democracy's most principled voices. "There are certain leaders one can respect, like the Dalai Lama," he says. "Although often they have no hope, they are still ready to sacrifice their lives and their freedom. They are ready to assume responsibility for the world—or the part of the world they live in. Courage means going against majority opinion in the name of the truth."

▲ Vaclav Havel, Czech Republic

Kek Galabru, Cambodia

E   There are around 600 to 900 people tortured by the police in custody every year to whom we give medical assistance," says Kek Galabru, 58.

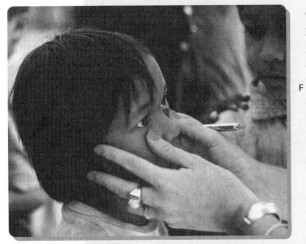

"Without us they would die." A medical doctor, Galabru played a key role in opening negotiations that led to the 1991 peace accords ending the Cambodian civil war, which left more than a million people dead.

F   Today, she monitors rights violations through the Cambodian League for the Promotion and Defense of Human Rights, which she founded. "Many times with our work, we are so depressed," she says. "It could be so easy for us to take our suitcases, take an airplane, and not look back. But then we say, 'Impossible, they trust us.' When a victim comes to see us and says, 'I know I would have died if you were not here,' that gives us more energy. If we only save one person, it's a victory."

▲ A young girl receiving medical treatment, Cambodia

Oscar Arias Sanchez, Costa Rica

G   "War, and the preparation for war, are the two greatest obstacles to human progress, fostering a vicious cycle of arms buildups, violence, and poverty," says Oscar Arias Sanchez, 60, the former

president of Costa Rica. Arias was awarded the Nobel Peace Prize in 1987 for his role in ending conflict in Central America. He continues to campaign for democracy and demilitarization worldwide. "Three billion people live in tragic poverty," he says, "and 40,000 children die each day from diseases that could be prevented. War is a missed opportunity for humanitarian investment. It is a crime against every child who calls out for food rather than for guns. The decisions we make about how to conduct our lives, about the kind of people we want to be, have important consequences. It is clear that one must stand on the side of life."

▲ Oscar Arias Sanchez, Costa Rica

Juliana Dogbadzi, Ghana

H   "When I was seven, my parents sent me to a shrine where I was a slave to a fetish priest for 17 years," says Juliana Dogbadzi, 26, referring to the

*After this article was written, former president Oscar Arias was re-elected President of Costa Rica in 2006.

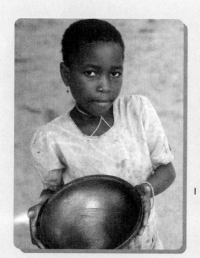
▲ A young *Trokosi* girl

religious and cultural practice known as *Trokosi*, in which young girls, mostly virgins, are sent into servitude to atone for the alleged crimes of their relatives. "Each day, we woke up at 5:00 A.M., cleaned the compound, prepared a meal for the priest, worked until 6:00 P.M. and returned to sleep without food," she says. Sexual services also were required, resulting in unwanted pregnancies. 90

"Unlike most of the others," says Dogbadzi, "I got over the fear instilled by the *Trokosi* system. This was my weapon." Today, after a daring escape, she travels the country speaking out against *Trokosi* and trying to win freedom for other slaves. "What I do is dangerous," she says, "but I am prepared to die for a good cause." 95 100

Source: "Courage Begins With One Voice" *Parade Magazine* (Kerry Kennedy) from *Speak Truth From Power* (Kerry Kennedy)

After You Read

IDENTIFYING THE VOICES IN A READING

An author sometimes presents different voices in an article by quoting (repeating) the exact words of other people. This adds interest and variety to the reading. It is important to notice when the author speaks and when it is someone else.

3 **Identifying the Voices** In this reading, all five of the human rights heroes are quoted. Read the quotations from the reading and match the letter of the correct speaker to each quotation.

    a. Kailash Satyarthi, India

    b. Vaclav Havel, Czech Republic

    c. Kek Galabru, Cambodia

    d. Oscar Arias Sanchez, Costa Rica

    e. Juliana Dogbadzi, Ghana

    _____ **1.** "War, and the preparation for war, are the two greatest obstacles to human progress, . . ."

    _____ **2.** "I have faced threats, and two of my colleagues have been killed . . . But I think of it all as a test."

    _____ **3.** "The post-communist world presented a chance for new moral leaders. But gradually people were repressed, and much of that opportunity was lost."

_____ **4.** "Each day, we woke up at 5:00 A.M., cleaned the compound, prepared a meal for the priest, worked until 6:00 P.M. and returned to sleep without food, . . ."

_____ **5.** "Many times with our work, we are so depressed, It could be so easy for us to take our suitcases, take an airplane, and not look back."

USING NOUN SUFFIXES TO CREATE NEW WORDS

Various suffixes (*-ance, -ence, -itude, -ity, -ment, -tion, -sion*) are commonly added to verbs or adjectives to turn them into nouns. Some examples include: *performance, gratitude, clarity, commitment, examination, confusion.* Sometimes small spelling changes are also necessary, as when we change *accountable* to *accountability.*

---

4 **Using Noun Suffixes to Create New Words** Read the sentences below. In each blank write the correct noun that is described in parentheses, using the italicized word plus a suffix. The nouns are from the reading.

1. That (way to *perceive*) _____perception_____ is wrong.

2. From free (action to *express*) _____ to women's rights, . . .

3. Their determination, valor, and (choice to *commit*) _____ in the face of overwhelming danger . . .

4. . . . and a writer of compelling essays on (act to *repress*) _____ and dissent.

5. They are ready to assume (the attitude of being *responsible*) _____ for the world . . .

6. . . . we give medical (action to *assist*) _____, . . .

7. A medical doctor, Galabru played a key role in opening (actions to *negotiate*) _____ . . .

8. War, and the (action to *prepare*) _____ for war, . . .

9. He continues to campaign for democracy and (the act to *demilitarize*) _____ worldwide.

10. War is a missed opportunity for humanitarian (action to *invest*) _____.

11. The (choices to *decide*) _____ we make . . .

12. . . . young girls, mostly virgins, are sent into (obligation to *serve*) _____ . . .

5 **Focusing on Words from the Academic Word List** Use the most appropriate word from the box to fill in each of the blanks below in the paragraphs taken from Part 2. Do NOT look back at the reading right away; instead, first see if you can remember the vocabulary. Check your answers on page 163.

assistance	depressed	founded	monitors	role
civil	energy	medical	promotion	violations

E   "There are around 600 to 900 people tortured by the police in custody every year to whom we give medical _____," says Kek Galabru, 58. "Without us they would die." A _____ doctor, Galabru played a key _____ in opening negotiations that led to the 1991 peace accords ending the Cambodian _____ war, which left more than a million people dead.

F   Today, she _____ rights _____ through the Cambodian League for the _____ and Defense of Human Rights, which she _____. "Many times with our work, we are so _____," she says. "It could be so easy for us to take our suitcases, take an airplane, and not look back. But then we say, 'Impossible, they trust us.' When a victim comes to see us and says, 'I know I would have died if you were not here,' that gives us more _____. If we only save one person, it's a victory."

6 **Guided Academic Conversation: How Do You Measure Courage?**
Not all questions have correct answers; some answers are a matter of opinion. It is often interesting to exchange opinions with others. Discuss the following questions with two or more classmates. Use specific points and examples from the reading to support your point of view. Then compare your opinions with those of other groups.

1. Judging from what you have read in the article, which of the five people mentioned has faced the most danger? Why? Who are the enemies of that person and why do they want to do harm to him or her?

2. Which of these people has the most difficult life? Do you think that his/her life will improve in the future or not? Explain.

3. Most people want to be happy. Are these people happy or not? What motivates them to keep on doing the work they are doing? Would you want this kind of life for yourself? Why or why not?

4. In your opinion, which of these people is the most courageous? Why?

<table>
<tr><td>Part 3</td><td>Tying It All Together</td></tr>
</table>

 1 Making Connections Work by yourself or with a partner on one of the following research tasks. Look on the Internet or in the library for specific examples to answer the questions and find interesting facts to report back to the class.

1. **Confucius in the World Today.** How do modern Chinese people view the teachings of Confucius? Are his books still selling? Does he influence movies or popular culture? Does his influence extend to other countries besides China? What other Chinese philosophers are popular now?

2. **Update on Courage.** Look up any one of the people presented in the article, "Courage Begins with One Voice" and find more information on what they are doing. What are their most recent activities? If that person has died, are there other people continuing their work? What is the popular opinion about them and their work? Are there any people who speak against them? Explain.

3. **A Hero (or Heroine) from My Own Culture.** Find a hero or heroine from your own culture who is alive today or whose influence continues on, even if he or she has died. You may choose a philosopher, writer, politician, entertainer, sports star—anyone you admire. Explain why this person is remarkable and how he or she has influenced others.

Responding in Writing

WRITING TIP: USING A VENN DIAGRAM TO COMPARE AND CONTRAST

To write a paper that compares and/or contrasts two things or people, start by making three lists: one about the qualities unique to one thing or person, one about the qualities unique to the other, and one about the things they have in common. Using a Venn diagram will help you to better visualize the comparison and the contrast. (Put the similarities in circle C and the different traits of one individual in circle A and of the other individual in circle B.) Hand this in with your finished essay so your teacher can see the process you used to prepare for writing.

2 **Comparing and Contrasting Two Leaders** Choose any two of the leaders you have learned about in this chapter and that you think would be interesting to compare and contrast. You can choose them from the readings or from the research you did on the Internet.

Step 1: List the most important similarities and differences between these two remarkable people. For this purpose, use a Venn diagram, like the one below, to set out your thoughts clearly on the similarities and differences.

Person 1: _____   Person 2: _____

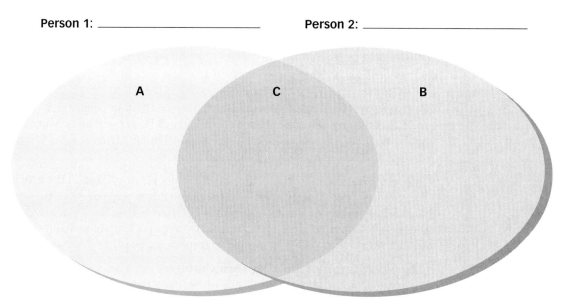

Step 2: Write an introduction paragraph describing each person and his or her importance and influence. Try to write a sentence to end this paragraph that expresses your view or the main overall point that you will want to make after considering the points you made in your diagram or list in Step 1.

Step 3: Write paragraph 2 describing similarities between the two. (You can include words such as: *similarly, like, in the same way*.)

Step 4: Write paragraph 3 describing the differences between the two. (You can include words such as: *on the other hand, but, unlike, in contrast to*.)

Step 5: Write a concluding paragraph summarizing your main point about these two leaders.

Step 6: After you have finished your paper, read and revise what you have written. Make sure that a sentence in the introduction does indeed express the direction you have taken in your conclusion. Be sure to think of a good title and write it at the center top of your essay. Your teacher may also want to see your Venn diagram and preparatory notes.

Focus on Testing

Sentence-Insertion Questions on Tests

For each reading on the TOEFL® Internet-Based Test (iBT), a one sentence-insertion question is asked. In the reading you will see four dark squares. Your job is to find the square that marks the best place to add the new sentence.
Here is an example of this type of question.

Example

Notice the four squares [■] that indicate where the following sentence could be added to the passage.

Most deep-vein coal mining is now done by machine, not by human workers.

Where would the sentence best fit?

Click on a square [■] to add the sentence to the passage.

Notice that you must click on a square within the reading passage, not within a list of options. This lets you actually see how the sentence fits into each of four contexts. After you have looked at all four possibilities, you should choose the place where it fits most smoothly and accurately.

Practice Read the following short passage about dangerous jobs. Answer the sentence-insertion question that follows.

The Most Dangerous Jobs in the U.S.

A   What is the most dangerous work you can do? In other words, which jobs give you the greatest chance of being harmed while at work? The Bureau of Labor Statistics (part of the U.S. Department of Labor) has issued reports that try to answer this question. It has drawn up a list of the top ten most dangerous jobs, based on the number of persons killed in various types of work.

B   One clear pattern in the statistics is that weather makes a big difference. No occupation in the top ten is an office-based or factory-based job. Instead, all of the most hazardous jobs involve working outside or in motor vehicles. Fishing is the most dangerous, more than 20 times as hazardous as the average job in the United States. Logging (cutting down trees) is almost equally dangerous. Workers in both of these jobs face tough weather conditions, including storms that can overturn boats, topple trees, or unleash deadly lightning bolts. Loggers also worry about trees that fall in an uncontrolled way after being cut. Getting struck by a heavy object is the leading cause of death among timber-cutters. ■

C   Crashes are the biggest threats to airplane pilots (3rd on the top-ten list) and truck drivers (9th). ■ Both problems could be reduced by performing better maintenance on vehicles and by reducing tiredness or stress in the pilots and drivers. ■ Icy, wet, or foggy conditions often contribute to the worst crashes. Other kinds of vehicle-related accidents—tractors falling over, construction machinery striking someone, etc.—are not actually crashes but can be deadly. They are the leading cause of death among construction workers (6th on the list) and farmers (10th). ■

D   Working in high places is very hazardous as well. Metalworkers on buildings (4th on the list), roofers (5th), and construction workers (6th) all need safer harnesses and other equipment to reduce the rate of falls. They also need to be more cautious when bad weather approaches, because they are often exposed to lightning strikes.

E   Finally, there are occupations that work with inherently dangerous things or people. Electricity has profound power, and it is no surprise that people who install electrical systems are on the list (8th). Taxi-cab drivers don't have to fear accidents as much as their own customers. Drivers who work at night are often the targets of violent criminals who hope to steal a driver's money. They are 7th on the list because so many of them are attacked by customers trying to rob them.

Question: Notice the four squares [■] that indicate where the following sentence could be added to the passage.

Working in the air or on the road involves exposure to weather hazards as well.

Where would the sentence best fit?

Click on a square [■] to add the sentence to the passage.

(NOTE: Because this is not a computer-based test, circle a square to add it to the passage.)

Self-Assessment Log

Read the lists below. Check (✔) the strategies and vocabulary that you learned in this chapter. Look through the chapter or ask your instructor about the strategies and words that you do not understand.

Reading and Vocabulary-Building Strategies

- ❏ Skimming for the general idea
- ❏ Figuring out words from structure clues
- ❏ Identifying key terms
- ❏ Forming new words from the same word family
- ❏ Matching words to their definitions
- ❏ Finding facts to support or disprove general statements
- ❏ Previewing to determine organization
- ❏ Using expressive synonyms
- ❏ Identifying the voices in a reading
- ❏ Using noun suffixes to create new words

Target Vocabulary

Nouns

- ❏ assistance*
- ❏ atrocities
- ❏ background
- ❏ childhood
- ❏ commitment*
- ❏ commoners
- ❏ cornerstones
- ❏ decisions
- ❏ defender
- ❏ demilitarization
- ❏ dynasty
- ❏ eloquence
- ❏ energy*
- ❏ etiquette
- ❏ expression
- ❏ (the) Golden Rule
- ❏ holocaust
- ❏ innovator*
- ❏ investment*
- ❏ lament
- ❏ negotiations
- ❏ notions*
- ❏ obstacles

- ❏ outlook
- ❏ perception*
- ❏ preparation
- ❏ prestige
- ❏ principality
- ❏ promotion*
- ❏ repression
- ❏ responsibility
- ❏ role*
- ❏ servitude
- ❏ tyranny
- ❏ valor
- ❏ violations*

Verbs

- ❏ atone
- ❏ conduct*
- ❏ eradicate
- ❏ founded*
- ❏ modernize
- ❏ monitors*
- ❏ permeated
- ❏ reared
- ❏ resigned

- ❏ sacrifice
- ❏ seized
- ❏ strive
- ❏ suppress

Adjectives

- ❏ benevolent
- ❏ civil*
- ❏ compelling
- ❏ Confucian
- ❏ depressed*
- ❏ diligent
- ❏ enduring
- ❏ governmental
- ❏ influential
- ❏ medical*
- ❏ overwhelming
- ❏ philosophical*
- ❏ political

Adverbs

- ❏ easily
- ❏ primarily*

Expression

- ❏ take up the torch

*These words are from the Academic Word List. For more information on this list, see www.vuw.ac.nz/lals/research/awl.

8

Creativity

In This Chapter

Exactly what makes a person creative? A precise answer to that question will always remain a mystery, but this chapter presents readings about people who work creatively in two very different fields, one as an architect and the others as singers. By learning about them, we can observe different kinds of creativity in action. Then toward the end of the chapter, the *What Do You Think?* section offers a brief opinion written by one of the world's best-known anthropologists on a controversial topic: Are men more creative than women?

❝ Poetry arrived in search of me. I don't know, I don't know where it came from, from winter or a river. I don't know how or when . . . and it touched me. ❞

—Pablo Neruda,
Nobel Prize-winning poet from Chile (1904–1973)

Connecting to the Topic

1 Who are the people in the photo? Where are they? What do you think they are doing?

2 In what ways can people express their creativity?

3 Do you think that creativity can be learned? Explain.

Guggenheim Museum, U.S.A.

Before You Read

Strategy

Understanding the Vocabulary of Shapes and Forms

Before reading an article on a subject with many visual references, prepare by connecting the key terms to illustrations and pictures.

When you read the following article, you will notice references to geometric forms (like the circle, polygon, and so on) and how they change in two or three dimensions. To understand the ideas of the architect of the Guggenheim Museum, it helps to have some vocabulary relating to these forms. Here is a brief review of the names of some basic shapes.

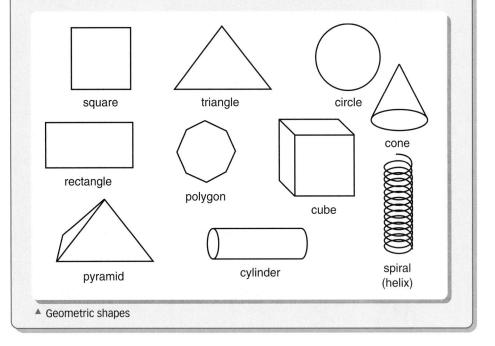

square   triangle   circle   cone

rectangle   polygon   cube

pyramid   cylinder   spiral (helix)

▲ Geometric shapes

1 Understanding the Vocabulary of Shapes and Forms Study the illustrations in the Strategy Box; then complete sentences 1 to 6 appropriately.

1. A square extended into three dimensions is a _____.

2. A _____ extended into three dimensions is a pyramid.

3. Any two-dimensional figure with four sides and four right angles is a

_____.

4. A closed, two-dimensional figure that usually has more than four sides is a

_____ .

5. The combination of a cylinder and a pyramid is a _____ . (Ice cream is often served in these.)

6. Some seashells (and bed springs and screws) are in the form of a

_____ ,

which may also be called a _____ .

2 **Guessing the Meaning of Adjectives and Adverbs** Use structure clues (such as finding a smaller word inside the larger one) or the context to guess the meaning of each italicized adjective or adverb in the phrases taken from the article. Choose the correct synonym(s) for each word.

1. In 1932, New York's Museum of Modern Art assembled what was clearly meant to be a *definitive* exhibition of modern architecture. (**Hint:** The verb *define* is inside the adjective *definitive*. To *define* is to give or describe the meaning of something. Which word comes closest to the idea of an exhibit giving the meaning of modern art?)

   Ⓐ beneficial   Ⓑ complete   Ⓒ negative

2. When his three co-exhibitors were still in grade school, he was already designing *remarkably* innovative houses. . . .

   Ⓐ charmingly   Ⓑ notably   Ⓒ unfortunately

3. By 1932, Wright's work had become highly *individualistic*. . . .

   Ⓐ classic   Ⓑ competent   Ⓒ personal

4. In the spirited and *energetic* atmosphere of the times. . . .

   Ⓐ active   Ⓑ boring   Ⓒ difficult

5. This is why he so often seemed more concerned with finding the *proper* form for an idea than with pleasing his clients. (**Hint:** The sentence suggests that this kind of form might not please clients.)

   Ⓐ entertaining   Ⓑ exact   Ⓒ practical

6. Wright was *continually* searching for natural forms appropriate to human needs. . . .

   Ⓐ constantly   Ⓑ occasionally   Ⓒ slowly

7. Wright *boldly* designed the new building in the shape of an inverted conical spiral. . . .

   Ⓐ angrily   Ⓑ courageously   Ⓒ shyly

8. In defense of his *stunningly* original design. . . .

   Ⓐ amazingly   Ⓑ horribly   Ⓒ probably

9. As a building, however, the Guggenheim Museum defines a magnificent space and has become a *compulsory* stop on even the most basic tour of New York.

   Ⓐ infrequent   Ⓑ necessary   Ⓒ unpleasant

10. The *startling* effect of the Guggenheim lies in its unusual form and stark simplicity.

   Ⓐ conventional   Ⓑ predictable   Ⓒ surprising

Introduction

A common characteristic of many creative works is innovation, the introduction of something new. This quality is apparent in the famous Guggenheim Museum of New York, as you can see by looking at the photos illustrating the following article. Although it opened in 1959, the museum still strikes the eye as new and unusual. The following article tells us about Frank Lloyd Wright, the architect who designed it.

- What kind of person do you think would design a building like this, and why?
- What great or beautiful building can you think of in your own city? In the world?
- In your opinion, what makes a building remarkable?

Guggenheim Museum, U.S.A.

A   In 1932, New York's Museum of Modern Art assembled what was clearly meant to be a **definitive** exhibition of modern architecture. It presented the work of Frank Lloyd Wright along with that of Le Corbusier,* Ludwig Mies van der Rohe, and Walter Gropius, two leaders of Germany's revolutionary design school, the Bauhaus.† On that occasion, Wright   5 commented, "I warn you that having made an excellent start, I fully intend not only to be the greatest architect that has ever been but also the greatest of all future architects."

B   Wright's pride in his own work was understandable. When his three co-exhibitors were still in grade school, he was already designing **remarkably**   10 innovative houses, any one of which could have established him as first among **contemporary** architects. With the help of devoted assistants, Wright had created dozens of these houses, year after year. By 1932, Wright's work had become highly **individualistic**—often with hints of expressionism‡ that would surface in his design for the Guggenheim Museum.   15

Le Corbusier (1887–1965) was a Swiss architect and city planner who lived in France. His buildings are characterized by daring and original design.

†A school of design founded in Germany in 1919 and continued in Chicago after 1937. The Bauhaus taught the importance of technical mastery and craftsmanship.

‡A style of painting developed in the 20th century, in which the expression of emotion is considered more important than the representation of reality. Colors and forms are often distorted or exaggerated.

C   Frank Lloyd Wright's childhood had been shaped by a New England heritage of liberal Protestantism and an acceptance of the "natural philosophy" that was expressed in the writings of Walt Whitman and Henry David Thoreau. These two American writers believed that much of modern human anguish was due to urban environments and loss of contact with nature. The human foot had been made to touch earth, not concrete, and human dwellings were meant to be in harmony with their natural surroundings. In the spirited and **energetic** atmosphere of the times, it is perhaps not surprising that Wright also developed that insistence upon absolute freedom of mind that marks the true **pioneer** as well as the renowned artist. This is why he so often seemed more concerned with finding the **proper** form for an idea than with pleasing his clients. To Wright, the artistic integrity of his work was far more important than its practical function. Once, when the owner of one of his houses called to say that rain was dripping on him from a crack in the ceiling, Wright is said to have suggested that the man move his chair.

▲ The Guggenheim Museum in New York

D   Both Wright's genius and **obstinacy** came to play their roles in his design for the Guggenheim Museum in New York City. In the early 1940s, Solomon R. Guggenheim, who was committed to the development of modern painting, found himself in need of more space to house a growing collection of pictures. He decided that a museum of modern art ought to be the work of a leading modern architect. Ironically, he turned to Wright, a man known to have little liking for twentieth-century painting, and commissioned him to design the new museum. Wright's creation is one of the most original buildings in the world, a museum with its own place in the history of art. Yet as a picture gallery, it is a failure. Ultimately, the only thing it displays well is itself.

E   Perhaps at the time that the plans for the Guggenheim were being drawn up, the administrators of the museum were unaware of Wright's growing rejection of **conventional** square and rectangular forms of city buildings and blocks. Wright was **continually** searching for natural forms appropriate to human needs, forms that he described as "organic architecture, opening onto the world rather than insulating people from it." So he had begun to explore the possibilities of the triangle, the polygon (recalling the form of mineral crystals), and even the circle. For some time, he had been ready to take the logical step from the circle to the spiral, the form of conch shells, "plastic and

▲ Frank Lloyd Wright

continuous." This form is more properly called a helix, and is really a circle carried to the third dimension. Wright **boldly** designed the new building in the shape of an inverted conical spiral, and convinced Solomon Guggenheim that this form would make a magnificent museum. 60

F The museum is essentially a long ramp that starts at ground level and spirals upward in five concentric turns, continually growing wider so that it opens out toward the top. Within the spiral is a vast central space, illuminated primarily by a huge skylight. At the first-floor level, the main spiral is joined with a smaller, round building, used for readings, lectures, and offices. A broad horizontal rectilinear base connects both elements and also relates the museum as a whole to its rectilinear environment of city blocks and conventional buildings. 65 70 75

G In defense of his **stunningly** original design, Wright declared that he was not merely playing a game with forms: He believed that the helix was really the best shape for a picture gallery. He claimed that the conventional manner of displaying paintings in one dreary room after another distracts the attention of visitors by making them concerned with the condition of their feet rather than the masterpieces on the walls. According to Wright, this museum **fatigue** was the result of bad architecture. At the Guggenheim, visitors would enter on the ground floor and be carried by elevator up to the top, where they would begin to slowly wind down along the spiral. Any **weariness** would be counteracted by the natural form of the shell, which would gently "spiral" visitors down to the first floor. As they descended, they would be able to study the paintings hung along the outward-leaning walls. In this way, each work of art would be viewed at an angle—as Wright believed the artist himself had seen it on the easel. But in reality, the museum is a challenge. Visitors must make their way down a ramp at an angle, studying paintings hung on a wall that both curves and slopes. 80 85 90

H As a building, however, the Guggenheim Museum defines a magnificent space and has become a **compulsory** stop on even the most basic tour of New York. The **startling** effect of the Guggenheim lies in its unusual form and stark simplicity. While it was under construction—and remaining upright in apparent defiance of gravity—Wright would **smirk** happily and say of his colleagues, "They'll spend years trying to work it out." 95

Source: "Guggenheim Museum, U.S.A." *Individual Creations* (Flavio Conti)

After You Read

Strategy

Making Inferences About a Person
Sometimes an article does not describe directly the character of a person.
Instead, it quotes the words of that person and tells what he or she did. From the
quotes and the actions of the person, we can then infer (draw conclusions about)
what the person was like. For example, someone who says he or she has no
friends and who never wants to talk in public is probably a shy person. Someone
who says he or she likes to paint pictures and write poetry is probably a creative
person.

 3 **Making Inferences About a Person** With a partner, read the following
statements taken from the article. What inferences can you make from them about Frank
Lloyd Wright and his relationships with people? After you finish, compare your inferences
with those of your classmates. The first answer is partially completed for you.

1. Wright commented, "I warn you that having made an excellent start, I fully
   intend not only to be the greatest architect that has ever been but also the
   greatest of all future architects." (lines 5 to 8)

   Wright has a lot of confidence in himself. He also . . .
   _____
   _____

2. With the help of devoted assistants, Wright had created dozens of these
   [innovative] houses, year after year. (lines 12–13)

   _____
   _____
   _____

3. Once, when the owner of one of his houses called to say that rain was dripping
   on him from a crack in the ceiling, Wright is said to have suggested that the
   man move his chair. (lines 35–37)

   _____
   _____
   _____

4 **Scanning for Words** Read the clues below and see if you can guess any of the words. For a word you are not sure about, scan the reading for it, and use the context to infer its meaning. (If you need to look back, the letter in parentheses indicates the paragraph.)

1. An adjective beginning with *c* that means *present-day.* (B) _____

2. A noun beginning with *p* that means *a person who goes before, preparing the way for others in a new region or field of work.* This word is often used to refer to early settlers of the United States who traveled in covered wagons to live in the wilderness in the 1800s. (C) _____

3. A synonym for *stubbornness* that begins with *o.* (D) _____

4. The opposite of *original* or *unusual*, beginning with *c.* (E) _____

5. Two synonyms for *tiredness*, one beginning with *f* and the other with *w.* (G)

_____ _____

6. Smiling is not always nice: a verb that begins the same way as the word *smile* but means *to smile in a way that is offensive, insulting, or irritating.* (H)

_____

5 **Guided Academic Conversation** In small groups, discuss the following questions. Afterwards, compare your answers with those of another group.

1. Exactly what is innovative about Wright's design for the Guggenheim? Why did he choose to build it this way?

2. Referring to the Guggenheim Museum, the article states: "Yet as a picture gallery, it is a failure. Ultimately, the only thing it displays well is itself." Is this a fact or an opinion? Explain. (For a brief explanation of the difference between fact and opinion, see page 95.)

3. When you travel to new cities, do you pay attention to the architecture? Does it have an influence on you? In which city or region has the architecture impressed you the most? Why?

4. If you have seen the Guggenheim Museum, describe your reaction to it. If you have not seen it, tell what you think of it based on the article and photos.

5. What other kinds of museums are there besides art museums? What museum(s) have you been in? What did you like about it (them)? Do you think that most people go to museums often? Should they? Why or why not?

Focus on Testing

Thinking Twice about Tricky Questions

The multiple-choice exercise is a common test format for reading comprehension. Usually it requires that you look back and scan for information. The items generally follow the order of appearance, so when you take the test, try looking for the answer to the first question at the beginning of the reading. Continue through the other items in that way.

You will see that question 1 is "tricky" because the answer is not given directly. You must make inferences. Look at each of the possibilities. Two of them relate to age, but the other is different. Check the reading section first. Is there evidence that Wright was "unknown" at that time? If not, how can you infer his age, compared to the other participants in the exhibit? Choose the best response, according to the reading selection "Guggenheim Museum, U.S.A."

1. When the exhibition of modern architecture was presented in New York in 1932, Frank Lloyd Wright was _____.
   - (A) the oldest of the participants
   - (B) the youngest of the participants
   - (C) unknown

Practice Complete the rest of the items in the exercise. Which ones are straight memory questions with answers given directly in the reading? Which ones are "tricky" and require inferences?

2. In his architectural work, Wright was most concerned with _____.
   - (A) expressing his heritage of liberal Protestantism
   - (B) finding the correct form for an idea
   - (C) making his clients happy

3. It is ironic that Solomon Guggenheim chose Wright to design his museum of modern art because _____.
   - (A) it is one of the most original buildings in the world
   - (B) he found himself in need of more space for his collection
   - (C) Wright did not like modern art very much

4. Wright was searching for an "organic architecture" that would use forms found in nature, such as the _____.
   - (A) square
   - (B) cube
   - (C) polygon

5. One of the strikingly original aspects of the Guggenheim Museum is that it follows the form of an upside-down cone in a _____.
   - (A) spiral
   - (B) pyramid
   - (C) rectangle

6. Another unusual characteristic of the Guggenheim is that _____.
   - (A) it is illuminated only by five huge skylights
   - (B) visitors view paintings while they walk down a ramp
   - (C) paintings are displayed in one dreary room after another

The Architecture of Shanghai and Dubai

A   **D**aring architecture in the 21st century is booming. Megacities throughout the world are tearing down the old and building the new. Two leaders in the competition for the most amazing city skyline are Shanghai, China, and Dubai, United Arab Emirates (U.A.E.).

▲ Shanghai's skyline

B   China, with its manufacturing boom, is rapidly razing old sections of its cities and building phenomenal skyscrapers. Some of the world's most imaginative buildings, topped off with balls, space needles, and observation decks, grace the skyline. Pudong, a district along the Huangpu River in Shanghai, boasts one of the world's tallest hotels, the 88-story Grand Hyatt Hotel. In a mere 12 years, Shanghai has built a skyline comparable to New York's, which took over 50 years to build. Architects from all over the world compete for contracts in this rapidly expanding city of 20 million.

C   Halfway around the globe in the U.A.E., the architecture of Dubai is in close competition with the cities of China. The building boom in Dubai is fueled by the oil economy. Buildings like the Emirates Towers and the Burj Juman Shopping Center combine state of the art architectural design with traditional Arab architecture. The Burj Al Arab is also one of the world's tallest hotels, standing at 321 meters, or 1,083 feet. The International Trade Centre, which can be seen for miles around the city, is a symbol of Dubai's rise in the business world. At ground level, off shore, the architects of Dubai have built a man-made island housing extremely expensive condominiums and hotels.

▲ Dubai's skyline

Shanghai and Dubai are not only architectural leaders, but economic   35
and cultural leaders in their sphere of the globe, and worldwide also.

1. Have you seen pictures of the skylines of Shanghai and Dubai before? Which skyline do you prefer? Why?

2. Of the large cities you have visited, or admired through pictures or films, which do you think has the best architecture? Why do you like it?

3. In order to make room for skyscrapers, sometimes older or historic neighborhoods are torn down. Often, people are displaced from their homes. How do you feel about this "down with the old, make way for the new" approach?

Part 2   Reading Skills and Strategies

Music Makes the World Go 'Round: Lila Downs, Nancy Ajram, and Don Popo

Before You Read

Strategy

Guessing the Meaning of Strong Verbs in Context
Strong verbs are verbs that express the action in a more complete, exact, or picturesque way than common verbs. Using strong verbs improves one's writing. The following selection uses many strong verbs. For instance, instead of saying that "Lila Downs grew up frequently going back and forth to stay in Mexico and the U.S.," the first sentence says that she "grew up *shuttling* between Mexico and the U.S."

1 **Guessing the Meaning of Strong Verbs** Read the sentences below and guess the meaning of the strong verbs from their context. Choose the synonym for each one.

1. Her childhood was spent *shuttling between* the United States and Mexico . . .
   - Ⓐ looking
   - Ⓑ (frequently going and returning)
   - Ⓒ moving slowly and carefully

2. . . . and passed a lot of time *grappling with* her cultural identity while she was growing up.

(A) being depressed by

(B) struggling hard with

(C) forgetting about

3. The pan-American make-up of her band has resulted in interesting combinations of traditional Mexican cumbia, bolero, ranchera, and songs that *experiment with* unexpected influences, such as reggae, jazz, and rap.

(A) play exclusively

(B) stay away from

(C) try out

4. Lila has even *dabbled* in cinema.

(A) worked from time to time

(B) listened to music

(C) made decorations

5. It took the young singer [Nancy Ajram] another three years to *launch* her second album.

(A) buy the songs for

(B) be successful with

(C) introduce publicly

6. The singer stressed the success of the album by *shooting* three of its songs in the form of video clips.

(A) firing at with a gun

(B) changing

(C) filming

7. Don Popo is a highly successful young man *rapping* his way up the ladder to international recognition.

(A) knocking down others as he climbs

(B) rushing very fast as he pushes

(C) becoming successful as he plays "rap" music

8. Don Popo himself started making music at the age of 13, two years after his own father was *murdered*.

(A) was killed by someone

(B) died from an illness

(C) left his family

2 **Finding the Basis for Inferences** Scan the sections of the reading indicated in parentheses to find the basis (facts that give support) for the following inferences. Write the words that suggest each inference and an explanation. The first one is done as an example.

1. Inference: Lila Downs is of mixed cultural background. (lines 1–3)

   Basis for inference: *Her father was a professor from the United States and her mother, a singer, was a Mixteca Indian from Mexico.*

2. Inference: Lila Downs knows at least a little of some of the indigenous (Native, American Indian) languages of Mexico. (lines 28–30)

   Basis for inference: _____

   _____

3. Inference: After her initial discovery, Nancy Ajram trained for her career as a musician through traditional channels. (lines 48–52)

   Basis for inference: _____

   _____

4. Inference: Don Popo sees himself as an activist to help young people who are poor. (lines 74–75; hint: more than one line could prove this inference.)

   Basis for inference: _____

   _____

5. Inference: Don Popo did not train in the traditional way for a career in music. (lines 100–102)

   Basis for inference: _____

   _____

Read

> ### Introduction
> Around the world, musicians express their creativity by developing genres of music with lyrics on new themes, derived from parts of their experience and cultural background. And how do these vocalists manage to get their creative works heard and rise to stardom? The following selection traces the stories of three emerging young singers from different countries, looking at their musical styles, their successes, and the side vocations and/or businesses that come out of their singing careers.
>
> - Do you know of any new young singers who have become popular recently?
> - How would you describe their musical style?
> - How did they rise to fame?

Music Makes the World Go 'Round: Lila Downs, Nancy Ajram, and Don Popo

Lila Downs

A   Lila Downs was born in 1968. Her father was a professor from the United States and her mother, a singer, was a Mixteca Indian from Mexico. Lila spent the first few years of her life in Mexico until her parents separated and she went to live with a relative in California. Her childhood was spent shuttling between The United States and Mexico and she passed a lot of time grappling with her cultural identity while she was growing up. She developed her ambition to study music early on, but her road to becoming a well-known, professional singer was long and circuitous. Lila started singing mariachi songs as a child and later grew to love and study classical music and opera. She studied voice in both the United States and Mexico, which has contributed to her unique style.

▲ Lila Downs, Mexican-American singer

B   Besides music, Lila also studied anthropology. In the early 1990's, she was hired to help translate documents related to the deaths of Mexicans who had died while crossing the Mexican/U.S. border. This experience prompted her to write songs to tell their stories. One of these songs, *Ofrenda*, is on her debut album, *La Sandunga*.

C   She has come out with three more high-profile albums over the past few years, that have earned her increasing critical acclaim. Her album, *Tree of Life*, includes songs in three of the indigenous languages of Mexico, Zapotec, Náhuatl, and Mixtec. Her album *La Linea*, deals with the subject of the border and features songs sung in English, Spanish, and Mayan. The pan-American make-up of her band has resulted in interesting combinations of traditional Mexican cumbia, bolero, ranchera, and songs that experiment with unexpected influences, such as reggae, jazz, and rap.

D   In addition to her musical achievements, Lila has also dabbled in cinema and appeared in the movie *Frida*, about Mexico's iconic artist, Frida Kahlo.

Nancy Ajram

E   Who would have imagined that the young girl born to Nabil and Rimonda Ajram on the 16th of May, 1983, in Al-Ashrafia, Lebanon, would be a famous singer by the age of 21!

F   She had quite a normal childhood with her small family. But when Nancy Ajram was twelve, she participated in a television program called "Nojoum Al-Mostakbal" and actually won first prize. Soon after, Ajram began studying music under the supervision of some of the finest teachers in her country. When she turned 18, she joined the Syndicate of Professional Artists in Lebanon—after they made an exception regarding her age.

▲ Nancy Ajram, Lebanese singer

G   Her first album, *Mehtagalak*, was released in 1998 and marked her first official step in the world of show business. But it took the young singer another three years to launch her second album, *Shil Oyounak Ani*, in 2001. Then her true hit came with her third and most famous album, *Ya Salam*, in 2003. The singer stressed the success of the album by shooting three of its songs in the form of video clips. The clips were a tremendous hit and gained popularity in such a short time that they gave the singer incredible fame in the Arab world. Her latest album *Ah we Nos* is witnessing the same success as the previous one.

H   As for other activities besides singing, the Lebanese diva has agreed to be the spokesperson for the international soft drink company, Coca Cola.
Source: yallabina.com

Don Popo

I   Don Popo, born Jeyffer Rentería, is a highly successful young man rapping his way up the ladder to international recognition. At the same time, he works hard to create opportunities for other Colombian youth to have lives free of drugs, violence, and crime.

J   The 27-year-old rap artist sponsors workshops where poor kids can rap and break dance, create graffiti or learn how to be a DJ. He also raises funds for festivals where young people can demonstrate their talents to a wider audience. To inspire kids in his old Bogotá neighborhood, he gives away his own CDs which appeared on the Sony Music label until he switched to smaller, independent labels. The message: Look kids, you can do this, too! His longtime dream is to open a kind of hip-hop academy in one of Bogotá's largest slums and mix music lessons with information about issues like safe sex and discrimination.

▲ Don Popo, Colombian rapper

K   This dream is closer to realization now that Don Popo has two sources of income. One is his musical career, which is a surprising experiment in the hip-hop world because he uses acoustic guitar, violin, and bass. His poetic talents yield lyrics that touch upon emotions as well as the political situation in his homeland. "I don't want to talk about the government, guerrillas, and paramilitary groups," he raps. "I want to talk about the little children who see their fathers murdered, about the hopelessness, about the feeling of having no future." Don Popo himself started making music at the age of 13, two years after his own father was murdered. It was the only way this silent young man could express his feelings.

L   The other source of income is a new clothing company headed up by Don Popo called La Familia Ayara. Like other Colombian rap artists and their families, he makes the pants at home. "I don't want to encourage employee anonymity," says Don Popo. "I want small-scale operations, not productions for the masses."

M   Colombian hip hoppers used to have no choice but to get their pants and shirts two sizes too big or buy smuggled goods from North America. Now there's an honest alternative, which can be purchased in Colombian shops. So why is this clothing so important? The sparkle returns to his eyes. "Clothing gives us recognition, our own identity."

Source: "Don Popo Raps About a Better Future For Colombia's Kids" *Ode Magazine* (Marco Visscher)

After You Read

3 **Understanding the Reading: Comparison** Which of the following details describes each of the three singers? Put a check mark in the correct column.

	Lila Downs	Nancy Ajram	Don Popo
1. Is a spokesperson for Coca-Cola.			
2. Sings about the U.S./Mexico border.			
3. Performs in a movie about Mexican artist Frida Kahlo.			
4. Comes from Bogotá, Colombia.			
5. Won a prize for singing on a television program.			
6. Works to create opportunities for young people in the community.			
7. Combines traditional Mexican forms with rap, jazz, and reggae.			
8. Uses acoustic guitar, violin, and bass to do rap and hip-hop music.			
9. Did video clips of songs which led to popularity in the Arab world.			
10. Heads a clothing company.			

4 **Matching Words to Their Definitions** Look at the list of words and definitions on page 190. The words or phrases on the left are listed in the order of their appearance in the reading. Match each word with the correct synonym or definition in the column on the right. For a word you are not sure about, scan the reading for it, and use the context to infer its meaning.

Vocabulary Words

_____ **1.** ambition

_____ **2.** circuitous

_____ **3.** debut album

_____ **4.** high-profile

_____ **5.** critical acclaim

_____ **6.** indigenous

_____ **7.** pan-American

_____ **8.** iconic

_____ **9.** show business

_____ **10.** spokesperson

_____ **11.** discrimination

_____ **12.** acoustic guitar, violin, bass

_____ **13.** guerrillas

_____ **14.** small-scale operations

_____ **15.** smuggled goods

Definitions and Synonyms

a. prestigious, well known, esteemed

b. from different parts of North and South America

c. prejudice, bigotry, intolerance

d. not straight, with many turns

e. representative, speaker for

f. the entertainment industry

g. companies with small production

h. first collection of songs released

i. revolutionary fighters who want to overthrow the government

j. symbolic, like an icon (representation)

k. musical instruments

l. goal, aspiration, desire to achieve

m. items that are imported or exported illegally

n. relating to cultures of the first inhabitants of a region

o. public praise, popular approval

5 **Focusing on Words from the Academic Word List** Use the most appropriate word from the box to fill in each of the blanks below in the paragraph taken from page 188 in Part 2. Do NOT look back at the reading right away; instead, first see if you can remember the vocabulary. Check your answers on page 188.

academy	funds	sex
create	income	sources
demonstrate	issues	
discrimination	label	

J   The 27-year-old rap artist sponsors workshops where poor kids can rap and break dance, _____ graffiti or learn how to be a DJ.

1

He also raises _____ for festivals where young people

2

can _____ their talents to a wider audience. To inspire

3

kids in his old Bogotá neighborhood, he gives away his own CDs which   5

appeared on the Sony Music _____. . . . The message:

4

Look kids, you can do this, too! His longtime dream is to open a kind of hip-hop _____ in one of Bogotá's largest slums and mix music lessons with^{5} information about _____ like safe

_____ and _____.
^{7} ^{8} ^{10}

K   This dream is closer to realization now that Don Popo has two

_____ of _____.
^{9} ^{10}

6 **Guided Academic Conversation** Work with two or more classmates to discuss Question 1, and then choose one other question to discuss. Take notes about the opinions of your group. Afterwards, be prepared to report your findings to the class.

1. **The Rise to Fame.** Nancy Ajram and Don Popo both started singing at 12 or 13 years old, but they started in very different ways and took very different paths as they embarked on their singing careers. Lila Downs went through several careers or areas of study on her way to her final career. Use the chain-of-events graphs below to fill in the first event and/or different areas of study or work that each of the three vocalists went through on their way to stardom. Be sure to include the *turning point* for each one, the moment that he or she really became famous. You may add boxes to the graphs to include as many events as you need for each vocalist.

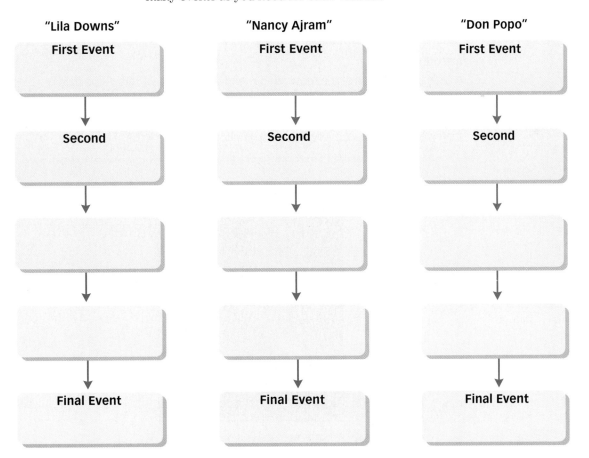

"Lila Downs"

First Event

Second

Final Event

"Nancy Ajram"

First Event

Second

Final Event

"Don Popo"

First Event

Second

Final Event

2. **Side Interests** Each of the three artists has some aspirations and activities besides just singing. Describe what this is for each of them. Do these all relate to their musical careers? How so? What do you think of these aspirations and activities? Is it important to have side interests or should people concentrate completely on their profession? Does this depend on what age a person is? Explain.

3. **Music as a Business** Think about the following questions. In your opinion, is music an art or a business? Or is it both? What does appearing in a video or starring in a movie do for the career of a vocalist?

   Why do you think Don Popo took his music off the Sony label and changed to a smaller independent label? Why does he want a small-scale operation for his clothing company? Do you agree with his way of thinking? Is making clothing locally in Colombia as important as he says?

4. **Music as Poetry** In olden times, people recited and listened to poetry. Nowadays, most people get their poetry from listening to CDs, attending concerts, or watching music videos on TV. What *lyrics* (words to songs) do you like? Are they only about love or are there other themes in the songs of your favorite vocalists and groups? In what languages do they sing? Can you explain why you like them?

What Do You Think?

7 **Discussing Creativity:** Read the selection by Margaret Mead and answer the questions that follow it.

Introduction
Margaret Mead, one of the most famous and widely-read writers in the field of anthropology, expressed her ideas on creativity in men and women. In the two following paragraphs, she gives her opinion on why men have achieved more than women in almost every field throughout history.

▲ Margaret Mead, anthropologist

Are Men More Creative Than Women?

A   Throughout history it has been men, for the most part, who have engaged in public life. Men have sought public achievement and recognition, while women have obtained their main satisfactions by bearing and rearing children. In women's eyes, public achievement makes a man more attractive as a marriage partner. But for men the situation is reversed. The more a 5 woman achieves publicly, the less desirable she seems as a wife.

B   There are three possible positions one can take about male and female creativity. The first is that males are inherently more creative in all fields. The second is that if it were not for the greater appeal of creating and cherishing young human beings, females would be as creative as males. If 10 this were the case, then if men were permitted the enjoyment women have always had in rearing young children, male creativity might be reduced also. (There is some indication in the United States today that this is so.) The third possible position is that certain forms of creativity are more congenial to one sex than to the other and that the great creative acts will 15 therefore come from only one sex in a given field.

Source: "Are Men More Creative Than Women?" *Some Personal Views* (Margaret Mead)

Questions

1. Do you agree with Margaret Mead when she says that "The more a woman achieves publicly, the less desirable she seems as a wife"? Why or why not?

2. What does Mead say about men who achieve publicly and their desirability as husbands?

3. What are the three possible positions given about male and female creativity?

4. Which of these positions do you think is correct? Can you think of any other position on this question?

Part 3   Tying It All Together

 1 Making Connections Research one of the following topics using the Internet. Share your findings with the class.

1. The Guggenheim Museum in Bilbao, Spain: its design, its uses, when, how and by whom it was built.

2. A famous architect in the world today, such as Zahar Hadid or I.M. Pei: his or her life and work.

3. Update on one of the three vocalists in the reading on pages 186–188: where are they living, what are they doing, and what is new in their career?

4. Choose another new, young aspiring musician or vocalist and find out some information about the creativity behind his or her style and rise to fame, as well as any aspirations or side businesses that he or she might have. Be prepared to report your findings back to the class.

Responding in Writing

WRITING TIP: DESCRIBING ART

To describe an object, first figure out a logical sequence for the details or ideas you will cover. Looking at the details you want to discuss, figure out how you will structure the description. Will you start at the top of the structure and move down, or move from left to right? Will you start outside (a building) and proceed inside? Will you start with colors and then move to patterns and images? Or some other pattern?

2 **Writing About Art** Find a work of art or architecture that you are interested in writing about, and bring a picture (or other illustration) of it to class, but do not show the picture to anyone. This work of art could be a painting, building, sculpture, tapestry, etc. Then write a one-to two-paragraph description of it following these steps:

Step 1: Do a cluster diagram (see page 151) to figure out all the points of the work that you will want to cover in your description. Imagine you are describing it to someone who has never seen this work.

Step 2: Write your description with as much detail as possible.

Step 3: Try to add a sentence at the beginning or at the end that sums up your whole outlook on the art work. Read and revise your description to make it as clear and descriptive as possible.

Step 4: Work in a group of five students. Put the pictures in the middle so everyone can see them but without showing who put each one there. Then take turns reading your descriptions aloud. After each one, it should be obvious which is the corresponding picture. Discuss how well the description matches the picture. From the description, did you have a good idea of what the art work would look like? In what ways, if any, does it look different from what you had expected? Who presented the most accurate description? The most interesting one? Why?

Self-Assessment Log

Read the lists below. Check (✓) the strategies and vocabulary that you learned in this chapter. Look through the chapter or ask your instructor about the strategies and words that you do not understand.

Reading and Vocabulary-Building Strategies

❑ Understanding the vocabulary of shapes and forms
❑ Guessing the meaning of adjectives and adverbs
❑ Making inferences about a person
❑ Scanning for words
❑ Guessing the meaning of strong verbs
❑ Finding the basis for inferences
❑ Understanding the reading: comparison
❑ Matching words to their definitions

Target Vocabulary

Nouns

❑ academy*
❑ acoustic guitar
❑ ambition
❑ bass
❑ critical acclaim
❑ debut album
❑ discrimination*
❑ fatigue
❑ funds*
❑ guerrillas
❑ income*
❑ issues*
❑ label*
❑ obstinacy

❑ pioneer
❑ sex*
❑ show business
❑ small-scale operations
❑ smuggled goods
❑ sources*
❑ spokesperson
❑ violin
❑ weariness

Verbs

❑ create*
❑ dabbled
❑ demonstrate*
❑ experiment

❑ grappling
❑ launch
❑ murdered
❑ rapping
❑ shooting
❑ shuttling
❑ smirk

Adjectives

❑ circuitous
❑ compulsory
❑ contemporary*
❑ conventional*
❑ definitive*
❑ energetic*

❑ high-profile
❑ iconic
❑ indigenous
❑ individualistic*
❑ pan-American
❑ proper
❑ startling

Adverbs

❑ boldly
❑ continually
❑ remarkably
❑ stunningly

*These words are from the Academic Word List. For more information on this list, see www.vuw.ac.nz/lals/research/awl.

Chapter

9

Human Behavior

In This Chapter

Human behavior can be viewed in many ways. Anthropologists, psychologists, and sociologists study human behavior. It has also been observed and recorded for centuries in literature. In this chapter, we start with a selection from an anthropology textbook that examines the way people evaluate their own culture and other cultures. Next comes a short story that focuses on how people are influenced by their environment.

❝ Let a person so act by day that he or she may rest happily by night. ❞

—Japanese proverb

Connecting to the Topic

1 Look at the photo. Where are these people? What do you think their relationship is to each other?
2 This chapter discusses how people evaluate their own culture and other cultures. What difficulties can arise when people do not understand and/or value other cultures?
3 In what ways are people influenced by culture?

Part 1 | Reading Skills and Strategies

Ethnocentrism

Before You Read

Reading Tip

Ethnocentrism is a term commonly used by anthropologists (people who study human cultures and customs), but the average English-speaking reader may not be familiar with it. In fact, the purpose of the article in Part 1 is to give the reader an idea of what this term means and why it is important.

1 **Skimming for the Main Idea** Skim the first two paragraphs of the article to find the author's explanation of *ethnocentrism* and write it here.

_____

_____

2 **Scanning for the Development of the Main Idea** Scan the article to answer the following questions.

1. Like most readings taken from textbooks, this one is written in rather long paragraphs. How many of the seven paragraphs begin with a sentence containing the word *ethnocentrism*? _____

2. The main idea is the meaning and importance of ethnocentrism. It is developed through examples. Put a check in front of the aspects of human culture that are discussed in the reading as examples of ethnocentrism.

_____ choice of clothing

_____ food preferences

_____ language

_____ marriage ceremonies

_____ myths and folktales

3 **Using Prefixes to Build New Words** Select the correct prefix to form the new word described in each sentence and based on the word in italics. All these new words are used in the article. Two of the prefixes are used twice. (See page 22 to review what prefixes are.)

Prefixes:
dis-, in-, ir-, non-, sub-, un

1. Certain groups of people live in both the *arctic* and the
   subarctic _____.

2. To some Westerners, it is not *conceivable* that many adults in Asia don't drink milk; it is simply _____.

3. Anthropologists study large *groups* of people which are divided into smaller

   _____.

198 Chapter 9 ■■▪

4. People have a tendency to think of those from their own culture as *human* and to view people from other cultures as _____.

5. Customs from our own culture seem *natural*, but customs from other cultures appear _____.

6. The way of thinking of our own ethnic group appears *rational*, but the way of thinking of another ethnic group appears _____.

7. The clothing and food of our own country seems *tasteful*, but the clothing and food of other countries seems _____.

8. It is often hard for someone from a *Western* society to learn the correct manners and customs of a _____ society.

Read

> ### Introduction
> The following reading about ethnocentrism is taken from an anthropology textbook used in classes for English-speaking students at the university level.
>
> - What do you think people learn by studying anthropology?
> - Have you ever taken a course in it? Would you like to? Why or why not?

Ethnocentrism

A   Culture shock can be an excellent lesson in relative values and in understanding human differences. The reason culture shock occurs is that we are not prepared for these differences. Because of the way we are taught in our culture, we are all *ethnocentric*. This term comes from the Greek root *ethnos*, meaning a people or group. Thus, it refers to the fact that our **outlook** or **world view** is centered on our own way of life. **Ethnocentrism** is the belief that one's own patterns of behavior are the best: the most natural, beautiful, right, or important. Therefore, other people, to the extent that they live differently, live by standards that are **inhuman**, **irrational**, **unnatural**, or wrong. 5

B   Ethnocentrism is the view that one's own **culture** is better than all others; it is the way all people feel about themselves as compared to outsiders. There is no one in our society who is not ethnocentric to some degree, no matter how **liberal** and **open-minded** he or she might claim to be. People will always find some **aspect** of another culture distasteful, be it **sexual** practices, a way of treating friends or relatives, or simply a food that they cannot manage to get down with a smile. This is not something we should be ashamed of, because it is a natural **outcome** of growing up in 15 any society. However, as anthropologists who study other cultures, it is something we should **constantly** be **aware** of, so that when we are tempted to make value judgments about another way of life, we can look at the situation **objectively** and take our **bias** into account. 20

C Ethnocentrism can be seen in many aspects of culture—myths, folktales, proverbs, and even language. For example, in many languages, especially those of **non-Western** societies, the word used to refer to one's own tribe or ethnic group literally means "mankind" or "human." This implies that 25 members of other groups are less than human. For example, the term *Eskimo*, used to refer to groups that inhabit the arctic and **subarctic** regions, is an Indian word used by neighbors of the Inuit people who observed their strange way of life but did not share it. The term means "eaters of raw flesh," and as such is an ethnocentric observation about cultural practices that were 30 normal to one group and **repulsive** to another. On the other hand, if we look at one **subgroup** among the Alaskan natives, we find them calling themselves *Inuit*, which means "real people" (they obviously did not think eating raw flesh was anything out of the ordinary). Here, then, is a contrast between one's own group, which is real, and the rest of the world, which is not so "real." Both 35 terms, *Eskimo and Inuit*, are equally ethnocentric—one as an observation about differences, the other as a **self-evaluation**. However, *Inuit* is now seen as a more appropriate term because of its origin.

D Another example of ethnocentrism in language can be found in the origin of the English term ***barbarian***. Originally a Greek word, the term 40 was used to refer to tribes that lived around the edge of ancient Greek society. The Greeks referred to these people as barbars because they could not understand their speech. *Bar-bar* was the Greek word for the sound a dog makes, like our word *bow-wow*. The Greeks, in a classic example of ethnocentrism, considered those whose speech they could not understand 45 to be on the same level as dogs, which also could not be understood. They did not grant such people the status of human being, much as the word *Eskimo* gives those people subhuman status.

E Shifting from language to myths and folktales, we find a good example of ethnocentrism in the creation myth of the Cherokee Indians. According 50 to this story, the Creator made three clay images of a man and baked them in an oven. In his haste to admire his handiwork, he took the first image out of the oven before it was fully baked and found that it was too pale. He waited a while and then removed the second image; it was just right, a full reddish-brown **hue**. He was so pleased with his work that he sat there and 55 admired it, completely forgetting about the third image. Finally he smelled it burning, but by the time he could rescue if from the oven it had already been burnt, and it came out completely black!

F Food preferences are perhaps the most familiar aspect of ethnocentrism. Every culture has developed preferences for certain kinds 60 of food and drink, and equally strong negative attitudes toward others. It is interesting to note that much of this ethnocentrism is in our heads and not in our tongues, for something can taste delicious until we are told what it is. We have all heard stories about people being fed a meal of snake or horse meat or something equally **repugnant** in American culture and commenting on how tasty it was—until they were told what they had just eaten, upon which they turned green and hurriedly asked to be excused from the table. 65

▲ In many western countries, meat from cows (beef) is a favorite food.

G Certain food preferences seem natural to us. We usually do not recognize that they are natural only because we have grown up with them; they are quite likely to be unnatural to someone from a different culture. In southeast Asia, for example, the majority of adults do not drink milk. To many Americans, it is **inconceivable** that people in other parts of the world do not drink milk, since to us it is a "natural" food. In China, dog meat is a delicacy; but the thought of eating a dog is enough to make most Americans feel sick. Yet we can see how this is a part of a cultural pattern. Americans keep dogs as pets and tend to think of dogs as almost human. Therefore, we* would not dream of eating dog meat. Horses, too, sometimes become pets, and horse meat is also rejected by most Americans, although not because of its taste . . . . On the other hand, we generally do not feel affection for cows or pigs, and we eat their meat without any feeling of regret. In India, a cow receives the kind of care that a horse or even a dog receives in our country, and the attitude of Indians toward eating beef is similar to our 95

70

75

80

85

90

▲ In India, cows are considered sacred and not eaten.

feeling about eating dog meat. On the other hand, in China, dogs are not treated as kindly as they are in the United States. Since they are not pets, the attitude of Chinese people toward dogs is similar to our attitude toward cows.

Source: "Ethnocentrism" *The Human Portrait: Introduction Of Cultural Anthropology, Second Edition* (John Freidl)

---

*The use of the pronoun *we* shows us that this excerpt is from a textbook used primarily in U.S. universities. The American author discusses the ethnocentrism of his own people.

After You Read

4 **Scanning for Words with Clues** Working alone or with a partner, scan the reading selection for the words that correspond to the following clues.

1. Two synonyms that mean *the way one looks at the world*

*outlook*_____

2. Two antonyms for *narrow-minded*, one beginning with *l* and one with *o*

_____

3. A short word beginning with *b* that means *subjective viewpoint or slanted opinion*

_____

4. A hyphenated term that means *an estimate about the worth or goodness of oneself*

_____

5. Two adjectives beginning with *r* and meaning the opposite of *pleasing*

_____

6. A noun that means *a crude, ignorant person* and has its origin in the sound made by a dog

_____

7. Another word for *shade* in reference to colors

_____

8. An adjective meaning *impossible to believe*

_____

5 **The Support Game: Finding Support for Main Ideas** How fast are you at finding information? Divide the class into teams of three to five players. Each team makes three lists of examples from the reading selection, one for each of the following main ideas. At a certain point the teacher calls "time" and each team reports on their findings. Which team is the winner? Who are the class experts on ethnocentrism?

1. Ethnocentrism is present in language.

2. Ethnocentrism is present in myths.

3. Ethnocentrism is present in food preferences.

6 **Focusing on Words from the Academic Word List** Use the most appropriate word from the box to fill in each of the blanks on page 203 in the section taken from the reading on pages 199–200. Do NOT look back at the reading right away; instead, try first to see if you can remember the vocabulary. The word *culture* will be used twice.

aspect	constantly	objectively
aware	culture	outcome
bias	liberal	sexual

B   Ethnocentrism is the view that one's own _____ is
1
better than all others; it is the way all people feel about themselves as
compared to outsiders. There is no one in our society who is not
ethnocentric to some degree, no matter how _____ and
2
openminded he or she might claim to be. People will always find some
_____ of another _____ distasteful, be
3   4
it _____ practices, a way of treating friends or relatives,
5
or simply a food that they cannot manage to get down with a smile. This is
not something we should be ashamed of, because it is a natural
_____ of growing up in any society. However, as
6
anthropologists who study other cultures, it is something we should
_____ be _____ of, so that when we are
7   8
tempted to make value judgments about another way of life, we can look at
the situation _____ and take our _____
9   10
into account.

7 **Guided Academic Conversation** In small groups, discuss the following
topics. Then compare your opinions with those of another group.

   1. **Culture Shock** What do you think is the meaning of this term (used in the
      first paragraph of the selection)? When does culture shock occur? Have you
      ever experienced this? Is it a good or a bad experience for a person to go
      through? Or can it be both? Explain.

2. **Examining Your Own Culture** What examples are there of ethnocentrism in the food preferences of your culture? What foods from other cultures are considered disgusting or repugnant? How do you feel about eating different types of food? Are there any words or phrases in your language which suggest a feeling of superiority with reference to other cultures? Tell the story of a popular myth from your culture. Is there anything ethnocentric about it?

3. **Purpose and Evaluation** In simple words, write what you think is the main purpose of the article. Do you feel that the author achieved his purpose or not? Why?

TOEFL® iBT

Focus on Testing

Questions About an Author's Purposes or Attitudes

The TOEFL® iBT includes "reading-to-learn" questions. These test your overall understanding of the reading, including implications, the author's purposes in writing, the author's feelings about a topic, how sure an author is about a certain point, or the interrelationships among several ideas. Here we will look at reading-to-learn questions about the author's purposes, implications, and attitudes.

Here are some questions like the "reading-to-learn" items on the TOEFL® iBT. These are based on the reading "Ethnocentrism" on pages 199–201.

1. *The author's attitude toward ethnocentrism is best expressed by which of the following?*

2. *What does the author mean by the phrase, it is a natural outcome of growing up in any society"?*

3. *Which of the following does the third paragraph most strongly imply?*

4. *Why does the author mention* dogs *in the fourth paragraph?*

To answer such questions, you have to consider the reading as a whole. Very often, the key sentence or phrase given in the question could, by itself, have many meanings. You must use other information from the reading to decide which possible meaning the author intends.

Practice Read the following passage about gestures and ethnocentrism. Then answer the reading-to-learn questions that follow it.

Gestural Ethnocentrism

A   Gestures are so naturally a part of any culture that they are almost automatic, used with little conscious thought about their meaning. Nonetheless, they are vital to communication. Even someone who learns the language of another culture communicates only poorly if the words are paired with the wrong gestures. A person who clings to his or her own system of nonverbal communication and fails to adapt to that of a host culture demonstrates a sort of "gestural ethnocentrism." When I wave my hand in a certain way, I expect the gesture to mean the same no matter where I go. That is pure narrowness on my part—and a big mistake.

B   To illustrate possible trouble arising from gestural ethnocentricity, we will look at what may happen when an American visits Malaysia. We will focus on the non-verbal messages of Malaysians who are ethnically Malay. Malaysians who are ethnically Indian, Chinese, Iban, European, and so forth have their own characteristic gestures but have probably also learned the dominant Malay set.

C   Malaysian handshakes communicate a tenderness and respect that seems absent from the typical European handshake. One holds out the right hand, just as in the Western version, but the palms touch only very gently. After a short contact period, Malaysians then disengage their right hands, which they bring up to the left side of the chest. There, the right hand is laid palm-down over the heart, much as an American might do while reciting the Pledge of Allegiance. The elegance, even nobility, of this gesture is impressive. Nonetheless, because it is far removed from the hearty, almost competitive, handshake that American visitors ethnocentrically expect, this beautiful gesture may be mistaken for something weak or unenthusiastic.

D   Malaysians, especially Malays, frequently hold hands with members of the same sex. It is not at all unusual to see two schoolboys walking down the street holding hands, or two men standing in line at a government office holding hands as they talk. The same would be true of two schoolgirls or two grown women. The gesture simply means friendship. Gesturally ethnocentric Westerners, especially men, often find the hand-holding disturbing because its meaning in their home societies is very different.

E   Westerners wrapped up in gestural ethnocentrism may do certain things that mean little to them but are very offensive to many Malaysians. Among these are standing with one's hands on the hips. To a Malaysian, it is likely to mean anger, and anger means insult. In Malaysian company, one should never hold up an index finger to say, "Come here." Such a gesture is reserved for animals or extremely naughty little children. Directed at an adult, it is a very harsh insult. Nor should one point at things with an index finger—a completely neutral gesture in the U.S. or Canada but a social mistake in Malaysia. To point things out, one should use the thumb or the entire hand, all fingers together. And never, never pound the fist of one hand into the palm of the other to emphasize a point. That is the equivalent of flashing a middle finger at another driver on the American roads.

1. Why does the author mention ethnic groups in Paragraph B?

A. to say which group of Malaysians use the best gestures

B. to show that Malaysian society discriminates against some ethnic groups

C. to emphasize that only Malays use and understand these gestures

D. to limit the discussion to one ethnic group's gestures

2. What is the author's attitude toward Malay handshakes?

A. They are too unenthusiastic.

B. They are too competitive.

C. They communicate warmth and respect.

D. They are used in reciting the Pledge of Allegiance.

3. What does the author imply about Western men in Paragraph D?

A. They see romantic love in a gesture that is meant to show friendship.

B. They have a hard time making male friends.

C. They never hold hands with anyone else.

D. They offend Malaysians by holding hands with members of the opposite sex.

4. What does Paragraph E imply about the gesture of pounding a fist into the palm of the other hand?

A. It is illegal.

B. It is exceptionally rude.

C. It is elegant.

D. It means "come here."

5. Throughout the passage, what is the author's attitude toward Malay gestures?

A. They are pleasant.

B. They are harsh.

C. They are meaningless.

D. They are not used anymore.

8 Around the Globe On pages 207–208 is a selection of ancient love poems from three different parts of the world. They allow us to examine some of the common themes about love that have come down to us through the centuries. In groups of three to five, read the three poems out loud and then answer the questions that come after the poems and compare your opinions of them.

▲ Love changes people's behavior

Introduction

The Strange Behavior of People in Love

What is it like to be "in love"? It is commonly said that those in love behave in strange ways: they focus all of their attention on the beloved one, to the detriment of everything and everyone around them. They tend to ignore work, friends, and family. "Love is a sickness that can only be cured by being with the beloved," is a phrase often heard.

- Do you agree with this? Explain your answer.

He drifts on blue water
under the clear moon
picking lilies on South Lake.
Every lotus blossom
Speaks of love,
Until his heart will break.

Li Po, 8th century, Chinese poet (male)

I lie awake, hot
the growing fires of passion
bursting, blazing in my heart.

Ono No Komachi, 9th century, Japanese (female)

> *The Sun Never Says*
> *Even*
> *After*
> *All this time*
> *The sun never says to the earth*
> *"You Owe Me"*
> *Look*
> *What happens*
> *With a love like that*
> *It lights the*
> *Whole*
> *Sky.*
>
> Hafiz, l4th century, Persian Sufi poet (male)

1. List briefly in your own words for each poem what you think is the main point or feeling expressed. Then compare and discuss your answers with your group.

2. Which of these three poems do you like best and why?

3. What emotions and themes are present in love poems (or songs about love) nowadays? Are they very different from these ancient poems or do they express the same eternal themes related to love? Can you give some examples?

Part 2   Reading Skills and Strategies

A Clean, Well-Lighted Place

Before You Read

The next story takes place in a café in Paris. It was written by the American writer Ernest Hemingway (1899–1961), who lived in Paris for many years. Hemingway is not the sort of writer who describes his characters in great detail. Therefore, the reader must infer a lot about the characters from what they say and do.

1 **Previewing for Characters and Plot** Skim the story to answer these questions.

1. How many characters are there in the story?

2. Which predominates (has a bigger place): dialog (speaking) or action?

3. Do you feel the general tone of the story is happy or sad? Why?

2 **Getting the Meaning of Words from Context** Read the following
excerpts from the story and decide from context which meaning corresponds best to
each italicized word. Even though some of the words are Spanish, the meaning should
still be clear from the context. Choose the correct answer.

1. "Last week he tried to commit suicide," one waiter said.
   "Why?"
   "He was in *despair*."
   "What about?"
   "Nothing."
   "How do you know that it was nothing?"
   "He has plenty of money."
   - (A) poor health
   - (B) a sad state of mind
   - (C) financial trouble

   (In this case, you are told the man has money, so *c* is not correct. Also, if the
   man were in poor health, the waiter would not have said he was in despair
   about "nothing," so *a* is not correct. That leaves letter *b*, the right answer.)

2. The waiter took the bottle back inside the café. He sat down at the table with
   his *colleague* again.
   - (A) client
   - (B) boss
   - (C) co-worker

3. "Finished," he said, speaking with that *omission of syntax* stupid people
   employ when talking to drunken people or foreigners. "No more tonight. Close
   now."
   - (A) shortening of phrases
   - (B) strange accent
   - (C) blurred speech

4. "Are you trying to insult me?" (younger waiter speaking)
   "No, *hombre*, only to make a joke." . . .
   "Each night I am reluctant to close up because there may be someone who
   needs the café." (older waiter speaking)
   "*Hombre*, there are bodegas open all night long." (Note: *hombre* is a Spanish
   word.)
   - (A) a funny insult
   - (B) a word you say to a friend
   - (C) the name of one of the waiters

5. "A little cup," said the waiter.
   The barman poured it for him. . . .
   "You want another *copita*?" the barman asked. (Note: *copita* is a Spanish word.)
   - (A) a small alcoholic drink
   - (B) a tiny saucer
   - (C) a spicy Spanish food

6. Now, without thinking further, he would go home to his room. He would lie in the bed and finally, with daylight, he would go to sleep. After all, he said to himself, it is probably only *insomnia*. Many must have it.

(A) a serious illness

(B) severe nervous depression

(C) the inability to sleep

Read

Introduction

Ernest Hemingway (1899–1961) is one of the most widely read of all modern American authors. His books have been translated into many languages. He always writes in a very simple, clear style, usually with a lot of dialogue, and with a deep and complex meaning hidden underneath. The following story, which traces the conversations between a customer and some waiters at a café near closing time, deals with loneliness, ageing, and compassion.

- Do you think people have a responsibility to be compassionate towards strangers, even if it puts them at an inconvenience?

- Why do some people become so lonely as they grow older? Is this a factor in some cultures and not much in others?

▲ Ernest Hemingway

A Clean, Well-Lighted Place

It was late and everyone had left the café except an old man who sat in the shadow the leaves of the tree made against the electric light. In the daytime the street was dusty, but at night the dew settled the dust and the old man liked to sit late because he was deaf and now at night it was quiet and he felt the difference. The two waiters inside the café knew that the old man was a little drunk, and while he was a good client they knew that if he became too drunk he would leave without paying, so they kept watch on him. 5

"Last week he tried to commit suicide," one waiter said.

"Why?"

"He was in despair." 10

"What about?"

"Nothing."

"How do you know it was nothing?"

"He has plenty of money."

They sat together at a table that was close against the wall near the door of the café and looked at the terrace where the tables were all empty except where the old man sat in the shadow of the leaves of the tree that moved slightly in the wind. A girl and a soldier went by in the street. The street light shone on the brass number on his collar. The girl wore no head covering and hurried beside him. 15

"The guard will pick him up," one waiter said. 20

"What does it matter if he gets what he's after?"

"He had better get off the street now. The guard will get him. They went by five minutes ago."

The old man sitting in the shadow rapped on his saucer with his glass. The younger waiter went over to him. 25

"What do you want?"

The old man looked at him. "Another brandy," he said.

"You'll be drunk," the waiter said. The old man looked at him. The waiter went away. 30

"He'll stay all night," he said to his colleague. "I'm sleepy now. I never get into bed before three o'clock. He should have killed himself last week."

The waiter took the brandy bottle and another saucer from the counter inside the café and marched out to the old man's table. He put down the saucer and poured the glass full of brandy. 35

"You should have killed yourself last week," he said to the deaf man. The old man motioned with his finger. "A little more," he said. The waiter poured on into the glass so that the brandy slopped over and ran down the stem into the top saucer of the pile. "Thank you," the old man said.

The waiter took the bottle back inside the café. He sat down at the table with his colleague again.

"He's drunk now," he said.

"He's drunk every night."

"What did he want to kill himself for?"

"How should I know."

"How did he do it?"

"He hung himself with a rope."

"Who cut him down?"

"His niece."

"Why did they do it?"

"Fear for his soul."

"How much money has he got?"

"He's got plenty."

"He must be 80 years old."

"Anyway I should say he was 80."

"I wish he would go home. I never get to bed before three o'clock. What kind of hour is that to go to bed?"

"He stays up because he likes it."

"He's lonely. I'm not lonely. I have a wife waiting in bed for me."

"He had a wife once too."

"A wife would be no good to him now."

"You can't tell. He might be better with a wife."

"His niece looks after him."

"I know. You said she cut him down."

"I wouldn't want to be that old. An old man is a nasty thing."

"Not always. This old man is clean. He drinks without spilling. Even now, drunk. Look at him."

"I don't want to look at him. I wish he would go home. He has no regard for those who must work."

The old man looked from his glass across the square, then over at the waiters.

"Another brandy," he said, pointing to his glass. The waiter who was in a hurry came over.

"Finished," he said, speaking with that omission of syntax stupid people employ when talking to drunken people or foreigners. "No more tonight. Close now."

"Another," said the old man.

"No. Finished." The waiter wiped the edge of the table with a towel and shook his head.

The old man stood up, slowly counted the saucers, took a leather coin purse from his pocket and paid for the drinks, leaving half a peseta tip.

The waiter watched him go down the street, a very old man walking unsteadily but with dignity.

"Why didn't you let him stay and drink?" the unhurried waiter asked. They were putting up the shutters. "It's not half-past two."

"I want to go home to bed."

"What is an hour?"

"More to me than to him."

"An hour is the same."

"You talk like an old man yourself. He can buy a bottle and drink at home."

"It's not the same."

"No, it's not," agreed the waiter with a wife. He did not wish to be unjust. He was only in a hurry.

"And you? You have no fear of going home before your usual hour?"

"Are you trying to insult me?"

"No, *hombre*, only to make a joke."

"No," the waiter who was in a hurry said, rising from pulling down the metal shutters. "I have confidence. I am all confidence."

"You have health, confidence, and a job," the old waiter said. "You have everything."

"And what do you lack?"

"Everything but work."

"You have everything I have."

"No. I have never had confidence and I am not young."

"Come on. Stop talking nonsense and lock up."

"I am of those who like to stay late at the café," the older waiter said. "With all those who do not want to go to bed. With all those who need a light for the night."

"I want to go home and into bed."

"We are of two different kinds," the older waiter said. He was now dressed to go home. "It is not only a question of youth and confidence although those things are very beautiful. Each night I am reluctant to close up because there may be someone who needs the café."

"*Hombre*, there are *bodegas* open all night long."

"You do not understand. This is a clean and pleasant café. It is well lighted. The light is very good and also, now, there are shadows of the leaves."

"Good night," said the younger waiter.

"Good night," the other said. Turning off the electric light he continued the conversation with himself. It is the light of course but it is necessary that the place be clean and pleasant. You do not want music. Certainly you do not want music. Nor can you stand before a bar with dignity although that is all that is provided for these hours. What did he fear? It was not fear or dread. It was nothing that he knew too well. It was all a nothing and a man was nothing too. It was only that and light was all it needed and a certain cleanness and order. Some lived in it and never felt it but he knew it all was *nada y pues nada y nada y pues nada.** Our *nada* who are in *nada*, *nada* be thy name thy kingdom *nada* thy will be *nada* in *nada* as it is in *nada*. Give us this *nada* our daily *nada* and *nada* us our *nada* as we *nada* our *nada* and *nada* us not into *nada* but deliver us from *nada*; *pues nada*. Hail nothing full of nothing, nothing is with thee. He smiled and stood before a bar with a shining steam pressure coffee machine. 130

"What's yours?" asked the barman.

"*Nada*." 135

"*Otro loco más*†," said the barman and turned away.

"A little cup," said the waiter.

The barman poured it for him.

"The light is very bright and pleasant but the bar is unpolished," the waiter said. 140

The barman looked at him but did not answer. It was too late at night for conversation.

"You want another *copita*?" the barman asked.

"No, thank you," said the waiter and went out. He disliked bars and *bodegas*. A clean, well-lighted café was a very different thing. Now, without 145 thinking further, he would go home to his room. He would lie in the bed and finally, with daylight, he would go to sleep. After all, he said to himself, it is probably only insomnia. Many must have it.

Source: "A Clean Well-Lighted Place" *The Short Stories of Ernest Hemingway* (Ernest Hemingway)

---

*Nada is the Spanish word for "nothing." *Y pues nada* means "and then nothing." The older waiter then recites the most famous of all Christian prayers, the "Lord's Prayer," which begins "Our Father which art in Heaven, hallowed be Thy name. . . ." However, instead of saying the correct words, he replaces many of them with the word *nada*. Afterward, he does the same with a small part of another prayer.
†Another crazy one

After You Read

3 **Making Inferences About Characters** Working alone or with others, make inferences about the characters in the story from the following words and actions. To express your inferences about the characters, you can use words like *maybe, perhaps, probably, must*.

1. We are told that the old man who is drinking tried to commit suicide the week before. (line 8) Finish the inference below.

   The old man:

   The old man must be very sad about something. He has problems. He is probably...

2. When asked what the old man was in despair about, this conversation follows:
   "Nothing."
   "How do you know it was nothing?"
   "He has plenty of money." (lines 12–14)
   The waiter who spoke last:

   _____

   _____

   _____

   _____

3. The younger waiter says, "He'll stay all night. . . . I'm sleepy now. I never get into bed before three o'clock. He should have killed himself last week." (lines 31–32)

   The younger waiter:

   _____

   _____

   _____

   _____

4. After the younger waiter has told the old man that the café is closed, the older waiter says, "Why didn't you let him stay and drink? . . . It's not half-past two." (lines 85–86)

   The older waiter:

   _____

   _____

   _____

   _____

5. After the man and the younger waiter leave, the older waiter stays for a while and thinks. He recites a prayer in his mind but substitutes the word *nada* for many of the important words. (lines 128–131)

The older waiter:

_____

_____

_____

_____

Strategy

Expressing the Theme

A story presents specific characters with their problems, feelings, and interactions. From these specifics, you can make a generalization about human behavior or human nature; this is the theme of the story.

 4 **Expressing the Theme** Here are three possible expressions of the theme of "A Clean, Well-Lighted Place." With a partner or a small group, decide which of the three you think is the best theme statement for the story, and why. If you do not like any of them, write your own theme statement.

1. Those who are sad and alone depend on the kindness of others to keep going.

2. Some people have understanding and compassion for others and some don't.

3. Very small details can sometimes make the difference between life and death.

 5 **Guided Academic Conversation** In small groups, discuss the following topics. Afterwards, compare your opinions with those of your classmates.

1. Your Own Interpretation At one point, the older waiter says to the younger one, "We are of two different kinds." What does he mean by this? Which one of them do you identify with more: the older waiter or the younger one? Why? Do you believe there are two different kinds of people? Explain.

2. The Hemingway Style Even today, many years after his death, Hemingway is a popular author whose books are read by people all over the world. It is said that his style is simple and clear and that his stories have universal meaning. In your opinion, what element is the most important in this story: the characters, the plot, or the setting? Explain. Why do you think that Hemingway included some Spanish words? Did you like the story? Why or why not?

6 **What Do You Think?** Read the paragraph below and discuss the questions that follow.

Manners

Manners apply to a distinctive way of acting or a social attitude towards others. A person can have good manners or bad manners. Some experts say that in the 21st century, we have lost our good manners and don't know how to act in certain social situations. We don't have respect for others, we don't eat properly, we don't dress properly, we don't behave properly.

1. Do you think that overall we have lost our good manners? Give some examples.

2. Do you think that manners from past generations were too strict and that nowadays we don't need those types of restrictions? Explain.

3. What manners would you change in your society? What manners would you change of foreigners you meet, or of those that visit your country?

▲ A person with bad maners is considered rude.

Part 3 Tying It All Together

1 **Making Connections** Choose one of the two topics below. Research the topic on the Internet and prepare some information on it to present to the class.

1. **Different Attitudes Toward Clothing and Styles** This may include head coverings, jewelry, ceremonial clothing, traditional costumes for different occasions (such as weddings or other ceremonies), or even hairstyles. Find examples of ethnocentrism in styles, where in some places certain items are used only by women but in others only by men, or where one culture would not permit the items used in another.

2. **The Importance of Hemingway** Look up some biographical and literary information about Ernest Hemingway. What other famous works has he written and what are they about? What are the main features of his style (in more detail than above)? Include some interesting facts about his life in your presentation. Or, as another alternative, read a different story by this famous author and describe its plot, setting, and characters.

Responding in Writing

WRITING TIP: CREATING A DIALOGUE
To write a dialogue, carefully select your speakers, make sure they stay in character, include their words in quotation marks, and follow a model for correct punctuation and formatting.

2 **Writing a Dialogue** In pairs, write a dialogue (a conversation) between two people about manners. Use the selection "A Clean Well-Lighted Place" as a model for how to format the speakers' words in quotation marks and how to use punctuation around quotation marks. Follow these steps:

Step 1: Carefully choose your two speakers. What different view on manners will each one represent? (i.e., Does one feel the younger generation is ruder than in the past and the other disagree? Does one feel that a certain way of behaving is appropriate and another feel that it is not? Be creative in making up their opinions.) List these two speakers' names along with their important characteristics, which might include such factors as age, gender, cultural background, appearance, etc.

Step 2: Decide on how the conversation should progress. Make a list of the main points that will be argued and of the examples that support each argument (or side.) Decide what the outcome will be. (Will one speaker win, will they continue to disagree in the end, or will they find common ground in their views?)

Step 3: Write the dialogue following the list of points you made in Step 2 and following the model for dialogue in the selection, "A Clean Well-Lighted Place."

Step 4: Read and revise the dialogue to make sure that each speaker stays "in character" (that is to say, that they say things that seem appropriate for their character as described in Step 1).

Step 5: Read your dialogues to another pair of classmates. Does the other pair have any critiques or comments about your dialogue that may help you revise a little more before handing in the assignment?

Step 6: Make final revisions and hand in your dialogue to the teacher.

Self-Assessment Log

Read the lists below. Check (✓) the strategies and vocabulary that you learned in this chapter. Look through the chapter or ask your instructor about the strategies and words that you do not understand.

Reading and Vocabulary-Building Strategies
- ❏ Skimming for the main idea
- ❏ Scanning for the development of the main idea
- ❏ Using prefixes to build new words
- ❏ Scanning for words with clues
- ❏ Finding support for main ideas
- ❏ Previewing for characters and plot
- ❏ Getting the meaning of words from context
- ❏ Making inferences about characters
- ❏ Expressing the theme

Target Vocabulary

Nouns
- ❏ aspect*
- ❏ barbarian
- ❏ bias*
- ❏ colleague*
- ❏ culture*
- ❏ despair
- ❏ ethnocentrism
- ❏ hue
- ❏ insomnia
- ❏ omission of syntax

- ❏ outcome*
- ❏ outlook
- ❏ self-evaluation
- ❏ subgroup
- ❏ world view

Adjectives
- ❏ aware*
- ❏ distasteful
- ❏ inconceivable*
- ❏ inhuman

- ❏ irrational*
- ❏ liberal*
- ❏ non-Western
- ❏ open-minded
- ❏ repugnant
- ❏ repulsive
- ❏ sexual*
- ❏ subarctic
- ❏ unnatural

Adverbs
- ❏ constantly*
- ❏ objectively*

*These words are from the Academic Word List. For more information on this list, see www.vuw.ac.nz/lals/research/awl.

Chapter

10

Crime and Punishment

In This Chapter

What causes people to commit crimes? Can criminals be reformed? And how should they be punished? To study the answers to these questions, we begin with a magazine article looking at some criminals who try to overcome what they see as their "crime addiction" through meetings and a spiritual program. This is followed by a fictional selection, a mystery story with a murder to be solved and a surprise ending.

❝ The way of justice is mysterious. **❞**

—Sanskrit proverb

Connecting to the Topic

1 Look at the photos below. What do you think is happening in each? What do you think happened after the last frame?

2 Have you ever been the victim of a crime? What happened?

3 Do you think that criminals can be reformed? Why or why not?

Hooked on Crime

Before You Read

Strategy

Identifying the Interviewees in an Article
Articles in a magazine or newspaper will often use interviews of key people and experts to get the story across. In this way, these people are similar to the "main characters" in a narrative. Sorting out who these "interviewees" are can help you understand better the overall story and its purpose.

1 **Scanning: Identifying the Interviewees** In this story, criminals are meeting around a table to talk about their "addiction to crime." Some of the people interviewed for the story are attending this meeting; others are "experts" in certain areas relating to crime.

Scan the article for the names below, and write a very short description of each person. (The first one is done for you as an example. You do not have to write everything, just enough to help you identify the person.)

1. Stan Mingo: *a man with a "crime addiction" who is starting the meeting*

2. Gary Johnson: _____

3. Rick A: _____

4. Benedikt Fischer: _____

5. George: _____

6. Rick B: _____

2 **Getting the Meaning of Specialized Terms from Context** Readings and discussions relating to crime include their own specialized vocabulary. Learning some crime-related terms will help you to read the selection and to discuss issues of crime and punishment.

Guess the meaning of each term or phrase in italics by breaking words into smaller parts or finding clues in the words that are nearby. Then match it with the correct definition in the column on the right.

Terms	**Definitions**

Terms

1. _g_ He has a *dependency* on alcohol. He drinks every day.

2. _____ It's in the city's *hard-luck* Downtown Eastside. You shouldn't go there alone.

3. _____ Her mind is *addled* by crack cocaine. She talks in a crazy way.

4. _____ They have been ground down by *homelessness*. At night they have nowhere to go.

5. _____ He was in jail for *robberies*. He took many things that didn't belong to him.

6. _____ He was in jail for *extortion*. He intimidated people.

7. _____ He was in jail for *assault*. He liked to hit people.

8. _____ He was in jail for *trafficking*. Many addicts made deals with him.

9. _____ He was in jail for small-time *cons*. He knew how to fool others.

10. _____ *Back when things were flush,* they bought many things.

11. _____ If a person takes *heroin* just a few times, it is very hard to leave it alone.

12. _____ He's been *clean* for four months and a day. Maybe he can get a job.

13. _____ *I did my time*, but that's not making amends.

14. _____ I did my time, but that's not *making amends*. There's still more I have to do.

15. _____ He knows some members will *backslide*. It's hard to learn good habits.

Definitions

a. thefts, stealing things

b. relapse, go back to old ways

c. fixing the wrong that was done

d. scaring people into paying money

e. buying and selling drugs

f. before, when there was money

g. condition of needing (and being controlled by)

h. tricks to cheat people

i. without drugs or alcohol

j. confused, mixed up mentally

k. fulfilled my sentence in prison

l. attacking or beating up someone

m. a place of misfortune, with people in tough situations

n. an addictive drug

o. living on the streets

Introduction

The following article from *Macleans Magazine* introduces some criminals from Vancouver (a city in Western Canada) who believe that they have an "addiction" (powerful physical and/or psychological urge) to crime. They meet regularly in the dining hall at the Salvation Army (a charity organization) to discuss this "addiction" and how to get over it and lead a life without crime.

- Do you think that crime can be an addiction? Why or why not?
- What do you think these people will do to try to prevent themselves from committing crimes?

Hooked on Crime
Vancouver Crooks Meeting to Talk About Their Compulsion to be Lawless

A   It's Tuesday evening, 7 P.M., and the last of the stragglers takes his seat. The lights in the Salvation Army dining hall are extinguished; candles are lit. A dozen men and one woman sit around a rectangle of tables waiting for Stan Mingo to start tonight's meeting. It's doubtful anywhere 5 in Vancouver tonight there is a larger gathering of career criminals, at least outside the prison system. The men range from their 20s to their 50s, and 10 from **clean-cut** to **jailhouse hard**. The woman, in her 50s, has a son up for robbery. They've got no proof, she says. The men nod politely, like 15 they've never heard that one before. The air smells of strong coffee. People drop coins into a cup making the rounds. "My name is Stan," says the **burly** guy at the head of the table. "I have a crime addiction."

▲ A group therapy session

B   With that, Mingo begins another weekly meeting of the founding chapter 20 of Crime Addiction Anonymous—dedicated to the **contentious** premise that crime can be an illness as tenacious as **dependency** on alcohol or drugs. The program was founded by Mingo, who washed up almost a year ago at the Salvation Army's Harbour Light Detox and Recovery Centre in the city's **hard-luck** Downtown Eastside. He was **addled** by crack cocaine, and ground down by **homelessness** and doubts about his abilities as a master criminal. He's spent more than half his 50 years in jail, for **robberies**, **extortion**, attempted murder, **assault**, **trafficking**, and small-time **cons**. Prison tattoos cover his upper torso like an illustrated criminal curriculum vitae*. The problem, he concedes, is crime can be thrilling. "It's fun to go in and rob a bank. It's a trip, man. It's a power trip to rob anybody, even with a knife in a back alley." There were few limits. He wouldn't harm old people, he says, "and most women, unless she acted and fought like a man."

C   **Back when things were flush**, he owned a home, a motorcycle, even a Vancouver restaurant, where the daily special was the **heroin** behind the counter. He called it *The Alibi*. Say what you want about Mingo, he has a sense of humour.

D   He **credits** Harbour Light with saving his life, and for providing the inspiration and wherewithal to **draft** the plan for CAA. The first meeting was held in May. A second **chapter** has since opened, also in the neighbourhood. The program's strength is that it was **created** by the members, not **imposed** on them, says Harbour Light associate executive director Gary Johnson. Asked if crime can be addictive, Johnson **responds** without hesitation: "Absolutely." There is some irony in the fact that the group steals heavily from the 12-step, spiritually based Alcoholics Anonymous program, started in 1935 and now used in more than 150 countries. A spokesman for AA's general service office in New York City, however, says other groups are welcome to share its traditions. They are spiritual **principles** we don't claim a right to if somebody wants to adopt them for themselves," notes Rick A.† who, in the AA **tradition**, asked his surname not be used. AA's principles have been applied to addictions from narcotics and nicotine to gambling and sex. As for crime, Rick concedes, "This is the first time I've heard of that."

E   Whether crime is, well, a legitimate addiction is an open question. "I'm very cautious in labeling anything with this very appealing and sexy label of addiction," says Benedikt Fischer, associate professor of criminology and public health at the University of Toronto, and research scientist with the Toronto-based Centre for Addiction and Mental Health. The term addiction is rather imprecise and often not "terribly helpful," he says. Crimes are committed for many reasons—economic need, compulsiveness, even an attraction to "the rush."

Curriculum vitae is a Latin expression that is used a lot in English and sometimes is abbreviated as CV. It means a document which lists information about a person's education, work experience, and qualifications. People applying for a job are usually asked to send in their CV.

†Since there were two participants named Rick at this meeting, they have been designated as Rick A. and Rick B. to help the reader to tell the difference between them.

F   Many of the men tonight are also fighting drugs or alcohol. They find crime similarly irresistible. Jason, in his 20s, says he's been **clean** for four months and a day. Money is tight. When he sees crack dealers, "I just want to take them out. Smash their heads and take their money." "The scary part is I like hurting people, too, you know." He pauses. "I'm hugely grateful for this meeting." 65

G   George, his dark hair streaked with grey, figures he's stolen or conned $80,000 from family members. "If you've ever seen the look in your family's eyes after you break their hearts," he says, "it's tough."

H   Tonight's topic is Step Nine: **making amends**. It's no easy task, they 70 agree. Where do you find all the people you've hurt? How do you pay all that money back? Rick B. lowers his shaved head, clasps his hands on the table. "How do you make amends to a dead person," he asks. "**I did my time**, but that's not making amends." Is prayer making amends? It's been 100 days, he says, "no crime, no dope." He's feeling guilt and shame for the 75 first time in years. "It's like we're thawing out, becoming human again."

I   Mingo knows the group faces skepticism. He knows some members will **backslide**. "For me, it's a new vision. I have strength and hope of recovery." The evening's **wrenching** hour of confession ends with arms linked in a group prayer. Some hurry into the night. Others help Mingo 80 rearrange the hall's furniture. He gathers his papers and asks about the collection cup, which usually adds about $5 to the group's **modest** coffers. It's gone. Ripped off, apparently, in mid-meeting.

J   Mingo, momentarily flummoxed, roars with laughter. What's a guy to do? He jabs a **meaty** finger at the writer's notebook. "That's crime 85 addiction, man," he says. "Write that down."

Source: "Hooked on Crime" *MacLeans Magazine* (Ken MacQueen)

After You Read

Strategy

Understanding the Setting

The setting of the story means where it takes place, and the same can apply to an article. If you don't understand where the action is occurring, it can be confusing to understand what is going on. When you read an article, try to identify where it takes place and who or what organizations are involved.

3 **Understanding the Setting** Fill in the blanks, using the context to understand the full meaning of the following names for organizations or places in the story.

1. The story mentions *Alcoholics Anonymous* (AA), a very well-known program with twelve spiritual steps that help people recover when they have been abusing _____. *Anonymous* means that people are not named or are unknown, so at meetings for these groups, the members' full names are _____ to each other.

2. *Crime Addiction Anonymous* is modeled after *Alcoholics Anonymous*, so it is a program with _____ spiritual steps that help people recover when they have a problem with _____. In this program also, the members' full names are _____ to each other.

3. The restaurant Mingo used to own was called *The Alibi*. An *alibi* is the story that an accused person tells to prove their innocence by stating that they were somewhere else when a crime was being committed. The article says that Mingo shows his "sense of humour" by this name for his restaurant because the food at this restaurant serves as an _____ to cover up the crime of also serving _____ (see line 35 in the story).

4. *Detox* is short for *detoxification*, the removal of a toxic or addictive substance (like excessive alcohol or drugs) from the body. *The Salvation Army* is a charity organization, and its *Harbour Light Detox and Recovery Centre* is a center where people can receive help getting over their _____. A *harbour* is a protected area on the sea coast where ships come, and harbors often have a *light* to guide ships in safely, so the center is called *Harbour Light* because _____. (**Hint:** use your imagination for this answer!) The article says Mingo "washed up" at the center because it is comparing Mingo to _____.

4 **Guessing the Meaning of Adjectives from Context and Structure**
Use your intuition, knowledge of word structure, and the context to select the best meanings for the words in italics in the phrases below.

1. Some of the men at the meeting are *clean-cut*.
- Ⓐ rough looking and menacing
- Ⓑ shaven and well groomed
- Ⓒ old and unhealthy

2. Some of the men at the meeting are *jailhouse hard*.
- Ⓐ rough looking and menacing
- Ⓑ shaven and well groomed
- Ⓒ old and unhealthy

3. Crime Addiction Anonymous is dedicated to the *contentious* premise (basic idea) that crime can be an illness as strong as dependency on alcohol or drugs.
- Ⓐ true
- Ⓑ debatable
- Ⓒ ridiculous

4. The evening's *wrenching* hour of confession ends with arms linked in a group prayer.

- Ⓐ unfair
- Ⓑ final
- Ⓒ difficult

5. The collection cup usually adds about $5 to the group's *modest* coffers (money boxes).

- Ⓐ fairly small
- Ⓑ substantial
- Ⓒ empty

6. He jabs a *meaty* finger at the writer's notebook.

- Ⓐ tiny
- Ⓑ dirty
- Ⓒ large

5 **Focusing on Words From the Academic Word List.** Use the most appropriate word from the box to fill in each of the blanks below in the paragraph taken from Part 2. Do NOT look back at the reading right away; instead, first see if you can remember the vocabulary. The word *principles* will be used twice. Check your answers on page 225.

chapter	credits	imposed	responds
created	draft	principles	tradition

D   He _____ Harbour Light with saving his life, and for
                    1
providing the inspiration and wherewithal to _____ the
                                                           2
plan for CAA. The first meeting was held in May. A second
_____ has since opened, also in the neighbourhood. The
         3
program's strength is that it was _____ by the members,   5
                                              4
not _____ on them, says Harbour Light associate
         5
executive director Gary Johnson. Asked if crime can be addictive, Johnson
_____ without hesitation: "Absolutely." There is some
         6
irony in the fact that the group steals heavily from the 12-step, spiritually
based Alcoholics Anonymous program, started in 1935 and now used in   10
more than 150 countries. A spokesman for AA's general service office in

New York City, however, says other groups are welcome to share its traditions. They are spiritual _____ we don't claim a right

7
to if somebody wants to adopt them for themselves," notes Rick A, who, in the AA _____, asked his surname not be used. AA's

8
_____ have been applied to addictions from narcotics

9
and nicotine to gambling and sex. As for crime, Rick concedes, "This is the first time I've heard of that."

15

IDENTIFYING SPELLING VARIATIONS

Spelling can vary in English depending on the country of origin. There are minor spelling differences between Canadian English and U.S. English. Canadians tend to spell words like *honour, cheque,* and *kilometre* in the traditional way as they do in Britain. Americans have altered these words to *honor, check,* and *kilometer,* often shortening or simplifying them.

---

6 **Identifying Spelling Variations** Change the following italicized words which are spelled in the American style to the Canadian style as they appear in *Hooked on Crime* (which came from a Canadian magazine).

1. recovery *center* _____

2. *Harbor* Light _____

3. sense of *humor* _____

4. in the *neighborhood* _____

7 **Guided Academic Conversation** In small groups, discuss five of the following six questions. Be prepared to report on the opinions of your group after you finish.

1. The reading says of Stan Mingo, "Prison tattoos cover his upper torso like an illustrated criminal curriculum vitae." What is a curriculum vitae? What does it normally list and for whom? Explain how Mingo's tattoos can be seen as a "criminal curriculum vitae."

2. Irony means a situation or event that is humorous because it is the opposite of what it seems it should be. So why does the article say, "There is some *irony* in the fact that the group steals heavily from the 12-step, spiritually based Alcoholics Anonymous program." What is ironic about this?

3. Why does Benedikt Fischer worry that the word *addiction* is a "very appealing and sexy label" for crime? Do you agree? What problems might arise from calling crime an "addiction"?

4. What other reasons do you think there might be for committing crimes, other than the "rush" mentioned here? List as many as you can think of. What do you think is the most common reason for committing crimes in the country you're living in? Would this be different in some other countries, and if so, why?

5. After talking about feeling guilt and shame, Rick B. says, "It's like we're thawing out, becoming human again." Is crime a "spiritual" problem?

6. What is Step Nine in the Crime Addiction Anonymous program, according to the article? Do you think it is a good idea for criminals to do this, and how do you think they should do it?

What Do You Think?

8 **Discussing the Death Penalty** Read the paragraph below and then discuss the questions.

Using the Death Penalty

"Capital punishment" is another way of saying "the death penalty." It means that when a person commits a crime such as murder, the state then has the right, under the law, to execute that person. Some countries—for example, Iran, China, Japan, Pakistan, and the Democratic Republic of Congo, have laws permitting this. In the United States, whether the death penalty is legal or not is decided by each state. Mexico, Canada, Australia, and most European countries do not have the death penalty. Increasing numbers of countries, like Taiwan, are considering abolishing the death penalty. Some people consider the death penalty unnecessarily cruel; others think it's fair punishment for certain crimes.

▲ A crowd protesting the death penalty.

1. Do you agree with the death penalty for certain crimes? Why or why not?

2. Do you think the threat of capital punishment stops people from committing murder? Explain.

3. Do you think killers should be kept in prison for the rest of their lives? Why or why not?

4. What are the various types of punishments for different crimes in your country?

Part 2 Reading Skills and Strategies

Eye Witness

Before You Read

1 Identifying Narrative Elements You may recall that the three elements of a narrative (story) are setting, characters, and plot (which starts out with a conflict). (See "The Luncheon" Chapter 6, Part 2.) In the detective story that follows on pages 232–236, the setting is New York City, about 60 years ago. Read the title, look at the illustration, and skim lines 1 to 25. Then answer these questions about the characters.

1. What does the title tell us about one of the main characters? What does he look like? What is his name? (You have to read carefully to find this out.) Why is he important? Whom does he want to speak to?

2. Who is telling the narrative? Is it the *omniscient narrator* (someone who knows everything), or is it one of the characters in the story? Explain. What is the narrator's name? You have to read carefully to find out this information.

3. Who is Magruder?

4. We are told at the beginning that the crime involved both a mugging (attacking someone with the intention to rob) and a murder. Who was the victim? What do we know about her?

2 Scanning for Specific Terms Scan lines 1–15 of the story for the specific details that the author uses to make his characters seem real. The references are listed in the order of appearance in the story. The first one is done as an example.

1. The sight of the murder has caused a physical change in the face of the man who saw it. It has given him a _____ *tic* _____ over his left cheekbone. (lines 2–3)

2. The narrator reacts to the eye witness' request to see the lieutenant and says, "None of us _____ will do, huh?" (line 12)

3. Magruder had been on the (police) force for a long time and was used to every type of person. But instead of saying *person*, the author uses police slang and says "every type of _____." (line 14)

4. Magruder uses slang to refer to the lieutenant. He asks, "You think maybe the

_____ would like to see him personally?" (lines 17–18)

5. The narrator thinks at first that the witness is being stubborn. But when he looks in his eyes he doesn't see stubbornness. He sees _____. (line 32)

6. The narrator tries to scare the witness into talking to him. He uses a legal term and says that not talking about evidence can make a person an

_____ *after the fact*. (line 37)

7. The author describes how the witness then thought about whether to talk with the detective or not. He uses a verb that means *considered, turned (something) over in his mind.* The witness _____ for another moment and then said . . . (line 60)

Read

Introduction

Murder mysteries present a murder and a number of suspects (people who may or may not be the murderers). These types of stories are also called *whodunnits* (bad grammar for "who did it?") because part of the interest is to guess which suspect is the murderer. Detective stories concentrate more on the reason for committing the crime and the process of solving it by the detectives or the police.

The following short story was written by Ewan Hunter (1926–2005) under the pen name of Ed McBain. One of the classic American detective authors, he wrote over 50 books and numerous short stories about crime. Many of his stories are based on true events that occurred years ago in the 87th precinct (police district) of New York. Read the story and follow the clues. Are you a good enough detective to discover who the murderer is?

Eye Witness

He had seen a murder, and the sight had sunken into the brown pits that were his eyes. It had tightened the thin line of his mouth and given him a tic over his left cheekbone.

He sat now with his hat in his hand, his fingers nervously exploring the narrow brim. He was a thin man with a moustache that completely ₅ dominated the confined planes of his face.

He was dressed neatly, his trousers carefully raised in a crease-protecting lift. . . . "That him?" I asked.

"That's him," Magruder said.

"And he saw the mugging?" ₁₀

"He says he saw it. He won't talk to anyone but the lieutenant."

"None of us underlings will do, huh?"

Magruder shrugged. He'd been on the force for a long time now, and he was used to just about every type of taxpayer. I looked over to where the thin man sat on the bench against the wall. 15

"Well," I said, "let me see what I can get out of him."

Magruder cocked an eyebrow and asked, "You think maybe the Old Man would like to see him personally?"

"Maybe. If he's got something. If not, we'd be wasting his time. And especially in this case, I don't think . . ." 20

"Yeah," Magruder agreed.

I left Magruder and walked over to the little man. He looked up when I approached him, and then blinked.

"Mr. Struthers?"

"Yes," he said warily. 25

▲ The scene of the crime

"I'm Detective Cappeli. My partner tells me you have some information about the . . ."

"You're not the lieutenant, are you?"

"No," I said, "but I'm working very closely with him on this case."

"I won't talk to anyone but the lieutenant," he said. His eyes met mine for an instant, and then turned away. He was not being stubborn, I decided. I hadn't seen stubbornness in his eyes. I'd seen fear.

"Why, Mr. Struthers?"

"Why what? Why won't I tell my story to anyone else? Because I won't, that's why."

"Mr. Struthers, withholding evidence is a serious crime. It makes you an accessory after the fact. We'd hate to have to . . ."

"I'm not withholding anything. Get the lieutenant, and I'll tell you everything I saw. That's all, get the lieutenant."

I waited for a moment before trying again. "Are you familiar with the case at all, sir?"

Struthers considered his answer. "Just what I read in the papers. And what I saw."

"You know that it was Lieutenant Anderson's wife who was mugged? That the mugger was after her purse and killed her without getting it?"

"Yes, I know that."

"Can you see then why we don't want to bring the lieutenant into this until it's absolutely necessary? So far, we've had ten people confessing to the crime, and eight people who claim to have seen the mugging and murder."

"I did see it," Struthers protested.

"I'm not saying you didn't, sir. But I'd like to be sure before I bring the lieutenant in on it."

"I just don't want any slip-ups," Struthers said. "I . . . I don't want him coming after me next."

"We'll offer you every possible protection, sir. The lieutenant, as you can well imagine, has a strong personal interest in this case. He'll certainly see that no harm comes to you."

Struthers looked around him suspiciously. "Well, do we have to talk here?"

"No, sir, you can come into my office."

He deliberated for another moment, and then said, "All right." He stood up abruptly, his fingers still roaming the hat brim. When we got to my office, I offered him a chair and a cigarette. He took the seat, but declined the smoke.

"Now then, what did you see?"

"I saw the mugger, the man who killed her." Struthers lowered his voice. "But he saw me, too. That's why I want to make absolutely certain that . . . that I won't get into any trouble over this."

"You won't, sir. I can assure you. Where did you see the killing?"

"On Third and Elm. Right near the old paint factory. I was on my way home from the movies."

"What did you see?"

"Well, the woman, Mrs. Anderson—I didn't know it was her at the time, of course—was standing on a corner waiting for the bus. I was walking down toward her. I walk that way often, especially coming home from the show. It was a nice night and . . ."

"What happened?"

"Well, it was dark, and I was walking pretty quiet, I guess. I wear gummies—gum sole shoes."

"Go on."

"The mugger came out of the shadows and grabbed Mrs. Anderson around the throat, from behind her. She threw up her arm, and her purse opened and everything inside fell on the sidewalk. Then he lifted his hand and brought it down, and she screamed, and he yelled, 'Quiet, you bitch!' He lifted his hand again and brought it down again, all the time yelling, 'Here, you bitch, here, here,' while he was stabbing her. He must have lifted the knife at least a dozen times."

"And you saw him? You saw his face?"

"Yes. She dropped to the ground, and he came running up the street toward me. I tried to get against the building, but I was too late. We stood face to face, and for a minute I thought he was going to kill me, too. But he gave a kind of moan and ran up the street."

"Why didn't you come to the police at once?"

"I . . . I guess I was scared. Mister, I still am. You've got to promise me I won't get into any trouble. I'm a married man, and I got two kids. I can't afford to . . ."

"Could you pick him out of a line-up? We've already rounded up a lot of men, some with records as muggers. Could you pick the killer?"

"Yes. But not if he can see me. If he sees me, it's all off. I won't go through with it if he can see me."

"He won't see you, sir. We'll put you behind a screen."

"So long as he doesn't see me. He knows what I look like, too, and I got a family. I won't identify him if he knows I'm the one doing it."

"You've got nothing to worry about." I clicked down Magruder's toggle on the intercom, and when he answered, I said, "Looks like we've got something here, Mac. Get the boys ready for a run-through, will you?"

"Right. I'll buzz you."

We sat around and waited for Magruder to buzz.

"I won't do it unless I'm behind a screen," Struthers said.

"You'll have a one-way mirror, sir."

We'd waited for about five minutes when the door opened. A voice 110
lined with anguish and fatigue said, "Mac tells me you've got a witness."

I turned from the window, ready to say, "Yes, sir." And Struthers turned
to face the door at the same time.

His eyebrows lifted, and his eyes grew wide.

He stared at the figure in the doorway, and I watched both men as their 115
eyes met and locked for an instant.

"No!" Struthers said suddenly. "I . . . I've changed my mind. I . . . I can't
do it. I have to go. I have to go."

He slammed his hat onto his head and ran out quickly, almost before I'd
gotten to my feet. 120

"Now what the hell got into him all of a sudden?" I asked.

Lieutenant Anderson shrugged wearily. "I don't know," he said. "I don't
know."

Source: *"Eye Witness" The McBain Brief* (Ed McBain)

▲ At the police station

After You Read

3 **Finding Descriptive Adverbs** Good writers use good adverbs to precisely describe the actions of their characters. Read the sentences below and note the clues in parentheses. Choose one of the adverbs from the box below to complete the phrases taken from the story.

abruptly	nervously	quickly	warily
carefully	personally	suspiciously	wearily

1. He sat now with his hat in his hand, his fingers (with tension) _nervously_ exploring the narrow brim.

2. He was dressed neatly, his trousers (with care) _____ raised. . . .

3. "You think maybe the Old Man would like to see him (in person) _____?"

4. "Yes," he said (with caution) _____.

5. Struthers looked around him (with doubt and mistrust) _____.

6. He stood up (in a sudden, rough manner) _____, his fingers still roaming the hat brim.

7. He slammed his hat onto his head and ran out (with a fast movement) _____. . . .

8. Lieutenant Anderson shrugged (in a tired way) _____.

Strategy

Understanding the Plot

The plot is the main sequence of events in a story. It is important to follow the main events and the order in which they occur to understand the story well. Begin with the *conflict*, then follow the *complications* which develop it to the *climax* (the point of highest tension), and then take special note of the *ending* that resolves the conflict, for good or for bad.

One way to understand the plot is to imagine the storyboard. A *storyboard* is a series of pictures that illustrates each part of a story's plot—like a sort of cartoon. It is used by directors who are making movies and it is shown to the actors to guide them. Storyboards may also include written descriptions along with the pictures that illustrate them.

---

 4 **Making a Storyboard of *Eye Witness* for TV** Work with a partner. Pretend that you are making a TV show based on the story *Eye Witness*. First you have to create a storyboard illustrating your story. Follow the steps on page 238 to help you complete the storyboard.

Descriptions:	Illustrations:
1.	1.
2.	2.
3.	3.
4.	4.

1. Draw a storyboard like the one above on a piece of paper. Be sure to make the boxes big enough for your descriptions and illustrations. Start by numbering the boxes on the left from 1–4. (You can add more boxes later if you need them.)

2. Next, decide what you think are the *main events* (or main scenes) in the plot that you want to illustrate; make a list of them on a separate piece of paper. Write a description of what is happening in each event in the column on the left (for example, "Detective Cappeli talks to Mr. Struthers"). You should have at least four events, but you may include more if you want.

3. Look over your list. A plot usually starts with a *conflict* or problem. Do you have a scene that shows this? Then come the *complications*, extra difficulties that make the tension grow. Then comes the *climax*, the moment of greatest tension, the moment that will decide how the story ends! When does that occur in the story? How can you show it? Finally, comes the *ending* that resolves the conflict (one way or the other).

4. Now illustrate each event in the square to the right of the description. (These may be stick figures or more elegant illustrations—you are the artists, so you decide.)

5. Exchange and compare storyboards with other classmates.
   - Did you all choose the same main events?
   - Were your scenes similar or different? How and why?

 5 You Are on TV! If time permits, work with a group and present the scenes from one of the storyboards to the class. One student should be the director and assign the parts. Remember, actors, to put your faces into the proper expression and use any props you can find (objects used in shows to make the story seem real). Your teacher will tell you how many minutes you have to prepare. Lights, camera, action!

6 **Guided Academic Conversation** In a small group, discuss the following topics.

1. **Solving the Murder** Who really murdered Mrs. Anderson? Do you all agree on who the killer is? Exactly how and when in the story did you know? Make a list of all the clues that point to the murderer. Are there any that occur early in the story? Are there any false clues? Was there really a mugging? What was the motive for this crime? Compare your ideas with those of other groups.

2. **Mystery or Detective?** Do you think this story was a murder mystery or a detective story? Or was it a combination? Explain.

3. **Getting Away with Murder** There is an expression in English to refer to someone who does something wrong and doesn't get caught. People say, "That guy got away with murder!" In this story, who "got away with murder"? Why? Does this happen in real life? If so, how and why does it happen?

4. **Why So Popular?** Since murder is such a terrible thing, why do you think that stories about it are so popular? Do people like to get scared? Or do they like to play detective and try to follow the clues to solve the crime? How can you explain this incredible popularity?

TOEFL® iBT

Focus on Testing

Prose Summaries on Tests

In the Focus on Testing section of Chapter 9, you learned about "reading-to-learn" questions on the TOEFL® iBT. You also practiced answering some multiple-choice questions of this type.

Another "reading-to-learn" question format is not multiple-choice. It involves piecing together a summary of a reading by dragging and dropping possible sentences for the summary. This is called a "prose summary" task.

Practice Read the following passage, then complete the "prose summary" task that follows.

Privatized Prisons

A   Research published by King's College London shows that the total prison population in 211 countries worldwide is about nine million. Of this number, about one-half are in three countries: the United States (2.1 million), China (1.6 million), and Russia (about 0.8 million). The pressure from such huge populations of imprisoned persons has stressed the prison systems in many countries, especially in the U. S. America imprisons a larger proportion of its residents than any other nation. Not enough resources are available to deal with all those prisoners. To solve the problem, many governments have contracted with private companies to operate prisons.

B   *Privatizing* a prison means turning its operations over to a business that hopes to earn a profit because it is paid by the government for its services. Advocates of privatization say that companies are more efficient than governments. Also, the private company bears the cost of providing pay and benefits to the prison guards and administration. This takes a great burden off the government. And a private company can move faster to establish a prison than the government can. In some cases, when the prison population in a state has suddenly jumped, private companies have been able to start up new prisons in just two or three weeks.

C   Critics of privatization say that quality in prisons drops when a private company takes over. Seeking greater profits, they say, a company is likely to cut corners. Too few guards, lack of medical care for prisoners, non-nutritious food, and many other faults may result as the company seeks greater profits. Also, critics say, private prison companies may take money from a state government or the Federal Bureau of Prisons and then spend it on something besides a prison. Executives get richer, critics contend, as prisoners suffer more. A further criticism of privatization holds that it encourages the courts to imprison criminals rather than seek their rehabilitation. Passing a drug-user to a company prison, for example, is a lot easier than treating the drug use as a sickness and helping the user recover. Privatized prisons are unlikely to spend much money on effective rehabilitation because the companies have an interest in keeping the prison population high.

D   Private prisons are not just a U.S. phenomenon. They have sprung up in Australia, Kyrgyzstan, Mexico, the United Kingdom, South Africa, and many other nations. The prison-operating companies are based overwhelmingly in the U.S. or the U.K. Prison populations are on the rise worldwide. From 1999 to 2005, they increased by 70 percent in Brazil, 40 percent in Japan, and 37 percent in Mexico. In the U.S., the increase was only 3.4 percent, but the prison population was large to begin with. With the pressures of ever more convicts to house and feed, governments are likely to provide a lot of money to these American and British contractors in the years to come.

Practice An introductory sentence for a brief summary of the passage is provided below. Complete the summary by selecting the three answer choices that express the main ideas in the passage. Some sentences do not belong in the summary because they express ideas that are not presented in the passage or are minor ideas in the passage. Write the letter of each of your choices on one of the blanks in the summary box.

Summary

Controversy surrounds the practice of contracting with private companies to run prisons that used to be run by national or local governments.

- _____

- _____

- _____

a. Critics of privatization argue that it results in lower-quality prisons.

b. Between 1999 and 2005, many nations experienced huge increases in their prison populations.

c. Supporters of privatization do not care about the health or safety of prisoners.

d. Privatization, its supporters say, saves governments a lot of money.

e. Privatization has been used in many countries around the world to deal with rising prison populations.

Part 3 Tying It All Together

1 Interpreting Charts Read the paragraph in the box. Then work with a partner: look at the chart on page 242, fill in the blanks, and answer the questions that follow. After you finish, compare your answers with those of the rest of the class.

The U.S. Prison Population

Some people feel that one problem with crime in the U.S. is that the administration and maintenance of prisons has become a big business. For many small towns, having a prison nearby is a source of jobs. Police officers, detectives, prison guards, lawyers, and court psychologists make a good living when there are lots of criminals. In the 1980s, new laws came in that made the simple possession of certain drugs a serious crime, punishable by imprisonment. By the end of the year 2000, one in every 137 people in America was behind bars! It used to be different. In 1973, only one in every 1,042 people in America was behind bars. This change did not happen because the rate of violent crime went up. In fact, it was just the opposite. The rate of violent crime went down considerably since the early 1970s.*

U.S. State and Federal Prison Population					
	Dec. 31, 1980	Dec. 31, 1990	Dec. 31, 2002	Dec. 31, 2003	% change from Dec. 31, 2002– Dec. 31, 2003
State	305,458	708,393	1,276,616	1,296,986	+ 1.6
Federal	24,363	65,526	163,528	173,059	+ 5.5
Total	329,821	773,919	1,440,655	1,470,045	+ 2

*Source: The U.S. Census Bureau

1. The chart gives statistics about changes in the U.S. prison population over a period of _____ years.

2. Did the number of prisoners in the U.S. go up or down in that period of time? It went _____.

3. Which changed more: the population in the State prisons or the population in the Federal prisons? _____

With your partner, discuss the questions below.

1. Do you think it is good for a country to have many people in prison? Why or why not?

2. How do you think this situation compares with that of your own country?

3. In your opinion, what, if anything, can the U.S. government do to lower the number of people in its prisons?

 2 **Making Connections** Choose one of the following four tasks to research. From the library or on the Internet, find information about that person or topic.

1. Give a brief description of a legendary person, political figure, or folk hero who commits crimes, such as Zorro, Jesse James, Dracula, or Robin Hood. This could be someone from any culture. Tell who he or she was and why some people feared or hated him or her. Also, describe the points of view of others who see this legendary figure in a positive light.

2. Following from the *What Do You Think* above (page 230), choose a country and research the view there on the death penalty and the reasons for this view. If the law there favors the death penalty, in which types of cases? If the law does not, what other punishment is used for serious crimes? Report on this to the class. If possible, tell about some famous case(s) in which the issue of capital punishment was important.

3. Who was the real Ed McBain? Was the name Ewan Hunter the name he was born with? How did he get started as a writer of crime stories? Give a report on his life and work.

4. Look up Sherlock Holmes or some other famous detective, real or fictitious, and describe what he looked like, how he became well known and what method he used to solve crimes.

▲ Famous fictional detective Sherlock Holmes might warn perspective criminals by saying "Crime does not pay."

Responding in Writing

WRITING TIP: DEVELOPING YOUR VIEWPOINT

Use a summary of something you have read as a lead into your viewpoint on the reading. Remember that the summary should not express your personal opinion of the event. Then you can use your summary of the event to connect to your personal viewpoint.

3 **Writing About a Real Crime** Find an article (in a newspaper or on the Internet) about a real crime that has been committed. Using that story, write two paragraphs on one of the two topics below. To develop your point of view, follow the steps that follow the topics.

Topics

1. What do you imagine were the reasons for this crime being committed and why? In your imagination, what really led up to this crime occurring?

2. From the information you have on this crime, what do you think should be the best punishment for this crime and why? What effects would this punishment have on the accused, the victims, on society?

Step 1: Write a brief summary of the article to begin your composition. Remember that a summary does not include your opinion (see page 75). It just repeats the main points that you have read.

Step 2: Using a cluster diagram (see page 149 and 151) or a list, outline all your main points on the topic.

Step 3: Write a sentence that sums up your main idea on the topic you have chosen. Write this sentence after the summary so that the summary leads into your opinion on the topic.

Step 4: Write the rest of the composition, using strong examples (see page 124) to support your position.

Step 5: Work with a classmate. Exchange your compositions and check them over for spelling, grammar, and punctuation. Are quotations and information listed with the source (name of the book or website)? Then read aloud to each other for the meaning. Are the ideas clear and in a good order? Give suggestions to each other. Revise your work again and sign at the bottom of your classmate's composition as *Reviewer*. Then hand in all of your work (including a copy of the original article, your cluster diagram or outline and notes) to the teacher.

Self-Assessment Log

Read the lists below. Check (✔) the strategies and vocabulary that you learned in this chapter. Look through the chapter or ask your instructor about the strategies and words that you do not understand.

Reading and Vocabulary-Building Strategies

- ❏ Identifying the interviewees in an article
- ❏ Getting the meaning of specialized terms from context
- ❏ Understanding the setting
- ❏ Guessing the meaning of adjectives from context and structure
- ❏ Identifying spelling variations
- ❏ Identifying narrative elements
- ❏ Scanning for specific terms
- ❏ Finding descriptive adverbs
- ❏ Understanding the plot
- ❏ Interpreting charts

Target Vocabulary

Nouns

- ❏ accessory
- ❏ assault
- ❏ chapter* (of an organization)
- ❏ cons
- ❏ dependency
- ❏ extortion
- ❏ fear
- ❏ heroin
- ❏ homelessness
- ❏ principles*
- ❏ robberies
- ❏ taxpayer
- ❏ tic
- ❏ tradition*
- ❏ trafficking
- ❏ underlings

Verbs

- ❏ addled
- ❏ backslide
- ❏ created*
- ❏ credits*
- ❏ deliberated
- ❏ draft*
- ❏ imposed*
- ❏ responds*

Adjectives

- ❏ burly
- ❏ clean (in the sense of "free from drugs")
- ❏ clean-cut
- ❏ contentious
- ❏ hard-luck
- ❏ jailhouse hard
- ❏ meaty
- ❏ modest
- ❏ wrenching

Adverbs

- ❏ abruptly
- ❏ carefully
- ❏ nervously
- ❏ personally
- ❏ quickly
- ❏ suspiciously
- ❏ warily
- ❏ wearily

Idioms and Expressions

- ❏ back when things were flush
- ❏ I did my time (do time)
- ❏ making amends (make amends)
- ❏ the Old Man

*These words are from the Academic Word List. For more information on this list, see www.vuw.ac.nz/lals/research/awl.

Outward Bound

Call Kim Ssang Su a man of the people. On a chilly night in the picturesque mountains south of Seoul, Kim, CEO of LG Electronics Inc., holds aloft a paper cup filled to the rim with *soju*, a clear, sweet potato-based Korean alcohol with a vicious bite. Surrounding him are a dozen of the 300 LG suppliers' managers whom Kim has spent the day lecturing and rallying. They have also been hiking up a snow-covered mountainside—necessary training, he says, for the grand plans he has for South Korea's second largest electronics firm. At the end of the day, he treats a group of LG Electronics employees to an outdoor barbecue of grilled pork and bowls of fiery red kimchi. "Great people! Great company!" he barks. "Great company! Great company!" they chant back, pumping their fists in perfect unison. Kim downs the *soju* in one gulp, then marches off to another table for another round of *soju* and another cheer. Then another, and another.

Eight tables and countless cups later, he is red faced, still screaming chants and bear-hugging an unfortunate reporter. When dancing girls in short skirts and blond wigs start jiggling to ear-numbing Korean pop music, the tireless Kim, 59, cavorts in a mosh pit of drunken workers near a makeshift stage. Later he ascends the stage himself, microphone in hand, to croon out a popular oldie called Nui (Sister). "We love our CEO," says Kim Young Kee, an LG executive vice president. "He shows us a good time."

CEOs rarely stoop to carouse with the common man in an Asia dominated by secretive business clans and élite old-boy networks. But Kim is no ordinary Asian boss. He began his career 35 years ago as a nondescript engineer at an LG refrigerator factory, climbed the ranks, and claimed the CEO post in October. Now he aims to duplicate the same feat with LG—lifting a con-

sumer-electronics company little known outside Asia into the stratosphere of global brands with Sony, Panasonic and Samsung. "I want to go down in LG history," says Kim. "After death, a tiger leaves its skin. A man leaves his name."

LG seems well on its way. While most of the electronics industry, including Sony, suffered sagging growth and profits in recent years, LG's market presence surged. Revenues jumped 18% last year, to $17 billion, and net profits rose 33%, to $556 million. LG has the electronics world bracketed. At the commodity end, low-cost plants in China make the firm a power in developing markets. At the big-bucks, high-tech end, LG's home in broadband-rich South Korea has fostered a focus at LG on design and function that fits perfectly into the emerging digital home. Last year LG was the world's largest seller of mobile phones operating on the CDMA standard (a type of mobile-phone technology). It makes dazzling flat-screen televisions and other leading-edge gadgets. LG.Philips LCD, a joint venture formed in 1999 with Royal Philips Electronics, became the world's biggest maker of the LCD panels used in flat-screen TVs and monitors in 2003, with 22% of the global market. The unit's operating profit soared 307% last year, to $935 million.

The growth has brought LG to the cusp of greatness but not quite into the industry's aristocracy. Still missing is the global brand name crucial for commanding high premiums and outpacing low-cost manufacturers in China. It is an accomplishment hardly any Asian corporations have managed to achieve. "We've had success at the foothills," says Woo Nam Kyun, president of LG's digital-TV operation. "Now we have to climb the mountain."

The climb LG has chosen is Mount U.S.A. This year LG is making its biggest thrust ever into the

U.S. market, with a $100 million budget for advertising alone. Last year LG spent $10 million refurbishing a billboard in New York City's Times Square into a giant flat-screen TV, and it helped renovate a Los Angeles concert hall. LG is also buffing up its U.S. product line. Last July, LG began introducing its first LG-branded flat LCD and plasma TVs in the U.S., and next year it will launch its first high-definition TVs with built-in hard-disc drives that can record movies. An LG refrigerator with an LCD TV set in the door is already on the market.

LG faces plenty of competition. Its biggest rival at home and abroad, Samsung Electronics, whose revenues of $36.4 billion are two times as large as LG's, has already hit the U.S.—and scored big successes. Samsung is also ahead of LG in developing a truly global brand. LG executives hope that competition from Samsung will make their company stronger. "Their presence as a very strong competitor in our neighborhood has always kept us alert and awake," says LG's Woo. "This has helped us compete in overseas markets as well. I can be more successful with Samsung's success."

LG's first crack at the U.S. market ended in disappointment. Beginning in the 1980s, LG sold cheap TVs under the brand Goldstar, after the company's former name, Lucky-Goldstar. In 1995, LG purchased American TV maker Zenith Electronics Corp. and began using that moniker on its products. But four years later, Zenith filed for bankruptcy, a victim of cutthroat competition. To avoid a repeat of that failure, LG was content until recently to supply other companies with appliances that sell in the U.S. under their own brands. Chances are, the average American may own an LG-made product but not know it. LG says it sells 43% of all room air-conditioners in the U.S., for example, but many under brand names like GE and Kenmore.

These days, however, a monumental transition is taking place in U.S. living rooms, and LG smells opportunity. Consumers are tossing aside boxy TVs and clunky VCRs in favor of wide, flat screens, DVD players and, eventually, computer-like systems with digitized video and music recorders and Internet services. With this emerging gadgetry, LG is surprisingly well positioned. LG.Philips has been a leader in developing large, flat displays, and LG makes 70% of all set-top boxes for receiving digital satellite TV sold in the U.S.

In this new digital world, LG has a distinct advantage in its ultra-wired South Korean home base. The demanding Korean market, where an amazing 84% of households using the Internet have high-speed access, propels LG to develop more advanced products and provides a testing ground for new technologies. LG has outpaced Nokia and Motorola in cramming the hottest new features into a mobile phone. One of its latest models, the SC8000, which came out in Korea in April, combines a PDA, an MP3 player, a digital camera and a camcorder. The advantage is paying off. In May, LG launched a new mobile phone in Korea with a 2-megapixel color screen simultaneously with Samsung. In the past, LG lagged at least several months behind its competitor's phone launches, missing out on higher prices and margins. LG became the largest supplier of mobile phones last year to service provider Verizon Communications.

It may seem odd that at this crucial time LG has turned over its top job to a farm boy from a tiny village in eastern South Korea. Kim Ssang Su spent his childhood knee-deep in the family's rice paddies. Even now, Kim is a bit of a fish out of water. He took over from the debonair John Koo, a senior member of LG's prestigious founding family. Kim has never worked outside Korea or, before becoming CEO, even at LG's glitzy Seoul headquarters, known locally as the "Twin Towers." He had spent his entire career buried in LG's stuffy bureaucracy at the company's main appliance factory in the industrial city of Changwon. He admits to being more comfortable in the field visiting factory floors and design centers than in his spacious office overlooking Seoul's Han River.

It would be wrong, though, to underestimate Kim, who has become near legend in Seoul for the turnaround he engineered at LG's appliance business. When he took over in 1996, LG was making washing machines and refrigerators that seemed little more than cannon fodder for low-cost Chinese companies like Haier. Kim sliced costs by moving production of low-end products to China. He proved there is room for innovation in basic white goods, introducing, for example, appliances like air-conditioners that can be controlled from the Internet. The result: sales reached $4.7 billion last year, more than twice the number when Kim took control.

Kim is infusing LG's other businesses with the same vigor. Called a "commander in the field" by executives, he storms about LG's factories and offices poring over details, issuing commands and spurring on the staff by giving them what he terms "stretch goals," or aggressive targets. Awake at 5:30 each morning for a brisk walk, he openly prefers "morning people" and holds 7 a.m. breakfast meetings with top executives. "I don't like the expression 'nice,'" Kim says. "I don't want LG to be perceived as nice. None of the great companies in the world are nice." Kim's relentless nature has put some executives on the defensive. "He likes to be heavily involved," complains a top manager. "I would prefer that he delegate a bit more."

Kim is backing up his tough talk with a strategy to augment the company's design and technology prowess. For instance, LG.Philips announced in March it would invest $22 billion with its suppliers in new flat-screen production facilities over the next 10 years. Kim is recruiting engineers at a furious pace, aiming to increase research-and-development teams to 60% of LG's total payroll by 2005, from 40% today. One recent afternoon at the LG Electronics Corporate Design Center in Seoul, young Koreans in jeans and hip black sweaters were packing up plastic models of computer monitors and microwaves to move to new offices. With the number of designers up 15% in the past year, to 390, the center has added an entire new floor. "As we emphasize our brand, design becomes more critical," says the center's president, Lee Hee Gook. "We're making ourselves more competitive."

Can Kim build LG into a global titan? Hurdles abound. LG still sometimes cuts prices to drive sales, softening both profit margins and its brand image. For example, LG sees 5% profit margins on its mobile phones; Samsung earns in excess of 20%. Nor does it help that LG Electronics is a member of one of South Korea's mammoth, family-controlled conglomerates, called *chaebols*, which are infamous for mysterious and convoluted business practices. In February the company broke a promise to investors by pledging $130 million to buy bonds of a nearly bankrupt affiliate, credit-card issuer LG Card. Kim says his company joined in because a failure at LG Card would have damaged LG's image.

Michael Lee, an executive vice president at LG Corp., the conglomerate's holding company, says affiliates had a "moral obligation" to help out and calls the LG Card case an exception. The LG *chaebol*, he says, has reorganized its shareholding structure to allow affiliates to be managed more independently. Because of concerns relating to its being a *chaebol*, LG—like many other Korean companies—is valued more cheaply than many of its international competitors.

Still, in Asia, LG has taken on the world's best and proved it can hold its own. In China and India, LG has become a preferred brand. In China, which Kim calls the "toughest marketplace in the world," sales last year rose 40%, to $2.8 billion. In India, LG has beaten out Sony and Samsung to claim the No. 1 market share in everything from TV sets to refrigerators to CDMA phones.

And in just a few months, LG is making inroads into the U.S. Its increasingly popular mobile phones hold fourth place in market share. Lisa Smith, general manager for appliances at U.S. retailer Best Buy Co., began carrying LG refrigerators and washers and dryers last July, and their jazzy designs, such as yellow and blue lights on dryer control panels that look like car dashboards, have made them a hit with younger shoppers. "[LG has] done a fantastic job of raising the bar in the U.S. market," Smith says. "The products are popular, and they continue to gain momentum."

In the end, Kim can take LG to the top only if he manages to solve that pesky branding problem. Its rival did it: four years ago, few in the electronics industry could have predicted the growing dominance of Samsung, despite its solid technology and financial clout. Samsung's surprise was its savvy at brand building. "In terms of the ingredients, LG has everything—the quality, the packaging, the global marketing reach," says Nam Park, an analyst at HSBC Securities in Hong Kong. "What's missing is the magic. It's missing that je ne sais quoi." If Kim finds it, he'll probably pour himself a glass of *soju* and let go a very, very loud cheer.

By MICHAEL SCHUMAN | SEOUL
Time Asia, Vol. 163, No. 25, June 21, 2004
Time, Inc. All rights reserved. Reprinted by permission.

Vocabulary Index

* These words are from the Academic Word List. For more information on this list, see
   www.vuw.ac.nz/lals/research/awl.

benefit*
cancer
communities*
compensation*
cuisine
demanding
diet
distinguish
eclectic
ecotourism
elite
enchanted
fiber
flock
found* (find)
frontiers
grain
heart disease
hence*
hippies
inappropriate*
indigenous
inexpensive
legumes
locals
monounsaturates
natural resources
peasant
physical*
prevent
prosperity
requests
stinginess
subculture
taboo
tourists
treats
up-front
virtually*

Chapter 5

benefits*
best-case scenario
braking
charge (batteries)
components*
computers*
craftsmen
data*

download
economy*
efficient
English-speaking
exhaust (from a car)
four-cylinder
    engine
fuel tank
gas pump
generator
global*
global warming
grassroots
greenhouse
    effect
handmade
hybrid car
Internet-enabled
Internet-linked
interwoven
knowledge-based
landmarks
large-scale
leapfroggers
locomotives
marketplace
medical*
mileage
network*
on the block
parallel*
propulsion rpm
    (rotations per
    minute) power
scenario*
service-based
shocked
speeds
tailpipe emissions
tech-savvy
telecenters (also
    spelled telecentres)
transmission*
twofold
upload
vehicle*
via*
well-educated
widespread*

Chapter 6

absentmindedly
affordable
amicable
anticipated*
boom
chain (as in a group of
    similar businesses)
convenience
drama*
effusive
enormous*
executive
flattered
found* (find)
franchises
globalization*
growth markets
imposing*
inadequate*
inclined*
management
marketing
maturing*
mentality*
modernizing
mortifying
multinational
outlets (as in
    individual
    businesses in
    a chain)
pizzeria
projected sales
prospered
specialties
startled
succulent
transform*
untapped market
vindictive

Chapter 7

assistance*
atone
atrocities
background
benevolent

childhood
civil*
commitment*
commoners
compelling
conduct*
Confucian
cornerstones
decisions
defender
demilitarization
depressed*
diligent
dynasty
easily
eloquence
enduring
energy*
eradicate
etiquette
expression
founded*
(the) Golden Rule
governmental
holocaust
influential
innovator*
investment*
lament
medical*
modernize
monitors*
negotiations
notions*
obstacles
outlook
overwhelming
perception*
permeated
philosophical*
political
preparation
prestige
primarily*
principality
promotion*
reared
repression
resigned

---

* These words are from the Academic Word List. For more information on this list, see
    www.vuw.ac.nz/lals/research/awl.

250

responsibility
role*
sacrifice
seized
servitude
strive
suppress
take up the torch
tyranny
valor
violations*

Chapter 8

academy*
acoustic guitar
ambition
bass
boldly
circuitous
compulsory
contemporary*
continually
conventional*
create*
critical acclaim
dabbled
debut album
definitive*
demonstrate*
discrimination*
energetic*
experiment
fatigue
funds*
grappling
guerrillas
high-profile

iconic
income*
indigenous
individualistic*
issues*
label*
launch
murdered
obstinacy
pan-American
pioneer
proper
rapping
remarkably
sex*
shooting
show business
shuttling
small-scale operations
smirk
smuggled goods
sources*
spokesperson
startling
stunningly
violin
weariness

Chapter 9

aspect*
aware*
barbarian
bias *
colleague*
constantly*
culture*
despair

distasteful
ethnocentrism
hue
inconceivable*
inhuman
insomnia
irrational*
liberal*
non-Western
objectively*
omission of syntax
open-minded
outcome*
outlook
repugnant
repulsive
self-evaluation
sexual*
subarctic
subgroup
unnatural
world view

Chapter 10

abruptly
accessory
addled
assault
back when things
    were flush
backslide
burly
carefully
chapter* (of an
    organization)
clean (in the sense of
    "free from drugs")

clean-cut
cons
contentious
created*
credits*
deliberated
dependency
draft*
extortion
fear
hard-luck
heroin
homelessness
I did my time
imposed*
jailhouse hard
making amends
meaty
modest
nervously
the Old Man
personally
principles*
quickly
responds*
robberies
suspiciously
taxpayer
tic
tradition*
trafficking
underlings
warily
wearily
wrenching

---

* These words are from the Academic Word List. For more information on this list, see
   www.vuw.ac.nz/lals/research/awl.

Skills Index

LITERARY CREDITS

Page 5 Excerpt from *Living in the USA, Fifth Edition* by Alison R. Lanier. Revised by Charles William Gay. © 1996 by the estate of Alison R. Lanier. Intercultural Press. Reprinted by permission of Nicholas Brealey Publishing, North American Group. **Page 18** "My Country" by Pierre Berton. Reprinted by permission. **Pages 29, 55, 77, 101, 127, 151, 171, 195, 219, 245** "Academic Word List Sublist One" by Averil Coxhead, as appeared on website www.language.massey.ac.nz/staff/awl/index. Reprinted by permission of Averil Coxhead. **Page 35** (Beckham: An Autobiography) "Football, La Vida" from *Beckham: Both Feet on the Ground* by David Beckham. Copyright © 2003 by Footwork Production, Limited. Reprinted by permission of HarperCollins Publishers and HarperCollins Publishers Ltd. **Page 39** Reprinted from *The Lighter Side of Campus Life* with permission of Bill Maul. **Page 43** "Outward Bound" by Michael Schuman, *Time Magazine*, June 21, 2004. Copyright 2004 by Time, Inc. All rights reserved. Reprinted by permission. **Page 59** "Who's Taking Care of the Children?" by Miki Knezevic. **Page 62, 133** CLOSE TO HOME, © 1995 John McPherson. Reprinted with permission of UNIVERSAL PRESS SYNDICATE. All rights reserved. **Page 63** Reprinted with permission from Encyclopaedia Britannica Almanac 2006, © 2005 by Encyclopaedia Britannica, Inc. **Page 67** From "70 Brides for 7 Foreigners" by S. Kuzina from *World Press Review*, July 1993, p.47. Reprinted by permission. **Page 81** "Eat Like a Peasant, Feel Like a King" by Andrew Revkin. Reprinted with permission from the March 1986 *Reader's Digest*. Copyright © 1986 by The Reader's Digest Assn., Inc. **Page 89** Chart "Some Benefits of Quitting Smoking" From *The World Almanac and Book of Facts 2004*. Copyright © World Almanac Education Group. All rights reserved. Reprinted with permission. **Page 93** "Here Come the Tourists!" by Deborah McLaren from *Rethinking Tourism & Ecotourism, Second Edition*, 2003. Reprinted by permission of Kumarian Press, Inc. **Pages 98** Table "World's Top 10 Tourist Destinations 2002" from *The World Almanac and Book of Facts 2004*. Copyright © World Almanac Education Group. All rights reserved. Reprinted with permission. **Page 99** Table "Top Countries in Tourism Earnings, 2002" from *The World Almanac and Book of Facts 2004*. Copyright © World Almanac Education Group. All rights reserved. Reprinted with permission. **Page 99** Table "Average Number of Vacation Days per Year, Selected Countries" from *The World Almanac and Book of Facts 2004*. Copyright © World Almanac Education Group. All rights reserved. Reprinted with permission. **Page 108** From "How Hybrid Cars Work" by Karim Nice as appeared on HowStuffWorks.com website. Courtesy of HowStuffWorks.com. **Page 117** From "Leapfrogging the Technology Gap" by Alexandra Samuel, which appeared on website www.ladlass.com, January 17, 2005. Reprinted with permission of the author. **Page 122** From *The Wall Street Journal* - Permission by Cartoon Features Syndicate. **Page 132** "Executive Takes Chance on Pizza, Transforms Spain" by Stephen Wade, as appeared in *Wisconsin State Journal*, May 29, 1994. Used with permission of The Associated Press. Copyright © 2004. All rights reserved. **Page 142** "The Luncheon" *Cosmopolitans* by W. Somerset Maugham, published by William Heinemann Ltd. Reprinted by permission of The Random House Group Ltd. **Page 156** "Confucius" from *The 100: A Ranking of the Most Influential Persons in History, Revised and Updated* by Michael H. Hart. Copyright © 1978, 1992 Michael H Hart. All right reserved. Reprinted by arrangement with Kensington Publishing Corp., www.kensingtonbooks.com. **Page 161** From "Courage Begins with One Voice" by Kerry Kennedy, *Parade* Magazine, September 24, 2000. © 2000 Kerry Kennedy. All rights reserved. Reprinted with permission. **Page 176** "Guggenheim Museum, U.S.A." from *Individual Creations* by Flavio Conti, Rizzoli Editore, SpA. Reprinted with permission. **Page 187** Biography of Nancy Ajram, www.arabicnights.com. **Page 187** "Don Popo Raps About a Better Future for Colombia's Kids" by Marco Visscher, *Ode* magazine, #19, December 2004, p. 6. Reprinted with permission of Marco Visscher, Managing Editor of Ode Magazine, www.odemagazine.com. **Page 193** From "Are Men More Creative Than Women?" by Margaret Mead from *Margaret Mead: Some Personal Views*. Copyright © 1979 by Mary Catherine Bateson and Rhoda Metraux. Reprinted by permission of Walker and Company, 435 Hudson Street, New York NY 10014, 1-800-289-2553. **Page 199** "Ethnocentrism" John Freidl and Michael B. Whittord, *The Human Portrait: Introduction Of Cultural Anthropology*, Second Edition, © 1988, pp. 39-41. Reprinted by permission of Prentice Hall, Inc. Englewood Cliffs, New Jersey. **Page 207** Ono No Komachi from *Introduction to Japanese Court Poetry* by Earl Miner translated by the author and Robert Brower, 1968. **Page 211** "A Clean Well-Lighted Place". Reprinted with permission of Scribner, an imprint of Simon & Schuster Adult Publishing Group, from the Short Stories of Ernest Hemingway. Copyright renewed © 1961 by Mary Hemingway. "A Clean Well-Lighted Place" from the First Forty-Nine Stories by Ernest Hemingway, published by Jonathan Cape. Reprinted by permission of The Random House Group Ltd. **Page 224** "Hooked on Crime" by Ken MacQueen, *MacLeans Magazine*, December 27, 2004. **Page 232** "Eye Witness" by Ed McBain, © 1982 by Hui Corp, originally published in *The McBain Brief*. Reprinted by permission of the author. **Appendix** "Outward Bound" by Michael Shuman, Time Asia, Vol. 163, No. 25, June 21, 2004. Time, Inc. All rights reserved. Reprinted with permission.

We apologize for any apparent infringement of copyright and if notified, the publisher will be pleased to rectify any errors or omissions at the earliest opportunity.